Unexpected Messiah

£4

REV. ROY BEVAN,
THE MANSE,
BRECON ROAD,
CRICKHOWELL
POWYS NP8 1SH
TEL: (0873) 811398

D1150498

Lucas Grollenberg

# Unexpected Messiah
*or*
How the Bible can be Misleading

SCM PRESS LTD

Translated by John Bowden from the Dutch
*Onverwachte Messias*
published 1987 by Uitgeverij Ten Have, Baarn.

© Uitgeverij Ten Have 1987

Translation © John Bowden 1988

All rights reserved. No part of this publication may be
reproduced, stored in a retrieval system, or transmitted,
in any form or by any means, electronic, mechanical,
photocopying, recording or otherwise, without the prior
written permission of the publisher, SCM Press Ltd.

*British Library Cataloguing in Publication Data*

Grollenberg, Lucas, *1916–*
    Unexpected Messiah, or, How the Bible
    can be misleading.
    1. Bible. N.T. Prophecies
    I. Title
    225

    ISBN 0–334–02402–1

First published in English 1988
by SCM Press Ltd
26-30 Tottenham Road, London N1 4BZ

Photoset by Input Typesetting Ltd, London
and printed in Great Britain by
Billing & Sons Ltd, Worcester

# Contents

# Preface

The plan for this book came about as a result of feelings of irritation and amazement. They followed each other quickly during a church service shortly before Christmas. The celebrant sang solemnly about Christ, 'Prophets foresaw and prophesied his coming.' That irritated me. We have long been aware that the prophets were not foretellers, certainly not of a distant future. Moreover, anyone who claims that is at the same time implying that the Jews must have been hard of heart and blind to reject a Messiah who was so clearly prophesied in their own Jewish Bible. At the same time I thought once again of the two splendid female statues which adorn the south porch of Strasbourg Cathedral. There is the synagogue, with a blindfold over her eyes, a broken staff in one hand and in the other a law book which she is almost dropping. Over against her stands the church with a triumphant look on her face, a crown on her head, bearing a chalice in her left hand and proudly holding out before her a cross in her right hand. All that flashed before my eyes. A few moments later I felt myself caught up in the ceremony with bread and wine, in memory of Jesus. At it the congregation, about one hundred and fifty people of all ages and backgrounds, sang a hymn about the living Jesus, the one who is part of us, who is proclaimed as living Lord and becomes our peace in the sharing of bread and wine. That is amazing. How did it come about that a pious Jew who lived two thousand years ago in Palestine was crucified as a criminal, and still brings people together now, all over the world, people for whom he is alive, and has to do with the depths of their existence? Could that perhaps be the beginning of what some Jewish prophets dreamed about, the dream of a humanity which is to be brought together by God to live in peace?

I am plagued by a kind of historical curiosity. Even when studying the Bible I asked questions like: 'What did the writers mean to communicate and record? What did their world look like? How did all these texts finally become one book, the Bible, and how did this collection of writings function over the course of centuries?'

This approach has also been fundamental to this book.

To make it easier to read, I have put references to the Bible and other writings at the back.

# 1 A 'Prescribed' Career?

The earliest descriptions of Jesus' life are the four books, almost booklets, which we call 'the Gospels'. Anyone reading them in an impartial way will get the impression that particular events in that life took place because they were foretold in the Holy Scriptures of the Jews, our Old Testament. Therefore they 'had to' happen as they did. They took place 'so that the scriptures should be fulfilled'.

This raises the question how the evangelists arrived at this view. Before we try to find an answer, we must first look rather more closely at the texts which have made the impression on us that I have indicated, taking each of the Gospels one by one. For the four books differ considerably, and also do so over this point. It is important for us to begin with the Gospel of Mark. Close comparison of this Gospel with those of Matthew and Luke shows that both the latter authors incorporated virtually all of Mark's account into their own much longer books. Most New Testament scholars accept that Mark wrote his Gospel around the year 70. Matthew and Luke will have followed his example some fifteen to twenty years later.

Mark begins his story about Jesus abruptly with a quotation from the Old Testament in which he finds an announcement of the appearance of John the Baptist in the wilderness. But he does not say explicitly that this event therefore 'has to' take place. Apart from the remarkable conversation that Mark relates in chapter 9, after his story about the 'transfiguration' of Jesus on a high mountain, the idea of a necessary fulfilment of the scriptures comes to the fore only in chapter 14, where his account of Jesus' passion begins. During the last supper with his disciples, Jesus tells them that one of them will betray him, the one who is dipping bread in the dish with him. Then he says: 'The Son of man goes *as it is written of him...*'

Shortly after this, when Jesus leaves the city with the group to

1

go to Gethsemane, he says: 'You will all fall away; *for it is written*: I will strike the shepherd, and the sheep will be scattered.'

In the garden of Gethsemane Jesus is arrested by a group of soldiers. He says to them: 'Have you come out as against a robber, with swords and clubs to capture me? Day after day I was with you in the temple teaching, and you did not seize me. But *that the scriptures may be fulfilled...*' The sentence is not finished. But the meaning is clear: this nocturnal attack can only take place because God had determined things in this way in the scriptures. Only here does Mark use the term 'fulfilment' for the scriptures. Perhaps there is a connection with the 'must' of which Jesus had spoken in chapter 8 when he announced his passion and death for the first time: 'The Son of man must suffer many things and be rejected.' The two evangelists who made use of Mark's account brought out these ideas more strongly, each in his own way.

### Luke: Must not the Messiah suffer all this...?

In the last chapter of Luke's Gospel there is one of his most attractive and therefore best-known stories, that of the disciples on the way to Emmaus. On the third day after the crucifixion and the death of Jesus these two disciples are returning to their homes tired and disillusioned. They tell the stranger who comes to join them what has happened in connection with Jesus the Nazarene, and also that women went to his tomb but did not find him there. Angels are said to have appeared to them who said that he was alive. Then the stranger says: 'O foolish men, and slow of heart to believe all that the prophets have spoken! *Was it not necessary that the Messiah should suffer all these things* to enter into his glory? And beginning with Moses and all the prophets, he interpreted to them in all the scriptures the things concerning himself.' Note that the word 'all' appears in these lines four times.

The same evening Jesus appeared to the whole group of disciples: 'Then he said to them, "These are my words which I spoke to you, while I was still with you, *that everything written about me* in the law of Moses and the prophets and the psalms *must be fulfilled.*" Then he opened their minds to understanding the scriptures, and said to them: "Thus it is written, that the Christ should suffer and on the third day rise from the dead, and that repentance and forgiveness of sins should be preached in his name to all nations."'

Where Luke earlier, in chapter 22, describes the last supper, he adds to Mark's account a number of sayings by Jesus which Mark and Matthew have in a different context. Only the last saying is peculiar to Luke and sounds rather mysterious. Jesus asks his disciples whether they had lacked anything when he had sent them out without purse and bag and sandals. Their answer is 'No!' Then he says: 'But now, let him who has a purse take it, and likewise a bag. And let him who has no sword sell his mantle and buy one. For I tell you that *this scripture must be fulfilled in me,* "And he was reckoned with transgressors"; *for what is written about me has its fulfilment.*' It is not clear what Jesus means by his advice to buy a sword. When the disciples show him the two swords that they have he says something like: 'Enough of that!' It is quite clear that the idea of the need for the scriptures to be fulfilled is expressed here, though not with the verb that is normally used for it. It is also remarkable that here Jesus relates to himself a quite specific statement from Isaiah 53: 'he was reckoned with transgressors'.

Luke also uses the same term 'fulfil' in Chapter 18, where he takes over Mark's third passion prediction. Mark wrote: 'Behold, we are going up to Jerusalem; and the Son of man will be delivered to the chief priests and the scribes, and they will condemn him to death.' Luke transcribes this as follows: 'Behold we are going up to Jerusalem, and *all that is written by the prophets* of the Son of man will be accomplished...' Here again we have the word 'all'.

*Matthew: This took place that the word of the prophet should be fulfilled...*

The Gospel of Matthew seems to have come into being in a Christian community which consisted largely of Jewish members, some of whom were very much at home in holy scripture and indeed were probably real scribes. For his Gospel works out much more richly and deeply than that of Luke the element that we found only in Mark's account at the arrest of Jesus, and then only in an incomplete sentence: 'But that the scriptures should be fulfilled...' In his rewriting of this account Matthew completes the sentence: 'But all this has taken place, that the scriptures of the prophets might be fulfilled.'

Just before that he added to Mark's story Jesus' warning that those who had taken the sword would also have to put it back again: '...for all who take the sword will perish by the sword. Do you think that I cannot appeal to my Father, and he will at once send me more than twelve legions of angels? *how then should the scriptures be fulfilled, that it must be so?'*

This last sentence is no surprise for those readers who began to read Matthew at the 'foreword'. 'Foreword' is a good description of the first two chapters; they are a kind of introduction in narrative form in which Matthew announces the most important themes of his work in true biblical fashion. First he gives the genealogy of Jesus from Abraham, three times fourteen generations, to Joseph, the husband of Mary, of whom Jesus is to be born. Then he describes how Mary appears to be pregnant without the knowledge of her husband Joseph. Joseph then dreams that an angel appears to him and reassures him: Mary's pregnancy is the work of God's Holy Spirit. Joseph must give the child the name Jesus, a name in which Greek-speaking Jews could clearly recognize the Hebrew name which means 'saviour, redeemer'. The narrative then goes on: '*All this took place to fulfil what the Lord had spoken by the prophet*: "Behold, a virgin shall conceive and bear a son, and his name shall be called Emmanuel" (which means, God with us).'

The fulfilment of the prophecy (from Isaiah 7) clearly relates to Mary's pregnancy, and not to the name Jesus that Joseph has to give the child. But Matthew evidently thinks that the name Emmanuel, which is alluded to, is appropriate for Jesus. He will make that clear in the course of his book, and have it expressed by Jesus himself in the very last sentence: 'Lo, I am with you always to the close of the age.' So Jesus gives an assurance that he will be God-with-us. Perhaps that is why Matthew does not use the name Jesus again in his prologue and goes on to speak only of 'the child'.

After the wise men from the East have been to Bethlehem to pay homage to the child, Joseph again sees an angel in his dream. This angel commands him to flee to Egypt with the child and his mother. He remains there until King Herod has died: '*This was to fulfil what the Lord had spoken by the prophet*: "Out of Egypt have I called my son."' The prophet meant is Hosea, who lived about 750 BC. Chapter 11 of the book of the Bible named after him begins with a word of God which relates to the very beginning of Yahweh's relations with Israel: 'When Israel was a child, I loved him, and out of Egypt I called my son.' That is remarkable. Hosea is referring to something that took place in the distant past, and Matthew regards this text as a prophecy which is fulfilled in Jesus.

Joseph had already escaped to Egypt with the child and his mother when King Herod became enraged because the wise men from the East returned home without seeing him, and thus cheated him. Thereupon in Bethlehem and its environs he had all the male children of two years old and younger murdered in order to get his newly-born rival out of the way. Matthew then writes: *'Then was fulfilled what was spoken by the prophet Jeremiah*:

A voice was heard in Ramah,
wailing and loud lamentation,
Rachel weeping for her children;
she refused to be consoled,
because they were no more.'

Anyone who looks up this passage in Jeremiah 31 will be amazed. In verse 15, which Matthew quotes, the prophet is recalling with a very poetic image what had happened more than a hundred years before his own time: in 721 the Assyrians conquered the northern kingdom, Israel, and deported the inhabitants to other parts of their great empire. According to the old sagas their inhabitants were descended from the patriarch Joseph, the son of Jacob's wife Rachel. The grave of the 'tribal mother' was pointed out in Rama, north of Jerusalem. The sensitive poet Jeremiah, who lived in Anathoth, not far from that tomb, could still hear Rachel weeping for her deported children. To her he goes on to say in the next verse, v.16, in the name of God, that she must stop her lamentation and crying, for 'your children shall return from the land of the enemy'. These words, which are about the future and contain a promise, in other words a 'prophecy', are *not* quoted by Matthew!

Already some centuries before Matthew Rachel's tomb was no longer located at Rama, north of Jerusalem, but to the south, on the road to Bethlehem. So Matthew could have the idea of relating Jeremiah's text to the massacre of the innocents. Here he does not use the formula 'this happened *that* it should be fulfilled'; in that case God would seem responsible for the crime. What was important to him was to show that even the pain of the mothers in Bethlehem had been 'foretold' in this verse about Rachel's pain. Then it had been the pagan Assyrians who had done away with her children. Here it was the king of the Jews who killed the little children of Israel because he could not accept any newborn king of the Jews alongside himself.

Matthew ends his prologue by relating that after the death of Herod, on the orders of an angel which appeared to him in a dream, Joseph returned to the land of Israel with the child and its mother. He avoided Judaea because one of Herod's sons was ruling over it, and again on divine instructions in a dream he went into the territory of Galilee. Having arrived there 'he dwelt in a city called Nazareth, *that what was spoken by the prophets might be fulfilled*, "He shall be called a Nazorean."' Unfortunately this statement is not to be found in any of the prophets nor in any other book of the Old Testament. That is a pity. For the name Nazoraean must have been very important for Matthew, otherwise he would never have ended his profound 'prologue' in this way.

This prologue is followed by the Gospel narrative proper which, in accordance with its model in Mark, begins with the appearance of John the Baptist, followed by the baptism of Jesus and his stay in the wilderness, where after his encounter with the devil angels come to minister to him. Then Matthew writes:

When Jesus heard that John had been arrested, he withdrew into Galilee; and leaving Nazareth he went and dwelt in Capernaum by the sea, in the territory of Zebulun and Naphtali; *that what was spoken by the prophet Isaiah might be fulfilled*:

The land of Zebulun and the land of Naphtali,
toward the sea, across the Jordan,
Galilee of the Gentiles
the people who sat in darkness
have seen a great light
and for those who sat in the region and shadow of death,
light has dawned.
From then on Jesus began to preach, saying, 'Repent, for the kingdom of heaven is at hand.'

Anyone who turns up this text in the book of Isaiah (8.23; 9.1) wil notice a number of things. First, that it clearly refers to the northern part of Palestine, which was conquered and plundered by the Assyrians around 730 BC. The way to the sea seems to denote the coastal area, and in addition to Zebulun and Naphtali, Transjordan was also included in this. Galilee is the district or

6

the region of the Gentiles. Matthew has taken over only the geographical details of the first part. He has already mentioned two of them, Zebulun and Naphtali, in order to locate the town of Capernaum, which moreover is by 'the sea' = the Sea of Galilee. For him the stress is on the term 'Galilee of the Gentiles', those who sat in the darkness and for whom a great light has now dawned, namely through Jesus' proclamation of the kingdom of heaven.

Anyone who is at all at home in biblical geography will also note something else. Capernaum was in the old tribal territory of Naphtali, not of Zebulun. But Nazareth was in it, the place which Jesus has now left for Capernaum. It has been supposed that even before Matthew, Christians saw in the Isaiah text an allusion to Jesus' preaching in Galilee, the tribal territory of Zebulun and Naphtali. Matthew would then have kept this interpretation, even if it did not fit precisely.

As already becomes clear in Matthew's prologue, the first Christians were not concerned with what the authors of the ancient text had wanted to say. That is something that we moderns ask about. They inferred the meaning of the ancient text from the events brought about by God in which they themselves were involved.

After the Sermon on the Mount, in chapter 8 Matthew narrates three healings: of a leper, of the servant of a centurion and of Peter's mother-in-law. Then he writes: 'That evening they brought to him many who were possessed with demons; and he cast out the spirits with a word, and healed all who were sick. *This was to fulfil what was spoken by the prophet Isaiah*, "He took our infirmities and bore our diseases."'

After Matthew has repeated Mark's account of Jesus healing a man with a withered arm in the synagogue on the sabbath, in his own way, in chapter 12, he also describes how the Pharisees then resolved to do away with him. Then he goes on to say: 'Jesus, aware of this, withdrew from there. And many followed him, and he healed them all, and ordered them not to make him known. *This was to fulfil what was spoken by the prophet Isaiah*:

Behold my servant whom I have chosen,
my beloved in whom my soul is well pleased.
I will put my Spirit upon him,
and he shall proclaim justice to the Gentiles.

He will not wrangle or cry aloud,
nor will any one hear his voice in the streets;
he will not break a bruised reed
or quench a smouldering wick,
till he brings justice to victory;
and in his name will the Gentiles hope.

These are the famous opening lines of Isaiah 42 in which God presents his servant or slave, in Greek *pais*, a word which can also mean child and son. This is the longest quotation from the Old Testament in the Gospel of Matthew. It gives us much to think about. It recalls what happened at the baptism of Jesus in the Jordan when the voice from heaven said: 'This is my beloved Son in whom I am well pleased.' The voice was heard after the spirit of God had descended on Jesus like a dove. This beloved of God has nothing about him of a glorious and spectacular Messiah but on the contrary concerns himself with those who are broken and almost extinguished. In so doing he makes the 'justice' of God manifest. That is what he will proclaim to the Gentiles. This suggests the manifestation of God's 'righteousness' of which Paul speaks.

In chapter 13 Matthew takes over the series of parables from Mark 4, which he expands with new parables in order to arrive at the number seven. Mark describes what happened when Jesus had told the first parable to the many listeners or bystanders, about the sower who went out to sow: 'And when he was alone, those who were about him with the twelve asked him concerning the parables. And he said to them, "To you has been given the secret of the kingdom of God, but for those outside everything is in parables; so that they may indeed see but not perceive, and may indeed hear but not understand; lest they should turn again, and be forgiven."'

In this incomprehensibly harsh saying Mark makes Jesus cite a word of God from the book of Isaiah without indicating that that is what it is. It is in chapter 6 of that book of the Bible, the chapter in which the prophet describes his calling and the task that was laid upon him at it. This involved the need to preach to people who just did not want to listen, so that his words would harden them even further in their resistance against God. Matthew the scribe also gives the biblical text, but only after he has made some changes in the text of Mark. He makes Jesus speak about the mysteries of the kingdom of God in the plural, has Jesus go on to repeat a saying which also occurs elsewhere in the Gospel, and then writes: 'This is why I speak to them in parables, *so that* seeing they do not see, and hearing they do not hear, nor do they understand. *With them indeed is fulfilled the prophecy of Isaiah which says*:

You shall indeed hear but never understand,
and you shall indeed see but never perceive.
For this people's heart has grown dull,
and their eyes they have closed,
lest they should perceive with their eyes,
and hear with their ears,
and understand with their heart,
and turn for me to heal them.'

Later on in this book we shall discuss what role this saying of Isaiah played in the reflection of the first generations of Christians.

In the same chapter 13 the fulfilment formula occurs once again, now in the complete form. After the parables about the mustard seed and the leaven Matthew writes:

All this Jesus said to the crowds in parables; indeed he said nothing to them without a parable. *This was to fulfil what was spoken by the prophet*:

I will open my mouth in parables,
I will utter what has been hidden since the foundation of the world.

The words quoted are to be found in the opening of the long Psalm 78, a long reflection on Israel's past, seen as a history of constantly repeated ingratitude in the face of God's good deeds and infidelity towards him. Thus even a psalm text can be 'prophecy'.

In chapter 11 of his Gospel Mark describes the entry of Jesus into Jerusalem, on what we call Palm Sunday. When Jesus approaches the city he sends two disciples to a village nearby and says that they will find there the foal of an ass, tied up, on which no one has yet sat. They find the foal, bring it to Jesus, put their clothes on it and then he gets on the foal. Many people spread their garments in the way, others tear down branches, and in this way the procession moves off to Jerusalem to cries of 'Hosanna!

Blessed is he who comes in the name of the Lord! Blessed is the kingdom of our father David that is coming! Hosanna in the highest!'

In his chapter 21 Matthew has the same account, but with the difference that the disciples are to find in the village an ass tied and by her a foal. Then Matthew solemnly writes:

This took place *to fulfil what was spoken by the prophet, saying,*

Tell the daughter of Zion,
Behold, your king is coming to you,
humble, and mounted on an ass,
and on a colt the foal of an ass.

Then Matthew describes how the disciples bring the ass and the foal to Jesus, how they lay their clothes on the animals and how he sat on them. There is no doubt that the first people who told this story and also Mark were thinking of the prophecy from the book of Zechariah. But it is Matthew the scribe who says this again explicitly, and for whom the fulfilment must be so literal that Jesus rides on both animals, something that is difficult to imagine.

The first line of the quotation from the prophet is not in the Zechariah text but is a summons that may come from Isaiah 62.11. Matthew introduces a much more complicated combination of different texts into the beginning of his chapter 27, where he tells about the suicide of Judas and what the high priests did with the money that he had thrown down in the temple. With it they bought the piece of land that was given the name of 'the field of blood'. Then Matthew writes:

*Then was fulfilled what had been spoken by the prophet Jeremiah,* saying, 'And they took the thirty pieces of silver, the price of him on whom a price had been set by some of the sons of Israel, and they gave them for the potter's field, as the Lord directed me.'

In fact the first part of this text is a free quotation of Zech.11.12f., amplified with details from Jeremiah, i.e. his purchasing of a field (32.6f.) and his symbolic action near the Gate of the Potsherds (19.1f.).

*John: The Messiah about whom Moses wrote*

The Fourth Evangelist twice interrupts the profound prologue to his work to say emphatically that John the Baptist was sent only to bear witness to Jesus. This is also the subject of the narrative that follows the prologue. The Baptist bears his witness to those who had been sent by 'the Jews'. Then he sees Jesus and recognizes in him the lamb of God and the son of God. Subsequently he refers his disciples to Jesus. They relate their discovery to one another: 'We have found the Messiah', and also: 'We have found him of whom *Moses in the law and also the prophets wrote*, Jesus of Nazareth, the son of Joseph.' Finally Nathanael says to Jesus himself: 'Rabbi, you are the Son of God, the king of Israel!'

In chapter 5, towards the end of his first long discourse to 'the Jews', Jesus says: 'You search the scriptures, because you think that in them you have eternal life; and it is they that bear witness to me.' And at the end: 'If you believed Moses, you would believe me, *for he wrote of me.*'

But John uses the formula about the fulfilment of the scriptures only when in chapter 12 he has completed his account of Jesus' public ministry. He then writes:

> Though he had done so many signs before them, yet they did not believe in him; *it was that the word spoken by the prophet Isaiah might be fulfilled*:

> Lord, who has believed our report,
> and to whom has the arm of the Lord been revealed?
> Therefore they could not believe.
> For Isaiah again said,
> He has blinded their eyes and hardened their heart,
> lest they should see with their eyes and perceive with their heart,
> and turn for me to heal them.
> Isaiah said this because he saw his glory and spoke of him.

John, too, changes this text from Isaiah 6 in which the prophet describes his call, but he does not do so in the same way as Matthew. In Isaiah it is the prophet who has the task of making the heart of his people fat, unfeeling, its ears deaf and its eyes blind, as a result of his proclamation. John changes this by writing (he leaves out the ears) that he has blinded their eyes and has hardened their heart. In the last line the 'I' certainly refers to God.

Is this then also the one who causes the blinding of the Jews? So what is it that 'the Jews' *could* not believe?

Anyone who has meditated on the Gospel of John often will have difficulty here: in all kinds of ways the evangelist says that God loved his world and his people and will give them his 'salvation'. Hence there are those who suggest that John uses 'he' to refer to the devil; in other places he calls the devil the arch-deceiver, and also the one who had implanted his evil plan in Judas.

In chapter 13 John describes what Jesus did when he was going to have a meal with his closest disciples for the last time. He got up and washed their feet, a task which might be performed only by a slave in the society of the time. Afterwards he explained to them that those who addressed him as their Lord had to serve one another in this way, because 'a servant is not greater than his master; nor is he who is sent greater than he who sent him. If you know these things, blessed are you if you do them. I am not speaking of you all; I know whom I have chosen; it is *that the scripture may be fulfilled.* "He who ate my bread has lifted his heel against me." I tell you this now, before it takes place, that when it does take place you may believe that I am he.'

Jesus quotes a line from Psalm 41 in which the person who prays, a sick person, complains that those around him have now become his enemies, indeed 'even my bosom friend in whom I trusted, who ate of my bread, has lifted his heel against me'; as we might put it: 'rebels against me'. Thus Jesus makes it clear that he knows what will happen to him; so the disciples should not be shocked by these terrible things and should believe that he is the one in whom God reveals himself, the one who refers to himself as 'I am'.

In his second 'farewell discourse', at the end of chapter 15, Jesus speaks of the unbelief of 'the world', which in the terminology of the evangelist often coincides with the Jews who do not accept Jesus. 'If I had not done among them the works which no one else did, they would not have sin; but now they have seen and hated both me and my Father. *It is to fulfil the word that is written in their law,* "They hated me without a cause."' This short sentence occurs in two psalms, 35 and 69, in which a righteous man complains about those who have treated him unjustly. Evidently for the evangelist here the whole of Holy Scripture falls under the concept of 'law' and he speaks of it as 'their' law, i.e. the Holy Scripture of the community of Jews in which he no longer includes himself.

In the long prayer with which Jesus ends his farewell in chapter 17 he says that he has preserved those whom the Father has given him: 'I have guarded them; and none of them is lost but the son of perdition, *that the scripture might be fulfilled.*' In authentically Hebrew fashion the word son is used here to indicate a belonging, a link, deep affinity: the person of Judas was as it were bound up with this downfall; that had at any rate been stated in scripture. Therefore Jesus could not prevent Judas from being lost.

Finally, John uses the formula several times in his account of the crucifixion. The four soldiers who carried this out divided Jesus' clothes among themselves: 'So they said to one another, "Let us not tear it, but cast lots for it to see whose it shall be." *This was to fulfil the scripture*, "They parted my garments among them, and for my clothing they cast lots." So the soldiers did this.'

Mark only said that the soldiers crucified Jesus and divided his garments among them by lot. Matthew and Luke took over this sentence with slight stylistic improvements but without a reference to the verse from Psalm 22 that John here sees fulfilled so explicitly and in detail.

After the evangelist has narrated how Jesus from the cross entrusted his mother and his beloved disciple to each other he writes: 'After this Jesus, knowing that all was now finished, said (*to fulfil the scripture*), "I thirst." A bowl full of vinegar stood there; so they put a sponge full of vinegar on hyssop and held it to his mouth. When Jesus had received the vinegar, he said, "It is finished"; and he bowed his head and gave up his spirit.'

In Psalm 69, the lament of a righteous person who is undeservedly hated by his neighbours, the person praying says that people had put poison in his food, and gave him vinegar to drink when he was thirsty. This word of scripture had also to be fulfilled before Jesus could say that he had completed, fulfilled everything.

After the death of Jesus soldiers come to break the legs of the three crucified men. 'But when they came to Jesus and saw that he was already dead, they did not break his legs. But one of the soldiers pierced his side with a spear, and at once there came out blood and water. He who saw it has borne witness – his testimony is true, and he knows that he tells the truth – that you may also believe. For these things took place *that the scripture might be fulfilled*: "Not a bone of him shall be broken." *And again another scripture says*, "They shall look on him whom they have pierced."'

It is not clear whether John is thinking of the passover lamb, not a bone of which could be broken, or of Ps.34, of which the writer says that God is watching over the end of the righteous, and that no bone of his will be broken. The second scriptural statement stands in a passage of the book of Zechariah, chapter 12, in which it is not clear who is meant by those who have pierced him. It does, however, say that they raise a lament over him as those who lament over an only son, and lament over him as people lament over a firstborn.

## Questions

The four Gospels, and above all that of Matthew, have had a decisive influence on Christian thought. Until modern times people usually regarded Mark as an abbreviated version of Matthew. Therefore Mark was rarely read out in church services. Virtually all of Mark was contained in Matthew more clearly and at greater length. So Mark came to take second place. A further influence may have been that the first words of Matthew ran: 'The book of the "genesis" (origin, birth) of Jesus Christ'.

But even before the work of Matthew became authoritative throughout the churches, the Christians read the Jewish Bible as 'prophecy' of all that Jesus had done and suffered, or better, of what the God of Israel had begun with and through him. So they found an increasing number of allusions to him in the Jewish Bible, which they began to call the Old Testament.

After the Middle Ages the approach became more systematic, and so there came into being a list of the clearest prophecies of the Redeemer. The texts were used down to our time in teaching the faith. His coming was already intimated in the account of paradise. God told the serpent that the woman's seed would trample his head: that 'seed' meant Christ. After that came the promises to the patriarchs, some sayings of Moses and the pagan prophet Balaam, and also many prophetic sayings, from Nathan up to and including Daniel with his Son of Man. The expectation of Christ was also seen to be expressed in a number of 'Messianic' psalms. Hence the deep conviction of Christians that Christ was clearly prophesied in the Old Testament and thus that the Jews must have been blind and hard of heart when they continued to refuse to recognize what was so unmistakably written in their own Bible.

The historical approach to the Bible has also disturbed this age-old conviction and thus raised the question: how did the first Christians arrive at this interpretation of the Bible? They were Jews. How did it come about that so many other Jews rejected this interpretation?

# 2 The Preliminary History

## (a) 'Politics'

Jesus of Nazareth is sometimes called a genius. According to the dictionaries the term 'genius' indicates a special endowment and originality which enables a person to accomplish extraordinary achievements. It is also characteristic of a genius that such a person makes a sudden appearance, as an astonishing freak of nature. But at the same time the genius is conditioned by the environment in which he or she appears. The brilliant young Wolfgang Mozart did not develop as a painter: music was all around him.

Jesus emerged from a people which unlike others depended only on one particular religion. His people defined itself in terms of its religion: we are the people of the one God, Creator and Lord of all that exists. Only to Israel had God communicated his plans for his creation and his people, since through him Israel had been called to life to be his own people, ally, partner... That was the people in which Jesus was born: religion was all around him; everything had to do with this relationship to God. It was here, in this sphere, that his exceptional giftedness and originality appeared. Certainly he came into the world at a particular moment in the chequered history of his people. Circumstances at the time were such that his way of talking about God led to his execution. But there were also ideas which made it possible to interpret his ignominious death in a positive way and to give it universal significance.

The dominant factors in Jewish society at the time were known to the disciples of Jesus who talked about him after his death, and also to their audience. That was equally true of the writers who a generation later brought together the stories about Jesus in their 'Gospels'. Only Luke among them felt the need to give the emergence of John the Baptist and Jesus a 'historical' context. He begins his own account like this:

In the fifteenth year of the reign of Tiberius Caesar,
Pontius Pilate being the governor of Judaea,
and Herod being tetrarch of Galilee,
and his brother Philip tetrarch of the region of Ituraea and
Trachonitis,
and Lysanias tetrarch of Abilene,
in the high-priesthood of Annas and Caiaphas,
the word of God came to John the son of Zachariah in the
wilderness...

In the Old Testament important events were dated by the year
of the reign of the ruling king. That was usual in the cultural
environment of which the kingdoms of Israel and Judah were
part. There was no generally accepted way of reckoning time. So
at the beginning of the book of Jeremiah it is said that the word
of the Lord came to him, literally 'happened to him', in the
thirteenth year of King Josiah.

It is striking that Luke dates the call of John the Baptist by the
year of the emperor's rule in Rome. He also mentions the
emperor's governor in Judaea, some rulers – 'tetrarchs' – in the
northern areas of the country and finally the high priest Annas,
with whom the name Caiaphas is coupled. For the educated
Theophilus to whom Luke addresses his work, and all other
interested readers of this time, this historical context will have
been enlightening.

But a reader of our time needs some explanations. These can
only be really illuminating if they show how the many aspects of
Jewish society in the time of Jesus were the consequence of events
in preceding centuries. Hence the historical sketch which follows.
It seems useful to begin with Ezra and Nehemiah. One of the
reasons for this is that the history-writing of the Hebrew Old
Testament ends with the account of their activities. There is also
another reason: Ezra gave the faith of the Jews the form which it
was to defend at all costs during the tumultuous centuries which
followed, a faith which therefore became determinative for their
society in the first century of our era. Although it is difficult to
keep politics and religion completely separate, above all in the
history of the Jews, primarily political developments will be
outlined in the first part of this chapter and religious developments
in the second.

In 539 BC Cyrus, the first king of the Persians (spelt Kores in the Bible), conquered the capital of the Babylonian empire. In contrast to earlier semitic conquerors this ruler and his successors showed respect to subject peoples and their cultures. The Judaeans who had been deported by Nebuchadnezzar to Babylonia in 597 and 587 were allowed to return to their fatherland by Cyrus. Those who had then experienced the grim journey on foot to Babylon as twenty-year-olds were seventy-eight and sixty-eight respectively in 539, too old to make the laborious return journey home. So it was above all their children and grandchildren who returned to the land of their parents as groups in the years after 539. There in 520 they began on the rebuilding of the temple, which was completed in 515.

Many families had chosen to remain living in Babylonia, above all because they had established themselves there as craftsmen, businessmen or traders. So at this time one can already speak of what was later called by the Greek term *diaspora*, the dispersion of Jews among other peoples. From Babylon some moved to other parts of the Persian empire like Asia Minor. In the years before and after the defeat of 587 Judaeans had already emigrated to Egypt. Like the Jews in Babylonia they also spoke Aramaic there, the language which had already come into use in their fatherland alongside Hebrew, and which the Persian government also introduced elsewhere as an official means of communication for their officials and governors, 'imperial Aramaic'.

The influence of prominent Jews in what used to be Babylonia, mentioned above, is illustrated by the stories about Ezra and Nehemiah. The former was attached to the court of the Persian king as minister in charge of Jewish affairs. In the year 458 he received from Artachsasta, spelt Artaxerxes by the Greeks, the task of organizing the community in and around Jerusalem on the basis of 'the Law of the God of heaven', as the Law of Moses was called by the king. Ezra was able to collect money among the Jews in Babylonia to finance temple worship, and the king also contributed to it. Then he went with a group of Jews to Jerusalem. There he read out in the temple the Law which was also recognized by the king, the Torah, after which the community committed itself to observe it in the future. In so doing Ezra laid the foundation for the whole of the further history of Judaism, and he was rightly called 'the Father' of Judaism. One of his measures was strictly to forbid the Jews to marry women from outside their community, even those who had belonged to the former kingdom of Israel. Men who were married to such women were obliged to separate from them and their children. The aim was to make the community as pure as possible.

Nehemiah held the post of chief 'cup-bearer' at the Persian court. In 445 he was commissioned by the king to begin to rebuild the walls of Jerusalem and to go to Jehud, Judah, as governor of that province. Though with a good deal of difficulty, after some years he enabled the Jewish community to live its own life without hindrance, with the temple at its centre. It was thus a kind of theocracy, a nation governed by divine laws and priestly leadership. This rule was of course in the interest of the Persian kings, who were glad to see a subject population in a territory on the route to Egypt with a temple city around them, which at the same time became an economic centre for the wider surroundings. Jerusalem, rebuilt and functioning again, also had a large place in the hearts of Jews all over the Diaspora.

Little is known about the further fate of Jewish society under Persian rule. But a good deal happened in the 'spiritual' sphere. However, we shall be discussing that later. The political world of which Judah was a part was decisively changed when in 331 Alexander the Great had defeated the army of the last king of the Persians, having previously conquered Egypt. After his campaigns in the East, extending as far as India, Alexander suddenly died in Babylon in 323 BC at the age of thirty-three. His generals then began to fight for possession of his empire. Ptolemy laid claim to the kingdom of Egypt, with its new capital Alexandria which had already been founded by Alexander. Seleucus was able to seize Syria and Mesopotamia. He founded a capital close to the Mediterranean coast, and it was called Antioch after his eldest son Antiochus.

The line of communication between the two Hellenistic kingdoms ran through the strip of land between the Mediterranean and the Arabian wilderness, which the Greeks had long called Palestine: their seafarers named this unknown land after the coastal inhabitants that they first encountered, and these were the Philistines whom we know from the Bible. Precisely because it was a line of communication, the country remained a bone of contention between the successors of the generals I have mentioned, the Ptolemies in the south and the Seleucids in the north. At first the Ptolemies had a good deal of influence, but eventually, in 200, the Seleucids gained the upper hand.

Because of all this violence and war a large number of Jews had already left Judaea to seek a calmer abode in the many newly built cities of Alexander's empire; these were in search of inhabitants and sometimes offered favourable terms for settlement. So the Diaspora spread even wider, and did so with Jews who began to speak Greek. Here we come to a development which was of decisive influence on the environment of Jesus and the movement that he set in motion after his death.

### Hellenism

This development related first of all to the influence of the Greek language on the religious life of the Jews. Already under the first Ptolemies many of those in the densely populated Jewish districts of Alexandria could no longer follow the readings from the Torah and the other holy books in the synagogues: Hebrew was incomprehensible to them. This difficulty had already arisen in areas in which Aramaic had become the main language of the Jews. There people often resorted to interpreters, Jews who could translate the passage that was read out into Aramaic. They did this in a quite extemporary fashion, since it was not customary and perhaps not even permissible to write such a translation down. That is what will have happened at first in the synagogues of Alexandria. But there the need for a written Greek translation finally became too strong. So the Torah, the most important book, was translated. The prophets and the writings followed later.

It was very difficult to get the translation established. It was not really thought possible to translate the Torah, written in the language of God himself, into a pagan language like Greek! Perhaps it was wrong to communicate all these intimacies between the true God and his people to those who were uncircumcised. Someone then put into circulation the story that the great Ptolemy had sent a delegation to Jerusalem to ask the high priest for a copy of the Torah and skilled translators. So seventy-two scholars arrived at Alexandria, six from each tribe of Israel, and in a miraculous way they completed the translation of the Torah in precisely seventy-two days. This story was later made even more miraculous by the addition of the detail that each of these seventy-two people worked in a separate room; when their texts came to be compared it emerged that each matched the other word for word. This made it clear that the Greek translation was inspired by the Spirit of God and could be used as holy scripture. In this way it found its way into the synagogues of the Greek-speaking diaspora. On the basis of this popular story the Greek translation was called that of the seventy, Septuagint; in biblical commentaries it is often denoted, with Roman numerals, as LXX.

An increasing number of Jews also began to speak and to write Greek in Palestine: this language was indispensable both for major businessmen and for those with cultural interests. This soon led to a crisis: a serious division arose in the Jewish community. A powerful group of intelligent and influential Jews felt that Judaism had to adapt itself to the world-conquering culture of Hellenism. If the Jews wanted to hold their place in this modern world, they had to give up everything that distinguished them from other people like the weekly day of rest (as a result of which they were regarded as lazy), circumcision (a barbarous mutilation) and abstention from certain foods (a form of primitive superstition).

Over against these 'progressives' with their interest in becoming truly cosmopolitan stood a group of 'traditionalists', convinced of the divine origin of these ancient customs, and of their essential link with Israel's election as the true people of the one and only God. This opposition ended up in armed conflict when the 'progressives' secured the support of a Hellenistic prince.

As I have already said, in the year 200 Palestine came under the rule of Seleucids from the north, as the result of a successful expedition by Antiochus III the Great. The name of his son Antiochus IV (175-164) is associated with a decisive crisis in the Jewish community. Leading 'progressives', including the high priests Jason and Menelaus, did all that they could to make those Jews who were loyal to the law give up their ancestral customs and take part in the 'contemporary' forms of worship. In 167 BC this led to the attempt to erect an altar to Zeus Olympius in the temple of Jerusalem on the site of the old altar of burnt offering: the local God of Israel was incorporated into this supreme and universal deity! Elsewhere too in Jewish territory places for sacrifice were constructed and people were forced to take part in the new ceremonies. The supreme authority behind these reforms was, however, king Antiochus. Hence the pious Jews began to see this ruler as the Satanic opponent of God and his believing people, a kind of antichrist, whereas in fact the high priest Menelaus was the great evildoer.

A certain Mattathias, head of a priestly family in the city of Modein to the north-west of Jerusalem, lost control when he saw a Jew sacrificing on a pagan altar. He killed the man, and also the imperial official who had asked him to perform the sacrifice. Thereupon Mattathias and his five sons fled into the wilderness of Judah to begin a guerrilla campaign against the Syrian rulers, a movement which was soon joined by many of those faithful to the law, the 'pious'.

After Mattathias' death, in 166, his third son Judas took over the leadership of the opposition. He was given the name Maccabaeus. In 164 he succeeded in removing the pagan altar from the temple and precisely three years after the desecration of the altar of burnt offering in reconsecrating the temple. This event was from then on to be commemorated in the feast of the 'consecration of the temple', in Hebrew Hanukkah, which is celebrated annually.

But Judas, who died in the year 160, and his youngest brother Jonathan, who took over the leadership, still had to fight a great many fights and engage in diplomacy (also on the international level: relations with Sparta, Rome, Egypt) before Jonathan could be installed as high priest. He, too, died a violent death, in 143: at a meeting with the Syrians he was taken prisoner and killed. The second of the five brothers, Simon, became head of the movement and a year later managed to gain exemption from taxation by the Syrians. In so doing he succeeded for the first time since the exile in forming the Jews into an independent nation. For almost eighty years they were to be under descendants of the Maccabees, who are usually called 'Hasmonaeans' after their ancestor, 'Hasmon'. Already with Jonathan and Simon one can see a development which would repeat itself in later history: people motivated by religion forget their original ideals when they start to use means of power to realize their aims. The Hasmonaeans began increasingly to behave like Hellenistic princes, for example by waging their wars with mercenary soldiers, hired from other countries, who were therefore 'Gentiles' in the eyes of the Jews. A few events from the turbulent times of these princes need to be mentioned, since they affected Jewish society in the first century.

Those who soon parted company with the priest-princes were

the 'pious', the group from which the Maccabees had gained their first followers and who had fought at the risk of their lives to maintain Jewish customs and have freedom to live in accordance with the Torah. They were soon referred to as Pharisees, a name which is said to mean 'separated ones'. But it can also be connected with a term which means 'explain, expound'. At all events, these Jews wanted to live their life according to the Law and also persuade other Jews to do so through their example and their teaching. They often protested against the 'pagan' politics of their rulers.

In the first period of the Hasmonaeans we also already hear of the Sadducees, a group of priests, of course also concerned to fulfil the Torah. In their case, however, this was above all in connection with temple worship and the legislation that was bound up with it. They belonged among the better-off, whereas the Pharisees had closer links with the lower classes.

Finally another group of pious must be mentioned, the Essenes. They wanted to go even further than the Pharisees in living according to the Law. Their name is derived from an Aramaic word that means 'holy'. Their nucleus was formed by a group of priests who left Jerusalem because they felt that the sanctuary had become impure. They tried to live outside Jerusalem in a group which set out to fulfil as many as possible of the demands for purity which were laid upon priests. They therefore avoided contact with other Jews as much as possible. That will be the reason why they are not mentioned anywhere in the New Testament.

The Hasmonaean conquests also affected the situation of the rest of Jewish society in the time of Jesus. With the help of their mercenaries they compelled the inhabitants of the territories they had subjected to take part in Jewish worship, and therefore to have their males circumcised and to live in accordance with the Torah. Hyrcanus I did that with the Edomites, the people which in 587 had helped the Babylonians in the destruction of Jerusalem and which therefore, as many texts of the Bible indicate, were so intensely hated by the Jews. They had to withdraw from the part of their country that lay to the east of the valley of the Dead Sea. They were forced out of it by the Nabataeans, an Arabian people that dominated the caravan routes and was very powerful in the time of Jesus: the ruins of their capital Petra are still an eloquent testimony to this. The western part of what used to be Edom bordered on the south of Judaea, and in Greek was called Idumaea. Around 120 Hyrcanus conquered that country and imposed Jewish religion on the Idumaeans.

In the year 104 his successor Aristobulus did the same thing to the pagan population of Galilee which he had conquered. It was probably the Pharisees who instructed the people there in their new religion and perhaps made certain that Jews from Judaea faithful to the Law should settle there. So Galilee could become the land of Jesus and his first disciples and later the heart of resistance to the Roman rulers.

It is worth reflecting that the Hasmonaean priest-kings were really doing with their forcible Judaizing the same thing that had been attempted under the Hellenistic ruler Antiochus IV: imposing a new religion on a people with violence. In their zeal to expand the Jewish nation, the Hasmonaeans plundered or devastated a great many cities which had become centres of Hellenistic culture. But they themselves lived in the style of Greek princes.

Towards the end of his long reign the bellicose Alexander Jannaeus (103-76) had expanded the Jewish nation so far that at that period its area was four times as great as under his grandfather Simon. But on several occasions Jannaeus had to use his mercenary troops to put down rebellions of his own people. Tensions between the different classes were a factor here. On the one side were the members of the old priestly nobility, and on the other the ordinary people, under the influence and leadership of the Pharisees. Between the right wing and the left wing stood the middle classes, made up of the Sadducees and the rich merchants. When Jannaeus as high priest once wanted to make a sacrifice on the Feast of Tabernacles he was pelted with the lemons which those taking part in the feast had to bring, and there was a continuous barrage of abuse. He sent in his troops against the crowds, and more than six thousand Jews perished. He treated the leaders of the people, whom he captured after a campaign, very cruelly. According to the Jewish writer Flavius Josephus he had these eight hundred men crucified in Jerusalem and their women and children killed before their eyes. He watched the spectacle from the roof of his palace, where he was having a banquet in the midst of his harem. This is the first instance in history of a Jewish ruler punishing his fellow countrymen with crucifixion.

In the year 64, at the season of the Passover, there were again violent fights around Jerusalem, this time between two sons of

24

Jannaeus. One of them had involved the wily Antipater, an Idumaean, and he had seen an opportunity of getting an army of Nabataeans to support his candidate. During this unbelievably complicated situation in the siege of the capital news came that the Roman ruler Pompey had arrived in Damascus with a commission from the senate to organize the former empire of the Seleucids as a Roman province. Each of the warring parties resolved to go to Damascus to win over the Romans. There appeared before him in due humility not only the two brothers, each with his following, but also a third party, a delegation of the people; it was tired of the Hasmonaeans, did not want a king any longer and asked the Romans to restore the old situation as it had been under the Persians and even under Alexander the Great, namely a community of the people led by the priests.

Invited by the Jews to bring peace to their land, Pompey achieved this under the rule of Rome, making the country part of the province of Syria. That meant that from then on no one could emerge as a political leader without the approval of the government in Rome and without taking responsibility for his actions. This can be illustrated well from the person of Herod the Great. He is the first king whom the reader of the New Testament encounters when he or she begins to read the New Testament from the beginning and after the genealogy in Matthew comes across the story of his birth in Bethlehem 'during the reign of King Herod'.

### Herod the Great

Herod's father was the influential Idumeaean Antipater, and his mother was a Nabataean woman. Antipater was nominated a Roman citizen and governor of Palestine by Julius Caesar in 47. This gave his son Herod a function. When in the year 40 the Parthians, arch-enemies of Rome, invaded Palestine, Herod escaped to Rome and there on the Capitol was nominated king of Palestine. With the help of Roman troops he conquered Judaea, and after his troops had been further reinforced, he was finally able to take possession of Jerusalem after an enormous blood bath. That was in 37 BC.

It took some years for him to strengthen his position, extend and secure his territories and remove all probable or possible pretenders to the throne. As a 'friend and ally' of the emperor, who in 27 had taken the name Augustus (the holy, the exalted one), Herod, a true Hellenistic prince, began to equip many cities within Palestine and outside it with resplendent buildings, including temples which he dedicated to Augustus, his divinized patron in Rome. He changed the appearance of Jerusalem. Real Hellenistic buildings arose like a theatre, an amphitheatre and a hippodrome. Games were held every four years in honour of Augustus, which involved not only athletes and gladiators but also wild beasts. Around 24 he built an impressive royal palace the three courtyards of which were famous far and wide, both for their impregnable strength and for their lavish construction. Many Jews were offended at all this pagan splendour, at the killing of animals and even human beings to delight the public. But the greatest scandal was that the house of God, the temple, became increasingly insignificant alongside all these new buildings.

It is important for us to note what Herod began in the year 19. Although he himself was not a real Jew, he took the opportunity to convince the people of his good intentions. In a democratic way he laid plans ro replace the modest sanctuary from the years after the return from Babylon with a new one which would be like Solomon's temple in pattern, but would surpass it in magnitude and splendour. In the rebuilding he wanted to respect all sacred regulations and laws. Ten thousand workers cut the stones for it, and thousands of priests were trained in building work at his expense. That was for the central building, comprising the Porch, the Holy Place, and the Holy of Holies, and also the court in front of it, on which stood the great altar of burnt offering. This central sanctuary, which only priests might enter, was to be demolished stone by stone, each old stone being replaced with a new one which matched it precisely. In this way worship would not be interrupted for a single day. This rebuilding took eighteen months.

Moreover, the hilltop on which the temple stood was too small for building large forecourts around the temple. So Herod undertook the gigantic task of enlarging this hilltop with the help of subterranean vaults and earthworks, to produce the enormous temple area that is still astonishing, with its circumference of more than 1400 metres. This was bounded by wide colonnades in which a good deal of marble and gold was used, as it was in the central building. Although it still took years to complete subsidiary sections, the powerful complex evoked the wonder of visitors, like the disciples who came with Jesus to Jerusalem and looked down from the Mount of Olives: 'Master, what stones and what buildings!'

In the last years of his life Herod thought that all kinds of intrigues were going on among his many sons: he had ten wives. Moreover, in those years he was afraid of losing the favour of the emperor Augustus because he had gone beyond his authority as a king allied to Rome by beginning a war with the Nabataeans without informing the emperor. In the year 12 he asked permission from the emperor to kill two of his sons. This favour was at first refused, but finally he was allowed to do so on condition that the action took place outside Judaea. In the year 7 both sons were assassinated in Samaria, the city in which he had married Mariamne, their mother, whom he also had murdered later.

After many intrigues Antipater travelled to Rome to be confirmed there by the emperor as successor to Herod. Before he returned Herod sent a request to the emperor to be allowed to kill this Antipater. Then he fell seriously ill. The rumour circulated among the people that he had died, whereupon some Pharisees pulled down the golden eagle which Herod had had set up in the temple. That was a symbol of his monarchy, customary in the East but a scandal to pious Jews. But Herod was not yet dead, and he had the culprits burnt alive. When the warm springs on the north-eastern shore of the Dead Sea gave him no relief and he returned to Jericho even sicker, he gave orders for a number of prominent Jews to be arrested and then killed after his death, so that there would really be mourning in the land. Then he was given imperial permission to murder Antipater. This son too was killed at his father's request, five days before Herod's own death.

In his last, third, testament Herod had divided his territory among three of his sons whom he had still left alive. Archelaus was to get Judaea with Samaria and Idumaea. Galilee and Peraea were destined for Antipas, and Philip was to reign over the areas to the north and north-east of the Sea of Galilee. But all that had to be confirmed by the emperor, Augustus. After the incredibly ostentatious burial of his father, Archelaus travelled to Rome. Antipas also went there, because the third testament was more unfavourable to him than the second; he wanted to explain to the emperor that his father was by then already mentally disturbed. Other members of the family also undertook the long journey. Finally, a delegation of fifty went to the emperor to argue for annexation by the province of Syria. These members of the leading families got the support of more than eight thousand Jews living in Rome.

Meanwhile, such violent disturbances broke out in Jerusalem that the legate of Syria, Quinctilius Varus, had to advance with some legions in order to put down these revolts in Judaea. But shortly after his return to Syria he had to go back to Judaea with an even greater army because troubles had broken out again in Peraea and above all Galilee. It seemed that the death of the tyrant had enthused many people with a kind of sense of freedom. In Judaea there was a sturdy shepherd who set himself up as king. In Peraea, in Transjordan, a certain Simon gained a large following and began by setting Herod's palace in Jericho on fire. In Galilee there was Judas, the son of an upstart who was killed by Herod. Soldiers were attacked all over the country and collaborators were killed. According to Flavius Josephus during his action Varus had about 2000 rebels crucified.

The emperor Augustus evidently had his reasons for respecting the last testament of Herod. Archelaus got the territory that was meant for him but without the title of king; he was provisionally to rule over it as 'ethnarch', people's ruler. Antipas was given Galilee and Peraea with the title 'tetrarch', ruler of four, and Philip got most of the territory in the north-east with the same title.

Herod Antipas ruled from 4 BC to AD 39, when he was banished in disgrace to Gaul. This ruler occurs several times in the Gospel accounts, which refer to him as Herod. One of the stories can be compared with what is related by a contemporary of the evangelists, Flavius Josephus, who has already been mentioned. It seems useful to pause to look at this Jewish historian. His works used to be read zealously by Christians. They are almost the only source of what we know of the turbulent history of the Jews from the time of the Maccabees to the destruction of Jerusalem by the Romans in the year 70, a drama in which Josephus was intimately involved.

## Flavius Josephus

According to his autobiography, which he published around the year 100 in Rome, Josephus (his complete Hebrew name was Joseph ben Mattiyahu ha-Kohen) was born in Jerusalem in the first year of the emperor Caligula, which according to our chronology is the end of 37 or the beginning of 38, i.e. not long after Stephen was stoned in that city. His father came from a priestly family and his mother was related to the Hasmonaeans. The young man from this distinguished Jewish family seems to have been highly gifted. At the age of sixteen he was fully conversant with the Jewish religion and also how it was practised by various groups: Sadducees, Pharisees and Essenes. None of the 'philosophies', as he sometimes called them for the benefit of his non-Jewish readers, satisfied him. So he sought out a certain Bannus as a teacher in the religious life. Bannus led an ascetic life in the wilderness; he clothed and fed himself exclusively with what nature produced and bathed more than once each day in cold water, in order to remain as 'pure' as possible. Josephus spent three years learning from him and then returned to Jerusalem. There he joined the Pharisees.

He was twenty-six when he went on a journey to the imperial court at Rome to plead before the emperor Nero for the release of some priest friends who had been arrested by the governor Festus and sent to Rome. On this journey in the winter of 63/64 he had the same misfortune as that which according to the account in the book of Acts had befallen Paul some years earlier: his ship was wrecked and the survivors had to spend the whole night on the sea. The next day they were picked up by a boat from Cyrene and were able to land at the harbour of Puteoli. A Jewish actor who had a good reputation in court circles introduced Josephus to Poppaea, the wife of the emperor Nero, and in this way he secured the release of the prisoners.

In the spring of 66 he returned to his fatherland. Disturbances there had meanwhile increased and they led to an organized revolt against the Romans. This ended in the capture and devastation of Jerusalem by the Romans in the year 70. Josephus was soon involved in the rebellion because the Jewish authorities in Jerusalem sent him to Galilee to organize the revolt against Rome there. Having vainly sought to defend the city of Jotapata, about six miles north of Nazareth, against the Romans, in 67 he was taken prisoner by them. As a consecrated priest and an expert in the sacred scriptures of the Jews he then prophesied to the Roman general Vespasian, of the family of the Flavians, that Vespasian would be emperor in Rome. Thereupon Vespasian spared his life and Josephus was held prisoner until, two years later, his prophecy came true. That brought him freedom and at the same time great respect, both from the new emperor, who took him to Egypt when homage was paid to him there, and from his son Titus. The grateful freeman then adopted the family name of Flavius.

During the siege of Jerusalem Josephus offered his services as a negotiator and tried to persuade the populace to surrender, a task which caused him many difficulties with both sides, the besieged and the Roman fighters. After Jerusalem had been captured he went with Titus to Rome. There in the former abode of the new emperor he was able to devote himself without financial anxiety to historical studies and the writing of books. He saw there a new Rome rising on the ruins of the city which under Nero had been extensively burned and further afflicted by the civil war after his death. These new buildings included the Colosseum, the glittering forums of Vespasian and Titus, and the Temple of Peace, witnesses to Rome's indomitable vitality. Sometimes he had trouble with Jews who intrigued against him; they regarded him as a traitor to the national cause. But Josephus could convincingly refute all criticisms and thus retain the favour of the emperor, including that of Titus' brother and successor Domitian (81-96), who really had an abhorrence of scholars and philosophers.

Josephus' first publication covered the history of 'The Jewish War', a work in eight 'books', which is so valuable because he himself was involved in the war. He wrote the work in Aramaic, his mother tongue, clearly with the aim of convincing the Jews in the east, Mesopotamia and further afield, who also spoke Aramaic, of the impossibility of ever rebelling successfully against the Romans. A Greek version of the work appeared between 74 and 79.

Josephus published his greatest work towards the end of the century. It was about *Jewish Antiquities*, as the Greek title (*Archeologia joudaika*) is usually rendered, and was divided into twenty books, evidently on the model of a similar work which described the history of Rome from its origin in the world of the gods. In the first ten books Josephus relates the biblical history from the creation to the end of the exile, and incorporates many Jewish narratives and explanations into it. In the second ten books he goes from Cyrus to the year 66, the beginning of the Jewish war. Here he drew on works by earlier historians.

In this gigantic undertaking Josephus was guided and encouraged by his learned friend and patron Epaphroditus, a well-known literary figure, who had built up a library of 30,000 books. In it Josephus found, for example, the works of Nicolaus of Damascus.

This highly gifted Jew had long been the friend and counsellor of Herod the Great. He had made many journeys in Herod's service, as negotiator or mediator. After Herod's death in 4 BC he had settled in Rome and there among other things wrote a history of the world from the beginning up to and including the time which he himself had lived through. That work has been lost, apart from those parts of it which Josephus took over.

Josephus also dedicated to Epaphroditus the last of his works known to us, entitled *Against Apion*. This writer had contributed a good deal to the distortions, suspicions and blasphemies which were going the rounds in non-Jewish circles. Josephus describes and refutes all this and contrasts with it both the ancient origin and above all the spiritual and moral greatness of the Jewish religion. An opponent of Jewish nationalism, Josephus remained devoted heart and soul to the religion of his forefathers.

There is another remarkable thing to note. Josephus knows all about the many trends and groupings in the Palestine of his day. But neither in the *Jewish War* nor in the *Jewish Antiquities* does he mention the movement which was set in motion by Jesus of Nazareth and which was already expanding when as a young man he went in search of the heart of the religion in which he had grown up. There had long been Jewish 'Christians' in Rome when the twenty-six-year-old Josephus arrived there in 64. According to the Roman historian Tacitus they were denounced by the emperor Nero as the instigators of the fire which in that year reduced part of the city to ashes. Josephus says nothing about this fire nor about these 'Christians'.

It is worth our noting that if the Christian movement was already known to Josephus, it was not important enough for him to record. Its supporters saw the event of Jesus as something of world-shaking significance: God had begun to make an end of this world by beginning a new and definitive one in Jesus, over which he alone would rule. According to Mark, on the death of Jesus darkness fell over all the land for three hours in the middle of the day. At that time the curtain in the temple was split from top to bottom. In Matthew there is also an earthquake in which the rocks split open. People in Jerusalem were of course unaware of all this, for these phenomena are good biblical ways of expressing belief in the earth-shaking significance of Jesus' death.

Precisely because Josephus does not describe the Christian movement anywhere, although he twice refers to Jesus in passing, his work is of inestimable value for us. He describes the extremely tense political situation during the years in which Jesus proclaimed his message after his baptism in the Jordan and was finally crucified in Jerusalem. And he does so as 'objectively' as possible, as a historian. Of course he also had his particular perspectives and aims. But even so, he is generally regarded as one of the great historians of this period.

## Herod Antipas and John the Baptist

In Book 18 of the *Jewish Antiquities* Josephus describes the rule of Herod's son Antipas, tetrarch of Galilee and Peraea. There he relates that this prince had long been married to a Nabataean woman, a daughter of King Aretas. When he had to go to Rome again, on the way he stayed with a half-brother and there suddenly fell violently in love with his wife Herodias. He was so infatuated that he began to talk about a wedding. She agreed and promised to go to him as soon as he came back from Rome. Her condition was that he should put aside the daughter of Aretas. When that was agreed, he sailed for Rome. After his return his own wife, who had got wind of the affair, asked for an escort to go to the fortress of Machaerus, on the frontier between the territories of her husband and her father. She had already arranged everything: from Machaerus she went to her father Aretas in his capital, Petra. Thereupon Aretas embarked on a war against Herod, whose army was defeated by the Nabataeans. Herod sent to the emperor Tiberius a report on this which was very favourable to himself. Tiberius then told his general in Syria either to capture Aretas alive or else send his head, Then Josephus continues:

> But to some of the Jews the destruction of Herod's army seemed to be divine vengeance, and certainly a just vengeance, for his treatment of John, surnamed the Baptist. For Herod had put him to death, though he was a good man and had exhorted the Jews to lead righteous lives, to practise justice towards their fellows and piety towards God, and so doing to join in baptism. In his view this was a necessary preliminary if baptism was to be acceptable to God. They must not employ it to gain pardon for whatever sins they committed, but as a consecration of the body implying that the soul was already thoroughly cleansed by right behaviour. When others too joined the crowds about him, because they were aroused to the highest degree by his

sermons, Herod became alarmed. Eloquence that had so great an effect on mankind might lead to some form of sedition, for it looked as if they would be guided by John in everything they did. Herod decided therefore that it would be much better to strike first and be rid of him before his work led to an uprising, than to wait for an upheaval, get involved in a difficult situation and see his mistake. Therefore John, because of Herod's suspicions, was brought in chains to Machaerus, the stronghold that we have previously mentioned, and there put to death.

This narrative differs somewhat from what Mark 6 suggests was related in the circles of Jesus' disciples about the arrest of John the Baptist and his death. According to this version he was taken prisoner by Herod beause he had denounced Herod's marriage to Herodias: she was his brother's wife. There follows the piquant but cruel scene on Herod's birthday: the dance of Herodias' daughter who at the instigation of her mother asks as a reward the head of John the Baptist on a platter. It is also striking in Josephus' account that he does not connect the baptism of John with his preaching of an imminent judgment on Israel. Perhaps he (or the historian whom he consulted) knew nothing of this connection and therefore described John as a man who encouraged the Jews to live a virtuous life.

The most important supplement by Josephus to the Gospel narrative is his description of Herod's panic fear of a man motivated by religion who attracted the masses to him and might have become a popular leader. Even to allow an activity which only marginally could be the instigation for a revolt endangered his position as a 'manager' appointed by Rome.

## Judaea under Roman government

Herod's son Archelaus had been made ruler of Judaea with Samaria and Idumaea as an 'ethnarch'. He was to receive the title king when he was up to it. But his rule was a failure. As a result of his capricious replacement of high priests and his marriage to the widow of a half brother he intensified the hatred that the upper classes had for him. So in the year 6 another delegation went from their circles to Rome. The emperor summoned Archelaus to answer to him, confiscated his possessions and banished him to Vienne in the Rhone valley. After Herod's death the delegation of ten years earlier had asked for annexation by the province of

Syria; the new one got even more: Augustus made the country a kind of mandated territory directly under him which was to be ruled by a procurator, rather like a governor or better still an administrator. For the produce of this imperial territory went into the emperor's own treasury.

So there was a new division of the land into taxation districts. Each inhabitant had to go to the centre in his district to register his possessions: houses, land and other sources of income. This measure, a kind of census, was carried out under the supervision of Quirinius, who governed the province of Syria as a legate.

Of course this reorganization of taxation provoked a good deal of resistance from the people and the 'party' of the Pharisees. But there was no point in opposing the soldiers of Quirinius. There was, however, a violent revolt in Galilee. The people there, governed by Herod Antipas, were not directly affected by the imperial measure. But their anti-Roman feelings mounted. A certain Judas, a scribe, allied himself with the Pharisee Zadok. They raised a large force of young men to begin to sabotage the census in Judaea.

Josephus describes this movement of Judas the Galilaean as 'a fourth philosophy' alongside the three others, the Pharisees, Sadducees and Essenes. This fourth philosophy rejected the view of many Pharisees that Jews had to obey the Roman authorities if their orders did not clash with essential matters of Jewish belief. No, said Judas and his followers, Jews may not in any way obey an earthly ruler, because God alone is their ruler, and only to him do they owe obedience. This fierce anti-Roman movement found a good deal of sympathy with those Jews in Galilee who were faithful to the Law. They laid the foundation for the organized opposition of the 'Zealots' in subsequent years. It is understandable that the word 'Galilean' took on an anti-Roman connotation in the higher and conservative circles of Judaea.

There a 'procurator' remained only three years in office, then to give place to another. This was the policy of the emperor Augustus. After his death in 14 he was succeeded by Tiberius (14-37). Tiberius gave such senior officials the opportunity of staying at their posts longer. According to Josephus he explained the advantage of the new policy with the following story. A man lay by the road with open wounds. A passer-by wanted to drive away the flies that clustered round him. 'Do not do that,' said the man, 'for these flies have already had their portion of blood and are already somewhat lazy. If you drive them off, new ones will come which will start sucking more energetically, and then I shall be in a worse state than before.' Procurators had to see that the taxes went to Rome and therefore they themselves could also become rich. Thus according to the cynical story told by the emperor they were professional exploiters.

The first procurator appointed by Tiberius, Valerius Gratus, held this office from 15 to 26. He experimented with high priests until in the year 18 he found someone who seemed to him to be trustworthy, intelligent and influential, the ideal man to look after Roman interests as far as possible in that delicate position. The man was called Caiaphas and was a son-in-law of Annas, who had been deposed by Gratus shortly after his arrival. But Annas had become the most powerful man in the Sanhedrin and was to remain so during his son-in-law's rule.

Gratus was replaced in 26 by Pontius Pilate, who remained procurator until 36 and all those years had Caiaphas as high priest. Shortly after his arrival Pilate wanted to make clear to the Jewish population that Rome was master in their country. One night he had his soldiers march into Jerusalem with standards, banners on which the bust of the emperor was depicted. That caused great consternation among the inhabitants the following morning. According to the Jewish Law no image could be brought into the holy city. A large number of people went to Pilate's residence in Caesarea and asked him urgently to have the standards removed from the city. When he refused, they began to lie flat on the ground around his residence and stayed there for five days and nights. On the sixth day Pilate went to his judgment seat in the wide stadium and the crowd had to follow him there. There he gave his armed soldiers orders to surround them. Enclosed by the triple ring of soldiers the Jews were first petrified with terror. Pilate spoke, threatening that he would kill them if they did not accept the images of the emperor, and gave his soldiers orders to draw their swords. Thereupon the Jews as though by agreement all fell down on the ground and offered their necks, crying out that they would rather die than transgress the laws of their forefathers. Pilate was so deeply impressed by this ardent faith that he gave orders for the banners to be removed from the capital.

Some time later Pilate organized the construction of an aqueduct, a watercourse above ground, to bring water from a spring in the southern hill country to Jerusalem. This was to the advantage of the city. But the procurator had difficulties when he wanted to finance the enormous construction (more than twelve miles long!) from the temple treasury. A loudly protesting mass of people gathered round his judgment seat when he was back in the capital: the temple treasure was holy! Pilate had reckoned on this protest and spread a number of soldiers in civilian dress among the people with orders not to use their swords, but clubs. At a given sign they began to hit the Jews. Many lost their lives from the blows, and others died because they were trampled under foot by those who fled. That put an end to the protests.

Josephus does not say whether Pilate had made an agreement with Caiaphas over the aqueduct. But he does note elsewhere that the sacred garments in which the high priest had to be clothed at great festivals were kept in the citadel of Antonia, at the corner of the temple plain, i.e. under the superivison of the Roman garrison. The power of Rome reached that far.

## (b) 'Spirituality'

The experience of the Jews during the period that I have described had considerable influence on their thought about God and his guidance in the rule of his people. New insights and expectations developed. So in these centuries there came into being the spiritual framework with which the disciples of Jesus were familiar and which gave them opportunities for expressing their experiences, making it possible for them to discuss these experiences among themselves and with other Jews. We can only trace these developments in Jewish writings from this period. There are many of them: some are preserved in the Hebrew Bible, others in the Greek Bible, and yet others outside these collections. All I can do here is give a sketch of three themes from them, which are important for the subject of this book.

To begin with, I must say something about divine wisdom, imagined as a person. She appears first in the biblical book of Proverbs. This comes under the genre of 'wisdom literature'. One form of that consisted in the short and powerful formulation of all kinds of rules which a person had to observe in order to be able to live a happy life with his fellow men. This genre had long been practised in Egypt and Mesopotamia, when Israel emerged as a kingdom. There, too, literate people began to occupy themselves with wisdom. This literature was therefore an international phenomenon and expressed the experiences of people over the course of centuries, their 'wisdom'.

The biblical book of Proverbs contains two collections of two-line sayings, in total amounting to more than five hundred. Beyond question they come from the time of the kings. When God is mentioned in them – and that sometimes happens, since in these ancient cultures everyone had a deity, in Proverbs this is of course Yahweh, the God of Israel. But nowhere in the book is there any allusion to the exodus, the covenant, the election of David and of Jerusalem/Zion. So in one sense this is a generally human view of life. The two collections mentioned (not texts to read straight through!), together with some additions in a rather different style, form the second and largest part of the book (10-31). Later, probably in the Persian period, Jewish wise men added the first part as a kind of introduction (1-9). Here a teacher constantly addresses 'my son' or 'my sons', to whom he gives all kinds of instructions for living a sensible and wise life, being truly right-eous, and avoiding the ways of sinners. But already in the first chapter the author describes how wisdom appears in person, and raises her voice in the streets and squares and at the gates of the city. Then he recounts what she says to men. These are above all threats against those who disregard her admonitions, Only the person who listens to her need not fear disaster.

After the writer has again given many lengthy admonitions to his 'son', in ch.8 wisdom herself suddenly appears again; now too she calls along the roads and at the city gates. This time she talks above all about herself, and the riches that she has to offer. Then she begins to talk about her origin:

Yahweh created me at the beginning of his work,
the first of his acts of old.
Ages ago I was set up,
at the first, before the beginning of the earth.
When there were no depths I was brought forth,
when there were no springs abounding with water.
Before the mountains had been shaped,
before the hills, I was brought forth;
before he had made the earth with its fields,
or the first of the dust of the world.
When he established the heavens, I was there,
when he drew a circle on the face of the deep.

37

When he made firm the skies above,
when he established the fountains of the deep,
when he assigned to the sea its limit,
so that the waters might not transgress his command,
when he marked out the foundations of the earth
then I was beside him like a master workman;
and I was daily his delight,
rejoicing before him always,
rejoicing in his inhabited world
and delighting in the sons of men.

This moving poem has raised the question how the writer came to describe wisdom in this way: as a woman who had emerged from God before he created the world, who was closely involved in that work and who rejoiced above all in humankind. An answer has been sought in an ancient Near Eastern way of thinking. It was usual here to derive important elements of the culture from a 'mythical beginning', when human society was as it were sketched out in the world of the gods. In Israel, too, people were familiar with this way of thinking. The story of paradise is a good example. The actual situation of humankind, men and women, differing from animals, with the possibility of choosing between good and evil, and so on, was described, 'explained', by depicting what happened right at the beginning, in paradise.

People also thought in this way in later times. When those who had been deported from Judah settled in Babylon, they stood out by the fact that they were circumcised, a custom which was unknown there. So circumcision became a sign of their religious character, their belonging to Yahweh. They gave it a place at the beginning of their existence as a people by describing how God had already imposed circumcision on their ancestor Abraham as a sign of his covenant with him and his descendant, Israel (Genesis 17). Also during the exile, the old custom of the sabbath, not working on the seventh day, took on a new significance. For want of a temple God could no longer be worshipped with sacrifices, and the great feasts could no longer be celebrated liturgically. The weekly celebration of the sabbath took the place of these customs. It was soon thought to be so fundamental that its origin was put right at the beginning of everything. God created the world in six days and rested on the seventh (Genesis 1).

Possibly the wisdom teacher who wrote the poem I have quoted thought along these lines: all admonitions and rules for behaviour, all the attitudes of the book of Proverbs are aimed at the ideal human society which God envisaged when he created the world. Or to put it a slightly different way: out of chaos God and his wisdom made an ordered world, and only by coming to terms with him and with one another do people come to realize the wisdom of their creator, who has nothing but joy in that happy life together.

But there are biblical scholars who suppose that the Jewish poet found his model in a text from another culture, in which a goddess wisdom spoke about herself and commended herself to her worshippers, those who loved her. Of course there could be no question of a Jew regarding wisdom as a goddess in the strict sense of that word. The figure of wisdom could only emerge from the one creator God, but then it was as his first creature.

## Wisdom in the form of a book

Whatever may be the background to the poem I have quoted, it is certain that it had a great influence on Jewish thinking about the Torah. That is clear from the book of a certain Jesus son of Sirach. Around the year 190 BC this much-travelled Jewish teacher wrote a substantial book in Jerusalem, where he lived. It was in the form of Proverbs, but much more extensive and more carefully arranged in themes. In his day Hellenism had long been on the march, and as an educated Jew who doubtless read and spoke Greek, he of course came under its influence. But at the same time he sensed the danger of this modern 'culture' for the Jewish community of faith. With his book, which he did not write in the vernacular, Aramaic, but in the venerable Hebrew of the tradition, he wanted to defend the riches and the values of Jewish belief and the Jewish way of life. Philosophy, literally love of wisdom, was also part of the new culture which fascinated so many 'progressive' Jews. Greek philosophers had reflected on the divine, on the origin and the nature of the universe, the cosmos, on the place of human beings in it, on the conditions for a good society and so on, in short on everything with which thinking people are often concerned.

Over against this the son of Sirach set the conviction of the traditional Jews: we do not really learn anything from this philosophy of the Greeks; our God, the only God, has already enlightened us about all these things by revealing them to his servant Moses, who set them down in the Torah. Moses lived hundreds of years before Greek culture came into being, and at that time there were no such figures as philosophers.

In chapter 24 of his book Jesus Sirach expresses this conviction very tellingly in the wake of Proverbs by making 'Lady Wisdom' speak. She describes how she came forth from the mouth of the Most High and then went to seek a dwelling place on earth. She continues:

> Then the creator of all things gave me a commandment
> and the one who created me assigned a place for my tent.
> And he said, 'Make your dwelling in Jacob,
> and in Israel receive your inheritance.'

After she has celebrated her characteristics in a very poetic way wisdom invites men to come to her to be filled with her and with all the glory that she has to offer. Then the writer himself adds his conclusion:

> All this is the book of the covenant of the Most High God,
> the law which Moses commanded us
> as an inheritance for the congregations of Jacob.

What the son of Sirach says here can be put in another way: the Torah is the wisdom of God in the form of a book.

He was not alone in this conviction. That emerges from the book of Baruch which, like the work of Sirach's son, was preserved in the Bible of the Greek-speaking Jews, although it had originally been written in Hebrew. In it there is a poem about the wisdom of God which permeates all creation, but which is hidden from humanity. Only God knows her. And then:

> He found the whole way to knowledge,
> and gave her to Jacob his servant
> and to Israel whom he loved...
> She is the book of the commandments of God,
> and the law that endures for ever.
> All who hold her fast will live,
> and those who forsake her will die.

There follows a summons to the Jews:

> Turn, O Jacob, and take her;
> walk towards the shining of her light.

Do not give your glory to another,
or your advantages to an alien people.
Happy are we, O Israel,
for we know what is pleasing to God.

We can see from later texts how specifically Jews could envisage the Torah as the embodiment of wisdom who was with God 'in the beginning'. When on the sixth day he wanted to create people, says one of these texts, God suddenly began to speak in the plural: 'Let us make man.' Question: To whom was he talking then? Answer: To the Torah; she was already with him before he began to create. It was also said that God made everything 'for the sake of the Torah', and even that the Torah was as it were the instrument of creation: everything was created through her.

This was not just theory, speculative thinking. In their concern with the sacred text and the exposition of it, and in their quest for its significance for the present, pious Jews felt that God was close to them: where two people were occupied with the Torah, said an old saying, the Shekinah (God's dwelling) is in their midst. They experienced the Torah as the side of God which faced humankind, and the pious turned to it in love and obedience. They foud power and trust in the Torah. They also said of the Torah what is said of wisdom: that it is light and life, the bread by which people live, water which refreshes, and that it liberates and gives healing.

The book by Jesus Sirach was the popular reading of pious Jews down to the first centuries of our era. It was part of the library of the Essenes who lived on the shore of the Dead Sea. Fragments of it were found in a hiding place of Jews who continued to fight against the Romans. But it was not incorporated into the Hebrew Bible. Consequently in due course the original text was no longer copied and was lost. But the book by Jesus Sirach was preserved in another way. A grandson of his moved to Egypt in 132 BC. There he encountered 'a not insignificant spiritual life' in the Jewish community, which for him was a reason for translating his grandfather's work into Greek. It was so esteemed that it secured a place in the Bible of the Greek-speaking Jews, eventually to include the authors of the New Testament.

A kindred work entitled the Wisdom of Solomon was also included in the same Bible. That was written shortly before the beginning of our era by a pious Jew who had also come to live in

Egypt and had steeped himself in Hellenistic culture. In his book the figure of divine wisdom plays a major role, though she is not presented as being embodied in the Torah. She sits on a throne alongside God, is initiated into his knowledge and actively involved in all that he has done and continues to do in the cosmos and for his people. In chapter 10 the author describes how she had a hand in what we call 'biblical history' which begins with Adam. She was also the one who liberated God's people from oppression, led them through the Red Sea and then looked after them in the wilderness.

In a very poetic summary of her characteristics the writer calls her 'the maker of all', who is also at work in all things. She is 'a reflection of eternal light, a spotless mirror of the working of God, and an image of his goodness... She reaches mightily from one end of the earth to the other, and she orders all things well.'

Nowadays one would ask: does the writer want to indicate the feminine side of God? Or perhaps better: for him, does referring to God as a 'he' fall short of the fullness of life to which the word God points? At all events, a number of New Testament writers who reflected on the person of Jesus were also influenced by this book of their Jewish Bible.

### Life after death?

During the centuries after the exile believing Jews became increasingly preoccupied with questions about the conduct of God in his government of the world, humanity, nations and individuals. This came about as a result of all the things that no longer fitted the faith and expectations with which they had been brought up. First came the question of God's righteousness in respect of individuals. In ancient Israel people had lived with the perspective that after death a person ended up in the underworld, a kind of extension of the grave. There he existed with all the other dead as a mere shadow, without feelings and without thoughts, in complete silence and darkness. That 'land of oblivion' was the universal prospect. But it had been good to be able to spend life on earth in the great totality of the people that was bound up with Yahweh, with him on the way. He would continue to pursue this way with his people, but those sharing it in future would be other individuals. The righteousness of God was seen to be effective in the life of that people as a whole: national disasters like 'plague, hunger and war' were experienced as punishments from God for crimes of the king and the people, while universal prosperity, *shalom*, was seen as a proof of the blessing with which he responded to the conversion of king and people.

As far as the individual was concerned, the wise men of old had always taught that the sensible and honourable man would be blessed with a long and happy life whereas the evildoer would be punished with misfortune, misery and an early death. That was what is called wisdom: anyone who observed people could see that laziness, dishonesty, concupiscence and debauchery usually led to poverty, sickness, misery and an early death, whereas zeal and honesty towards others led to prosperity and respect along with good health. All this had already been noted by the ancient sages of Egypt and Mesopotamia. An Israelite saw the hand of Yahweh in this human destiny.

Shortly before the fall of Jerusalem some doubt was certainly cast on the correctness of this view. But it was only after the exile that more and more people found that this teaching did not match up with experience. Already in the time of Nehemiah Jerusalem and its temple also began to become an economic centre. Trade was furthered by the coinage that the Persians had developed. An increasing gulf between rich and poor thus came into being in the Jewish community. So the rich could not take into account all the precepts of the Torah in their profitable relationships with foreigners. Jews faithful to the Law had less chance of success in life and were increasingly to be found among those classes of people whose life was difficult, those facing bankruptcy or mounting debts, with no defence against exploitation, hunger and debilitating diseases. Hence the ever more pressing question how God deals with those who are faithful to him. In other words, how can a sorely tried pious person still defend and justify his belief in God?

This set of problems inspired a particularly gifted Jewish sage to write the book of Job. He began from a main character who, without himself knowing it, was the stake in a kind of wager between God and a heavenly 'tester', Satan, who wanted to deprive him of all his possessions and even his health. Then three friends come to 'comfort' him by presenting him with the traditional teaching: you have been afflicted, therefore you must have sinned. Job opposes this vigorously and in his conversations with the friends sometimes also attacks God and finally challenges God to demonstrate his, Job's, guilt. After a fourth friend has given his view, God speaks and puts to Job ironical questions about all kinds of mysterious phenomena in what we call 'nature'. Job has no answer to them; he recognizes that he has gone too far in calling God to account. But it is the three friends who are told by God that they and their traditional doctrine of retribution are not so true to God as is his servant Job.

A century or more later a Jewish sage tackled a similar set of problems. The Preacher, as he calls himself, tells how after a long life he has come to the conclusion that all reflection on God's governance of the world and human destiny is sheer vanity, fruitless and pointless. The only sensible thing that a person can do in his short life is to enjoy 'in the fear of the Lord' as much as possible of the life that God has given him for a short time before this life loses its power and disappears into the great nothingness.

Like the book of Proverbs, Job and the Preacher are silent about the distinctive features of Israel: exodus, covenant, Torah. The Jewish author of the book of Job presents his hero as a foreigner, nor are his four friends Jews. The Preacher introduces himself at the beginning of his book as Solomon, king over Israel in Jerusalem, but he does not revert to that. Thus these wisdom books also give the impression of treating 'universal human problems'. That might explain their attraction for people of our time. But the questions which the authors of both books discussed can arise only for those who accept a personal God as creator and governor of the world.

The question of the book of Job was: why does God allow evil to afflict good men, men who lead their lives in accordance with his explicit wishes? Along with this went the question: why do those who do not do this prosper so often, and enjoy all kinds of good things which are a blessing from God? Again, these questions arose out of the conviction that it was impossible for God to correct this perverse governance after the death of his people. For in the gloomy domain of the underworld they all became 'shadows', without feeling, no longer capable of happiness or unhappiness. Moreover, that domain fell outside the sphere of influence of Yahweh, the God of life.

Many petitions in the book of Psalms are governed by this vision of earthly life as a sphere in which the righteousness of God must be made manifest. Some psalms mention sickness, and see its wretchedness as a chastisement, a divine punishment, and therefore pray for God's forgiveness, of which recovery will be a sign. Another 'argument' in these prayers of those in need is that those who mock their piety (what does that faith of yours mean now?) will be proved right if God does not make the sufferers better. Moreover, if they are to die prematurely, what is the point of their having lived? The meaning of life is thanksgiving and praise of God, and shadows in the underworld cannot do that any more.

Psalm 37 is not a prayer but instruction in an artificial form: each verse begins with a new letter of the alphabet. The teacher wants to stress that God will severely punish the evil who prosper before their death and that the righteous can firmly count on his blessing, even though this fails to materialize. This is the theory of Job's friends, boldly held against the facts.

The poet of Psalm 73 relates how much difficulty he has had with the facts. Finally he found certainty in his faithful converse with God which is the real heart of his life. So much is this the case that death will not be able to put an end to this intimate relationship. God will 'receive' him, as he received Enoch and Elijah. The term 'receive' occurs once again in Psalm 49, which is difficult to translate: in it a sage contrasts the ultimate fate of the unscrupulous rich with that of the pious poor, with whom he seems to identify himself: 'But God will redeem me from the power of the dead, for he shall receive me.'

In texts like the one that I have quoted the idea and the hope are expressed that it may be possible to remain bound to God after this earthly life. However, many Jews will have held on to the idea of the retribution of good and evil as this is expressed by Job's friends and the teacher in Psalm 37: in rewarding good deeds and punishing evil deeds God is bound to the earthly life of men and women, and so this righteousness must be demonstrable there.

But finally, in the years after 168 BC, this idea clashed with the facts: young Jews who joined Mattathias and his sons in their fight for God and his Torah died on the field of battle or after cruel torture. Such an early death could no longer represent divine punishment. On the contrary, he would reward the faith and the courage of these young men by giving them a new and immortal life. For many people this became a certainty. We find it clearly expressed in the narratives of the two books of Maccabees which are included in the Greek Bible. These also express the idea that

45

the suffering of martyrs for the sake of God and his law can be 'redemptive', by taking away the guilt of the people.

## Apocalyptic visions

This new form of belief in the righteousness and fidelity of God towards each individual could not be separated from another development. Questions had also arisen about the action of God in his governance of humanity as a whole, the peoples of the world among which Israel was his special possession. He had chosen Jerusalem to dwell there, on Mount Sion, the most holy place on earth. There the expectation developed that this dwelling place of God would become the capital of the world, the centre from which his benevolent rule would extend over all people. We might think, for example, of the vision in Isaiah 2. All peoples would go to the house of Yahweh that would be raised above all hills and mountains: there they would learn how they could live together in peace. They would then beat their weapons of war into useful tools and would never again fight one another... That belief, too, ran counter to the facts.

After the exile the temple state of Jerusalem with the small province of Judah around it was an insignificant part of the vast Persian empire. With Alexander the Great a new power gained the upper hand, a power which was much more 'pagan' than the Persians. Jerusalem lay on the coastal route which linked the two mighty centres of this new world, Antioch and Alexandria, cities of unprecedented attraction and size. There decisions were made about the fate of the nations until this came to lie in the hands of Rome. Compared with these centres, the capital of the Jews, the dwelling place of God, was completely insignificant and powerless, and what the Hasmonaean priest-princes achieved there had nothing to do with the old dream of an ideal world-ruler from the house of David.

So there grew up among pious Jews the conviction that the world as it was was too evil ever to become the 'kingdom of God'. To bring that about, God would first put an end to 'this' world which had become so utterly evil, so utterly dominated by Gentile, anti-godly powers. There was only the handful of Jews who remained faithful to God, an island in this sea of godlessness. They would have a share in the new world which God would realize, a new world, so that in it he would be the only ruler, and

46

no evil power would be able to do anything to damage the happiness of his subjects.

It is understandable that these Jews also tried to imagine how things would develop, the annihilation of this evil world and the coming of a new world which could really be called the kingdom of God. How would that come about and when would it happen? To use a word which has again become topical in our time, the great and definitive turning point in history would assume 'apocalyptic' forms.

This future perspective is already evident in passages from the prophetic books which were the last to be written. One example of this is Ezekiel 38-39, about Gog from the land of Magog, a passage about the last great struggle which is difficult to understand but which is nevertheless impressive. Often this turning point is associated with enormous upheavals in the universe, the cosmos. The compilers of the book of Isaiah bring together a number of sayings of God about neighbouring peoples in chapters 13-23. As is well known, as a conclusion to these they add the remarkable collection of chs.24-27; this describes a disaster of cosmic proportions, in connection with the annihilation of a city which is not mentioned by name. In between we hear thanksgivings and psalms of the ransomed people of God. There is an unforgettable short passage about the banquet on Mount Zion in which all the nations of the world are to take part, in connection with the fact that Israel is saved:

On this mountain Yahweh of hosts
will make for all peoples
a feast of fat things,
a feast of wine on the lees,
of fat things full of marrow,
of wine on the lees well refined.
And he will destroy on this mountain
the covering that is cast over all peoples,
the veil that is spread over all nations.
He will swallow up death for ever;
and the Lord God will wipe away tears from all faces,
and the reproach of his people he will take away from all the
earth;
for the Lord has spoken.
It will be said on that day,

'Lo, this is our God; we have waited for him;
let us be glad and rejoice in his salvation.'

After the text of the prophetic books was definitively established, inspired Jews found a new way of envisaging the transform-
ation to come. Of course how and when it would come had
already been established from eternity in the plans of God. But
how could one discern that? Formerly there had been prophets to
whom God, as Amos put it, had communicated his decree, or
who, according to a saying of Jeremiah, had taken part in his
counsel. But the time of the prophets was past. However, the
book of Genesis related that when the sixth patriarch after Adam,
Enoch, was 365 years old, he did not die but was received up by
God. This man had thus been able to gain insights into God's
plans for the world. So there came into being among the Jews a
number of writings in which Enoch related something of what he
had been alllowed to see in the heavenly world. This related not
only to its nature, like the mysteries of the universe with its
heavenly bodies, but also and above all to the course of the history
of the human race and Enoch's own role in its consummation in
the coming kingdom of God.

Alongside Enoch yet other figures from the past were chosen
as authors of books in which they reported what they had seen
and heard in heaven: Adam, Abraham, Moses, Baruch. This
extensive Jewish literature from the centuries around the beginning of our era is usually referred to as pseudepigrapha, that is,
writings which are falsely attributed to a particular author. None
of these books, which were written in Hebrew or Aramaic, found
a place in the Jewish Bible, with one exception, the book of Daniel.
This can give the reader of the Bible some idea of the 'books of
revelation' or apocalyptic literature which went the rounds in
Jewish circles before and during the time of Jesus. The stories
about Daniel with which the book begins and the visions which
he himself relates in the second half of the book all have to
do with the crisis in the Jewish community which led to the
Maccabaean revolt. On the orders of king Antiochus the most
serious crime that a Jew could conceive of had been committed:
the most holy place in the world had been desecrated by official
idolatry! The writer of the book wants to show that this abomination, the height of wickedness, did not come as a surprise to
'heaven'. It had been foreseen long beforehand. But those in

48

heaven also knew what would happen next; God would destroy all pagan powers and himself begin to rule, over a world in which there would no longer be any room for evil, the 'kingdom of God'.

To show that, the writer did not choose Enoch, Isaiah or Baruch as his main character, but the legendary figure of Daniel. Stories were already in circulation about him, written in the vernacular, Aramaic, stories that could encourage the Jews in their belief. The author introduces Daniel as a member of the court of Nebuchadnezzar, the Babylonian ruler who in 587 and desecrated and destroyed the temple of Jerusalem. Along with three other young Jews who are faithful to the law, Daniel has to serve the king as a counsellor. Thanks to their belief in the one true God their 'wisdom' is on an infinitely higher plane than that of the wise men of Babylon. The author then goes on to describe how Nebuchadnezzar had a dream which disturbed him greatly. None of his counsellors could tell him what he had dreamed and therefore certainly could not say what this dream meant. Daniel knew very well. In his dream the king saw an enormous statue with a head of gold, chest and arms of silver, belly and loins of bronze, legs of iron and feet of iron mixed with clay. Then a stone rolled down and shattered this statue, after which the material was blown away by the wind. But the stone which had hit the statue grew into a mountain which covered the whole earth. Daniel explained: in this way God had made known to the king what would happen at the end of time. The head of gold is the king himself. But after him come other world empires. And without any name being mentioned the silver is interpreted as the kingdom of the Medes, the bronze as that of the Persians and the iron as that of Alexander the Great. The feet of iron mixed with clay are a reference to the disputes between the Ptolemies and the Seleucids, but they will soon come to an end. '*And in the days of those kings the God of heaven will set up a kingdom which shall never be destroyed, nor shall its sovereignty be left to another people.*'

This is followed in chapter 3 by the well-known story of the three young men in the burning fiery furnace: they had refused to prostrate themselves in worship to an idol that the king had erected and were therefore shut up in a burning fiery furnace. But God sent them an angel who saw that there was a cool space in the midst of the fire, so that they were not burned. This was an encouraging story for the Jews who refused to worship Antiochus as a god and thus risked their lives.

After two stories in which pagan rulers find themselves compelled to recognize the power of the God of the Jews, there follows the well-known story of Daniel in the lions' den. The Persian ruler Darius is forced by his satraps to decree that anyone who addresses prayers to anyone but Darius is to be devoured by lions. Daniel, caught praying to God, is thrown into the den and spared by a miracle. Then Darius has it proclaimed: '*The God of Daniel is the living God, enduring for ever; his kingdom shall never be destroyed, and his dominion shall be to the end.*'

Chapter 7 does not contain a story about Daniel; it has its own written account of a dream that is sent to him. Here, as with Nebuchadnezzar's dream, this is a dream about the four kingdoms which precede the establishment of God's glory, but they are now denoted by other symbols: there are four monstrous beasts who emerge from the sea, and here too the fourth receives most attention.

Then Daniel sees in the midst of a stream of fire and countless serving beings an 'ancient of days' take his place, who with his court of judgment passes a devastating judgment on these beasts. He goes on: '*I saw in the night visions, and behold, with the clouds of heaven there came one like a son of man, and he came to the Ancient of Days and was presented before him. And to him was given dominion and glory and kingdom, that all peoples, nations and languages should serve him; his dominion is an everlasting dominion, which shall not pass away, and his kingdom shall not be destroyed.*'

Daniel then describes how he asked one of those present, evidently an angel, what all this meant. He explains: '*These four great beasts are four kings who shall arise out of the earth. But the saints of the Most High shall receive the kingdom, and possess the kingdom for ever, for ever and ever.*'

Still not content with this, Daniel goes on to ask for an explanation of the terrifying fourth beast with its ten horns, and an eleventh beast which wages war on the saints and overcomes then. Then the angel gives an explanation in which without mentioning any names he refers quite clearly to the crimes of Antiochus IV against the Jewish community, the desecration of God's temple and the persecution of those Jews who were faithful to the Law. He also gives the assurance that this domination will not last long. The power of Antiochus will be annihilated and then '*the kingdom and the dominion and the greatness of the kingdoms under the whole heaven shall be given to the people of the saints of the Most High; their kingdom shall be an everlasting kingdom, and all dominions shall serve and obey them.*'

There are indications in the text that the details of the fourth beast which refer so clearly to Antiochus have been added to an earlier version of the vision. But these do not make it less fascinating. The four beasts emerge from the great sea, the primal ocean, which is described in many ancient biblical texts as a breeding-ground of all kinds of monsters, chaotic powers, who set themselves against the God who created order from chaos. They symbolize the inhumanity that was characteristic of the great world empires.

Over against the primal power of the ocean which brings forth monsters the author then sets the majesty of the throne-room in which the ancient of days is sitting, in a setting which suggests the vision with which the book of Ezekiel begins.

The one who receives rule over the world from God after the devastating verdict is one like a son of man. He does not come from below, from the oceans or the earth, but he comes with the clouds of heaven. In the Bible, clouds often occur where we are told that God 'appears' or makes his presence known in some other way. Does this mean that this 'one like a son of man' comes from God's presence?

At the same time he seems to be identified with '(the people of) the saints of the most high' to whom the same eternal rule will be given. The text leaves open who is meant by the saints. One might think of the Jews who in all their resistance to persecution remain faithful to God, and of Israel's destiny to be his holy people. But it is possible that at the same time the author had in view heavenly beings: the angels or the heavenly hosts. In this kind of literature they are often seen as being actively involved in the struggle for the kingdom of God.

In the next chapters of his book (8-12) the author develops his theme further in the same way. He narrates the history of the Persians, Alexander the Great and the Greek princes who fight with one another for the possession of Palestine, in the form of visions of the future, in veiled terms, symbolically. An angel explains their significance to the seer Daniel. In chapters 8 and 9 the angel is given a name, Gabriel. He says that Daniel must listen carefully: 'Understand, O son of man, that the vision is for the time of the end.' This angel Gabriel is mentioned elsewhere in the Bible only where he announces the births of John the Baptist and Jesus, at the beginning of the Gospel of Luke. Here the narrator clearly means to suggest that the coming of these two figures ushers in the 'end time', the kingdom of God.

Part of the fiction is that Daniel must keep secret what is revealed to him, including the mysterious indications of the times when the decisive events will take place. The writer seems to believe that the course of history was already known beforehand in heaven and that everything therefore 'had to' happen like that.

In Chapter 12, the last chapter, the angel announces that at the great reversal, in the 'end-time', many who sleep in the dust, the kingdom of the dead, will awaken, some to eternal life and others to discover the shame of eternal guilt. Then the wise and righteous shall shine like the brilliance of the firmament and sparkle like the stars for ever and ever.

### 'Messianic' expectations

The book of Daniel is one of the earlier writings of the many which were going the rounds in Jewish circles shortly before and also after the beginning of our era. Since the discovery of the 'Dead Sea Scrolls' (in 1947 and the years following) interest in this rich literature has steadily increased. From these books and pamphlets we can see how intensely the writers must have been occupied with all kinds of aspects of their faith. This was not merely a theological interest. Just as earlier the book of Job had come into being as the result of a 'spiritual' struggle because traditional faith was no longer able to cope with experience, the facts, so new political situations gave rise to the search for new perspectives among believers.

The abhorrent desecration of the temple had evoked in the author of Daniel the expectation that God would soon 'reveal', make tangible, his glory, when he had annihilated all the pagan powers. But that did not happen. On the contrary, the rulers of the Maccabeaan family extended the territory of the Jewish state enormously, to the satisfaction of those with 'nationalistic' aspirations. But quite apart from their cruelty to rebel subjects, the Hasmonaeans desecrated the office of the high priest and thus in effect the whole of worship. Thereupon a number of priests left Jerusalem and founded a 'holy' community on the shores of the

Dead Sea. When the Hasmonaeans had called on the Roman general Pompey for help in settling their various disputes in 65 BC they had put the Jewish nation in the grasp of the Romans. The Romans were concerned only for power. They did not understand anything of Jewish faith and their soldiers showed nothing but contempt and hatred for the Jews. The well-to-do did not suffer from this, nor did the priests who lived by the temple, but the less well-off did, and these included many 'pious'. The literature I have mentioned appeared in groups of such Jews. It is so varied that all that can be done here is to refer to some individual themes.

Several of the writers were occupied with the old question of people who believe in one God, creator and governor of all. He cannot be the cause of evil in the world, the evil under which they and their group had to suffer so much. Some saw the sin of Eve as the beginning of all misery; others pointed to Adam as the first culprit. But above all, attention was paid to what was narrated in Genesis 6: the 'sons of God' had intercourse with the 'daughters of men'. This led to the creation of perverse beings. Devils, legions of demons, joined the fallen angels. Some writers give proper names to the main figures of these satanic powers and forces. They were the real cause of the evil which was practised by the greater and lesser rulers of the world, and also of the misery that ordinary people experienced in body and soul, like sickness and possession. So this literature gives us some background to the many texts in the New Testament which speak of the devil and demons.

Another theme is the intense interest in the heavenly world: that of the heavenly bodies, stars and planets and their courses, but also that of God and his countless angels, as Daniel saw them in his vision: 'a thousand times a thousand served him and ten thousand times ten thousand stood before him'. Two kinds of knowledge, which we would feel to be totally different, come together among these writers: knowledge of the cosmos according to the popular science of the time, and the view of faith into the world of God, 'visions'. Prophets like Isaiah and Ezekiel had told how they were called by God. At their call they had been given a glimpse of his glory and then tried to describe something of this inexpressible experience. There are indications that pious men, particularly gifted in prayer and fasting, meditated on these texts and as a result fell into ecstasy. Where writers relate journeys through the heavenly world such mystical experiences may have been their starting point. In these circles it was not strange for someone to relate how he found himself outside himself and was taken up into the third heaven, and how he had looked on paradise.

But over against the heavenly world stood the earthly world, with its almost intolerable reality of oppression by those in power, the exploiters: real pagans, or Jews who acted like pagans. Here we come upon a third theme: among the pious there was the expectation that God would annihilate all the power of evil and would do so very soon. Then the 'glory' of the heavenly world would also stream out over the earthly world. This expectation could not disappear from Jewish hearts, rooted as it was in trust in their God and nurtured by their daily prayers to him, which often began with a hymn of praise to his eternal kingship. In these prayers they used expressions and sometimes whole sentences from the biblical book of Psalms, which they had made wholly their own. Of course these pious people also tried to imagine how God would do this, and realize his rule. He himself had already spoken about it in the books of Moses and the prophets. These last books in particular contain a confusing multiplicity of descriptions of this decisive event. We modern people draw a distinction between prophetic texts from the time of the kings, from the time of the exile and from subsequent periods. But for the Jews of the time all these texts were on the same level; all were words of God.

It could be deduced from this that the great turning point would be linked with cosmic upheavals; the sun and moon would no longer give light and the stars would fall from heaven; indeed the whole of the old world would be annihilated. As is clear from the first line of the Bible, 'heaven and earth' denote what we call the cosmos. Any mention of 'a new heaven and a new earth' therefore referred to a recreated world.

But the God of Israel was concerned above all with men and women, the society of his people. This was fundamentally corrupted by the powers of evil which seemed to predominate in it. When God's great day dawned, he would annihilate them all. Perhaps with fire from heaven or in the form of a gigantic battle between his armies and theirs, until everyone was defeated. And then? At all events then God himself would be king, over people who would live entirely in accord with his desires in a kingdom in which animals and plants were equally obedient, a paradise.

Anyone who expected a recreation of the cosmos could imagine it being inhabited by the righteous dead whose bodies would then be raised from the dead, in other words recreated. But in the imagination of others people would live a long and happy life in the world redeemed from evil until they died content and fulfilled, 'full of days', as the King James Version says of the patriarchs of Israel.

Thus there also came into being a confusing number of answers to the question whether God would involve others in the event of this great day, perhaps angels, the heavenly hosts or one figure: human beings, an individual or more. Among the prophets there was sometimes talk of a future ideal king from the dynasty of David, an 'anointed' or Messiah, destined by God to realize his kingdom of righteousness and everlasting peace. Hence all these expectations of the kingdom of God later came to be called messianic. That is misleading. For in the Jewish literature discussed here it is hardly ever possible to find a clearly defined messianic figure.

In some writings of the community founded by priests by the Dead Sea two messiahs seem to be expected, one from Aaron and one from Israel. The first, a priest, will get a much more important function than the 'Messiah of Israel'. The latter will appear only as 'prince' of the new people of God. But sometimes in addition to these two figures a third is expected, the one who was mentioned in Deuteronomy 18. There Moses forbids his people to listen to sorcerers and soothsayers, as was the custom of the inhabitants of Cannan. No, he says, 'The Lord your God will raise up for you a prophet like me from among your own brothers – him shall you heed.'

But there were other views in this community of the Essenes. In the remains of their library fragments have been found of a writing in which Melchizedek plays the leading role in the end-event. His name occurs in Genesis 14: Abraham encounters him as 'king of Salem', who is also 'priest of God most High' and gives Abraham his blessing. The author seems to have developed this Melchizedek, who is also mentioned in Psalm 110, into a heavenly figure, leader of the hosts of angels. In a decisive blow he is to annihilate the powers of evil, the arch-enemies of God and his faithful. The hosts of evil are commanded by Belial, the prince of all the 'sons of darkness'.

One of the other Dead Sea Scrolls contains a work which has

been called the War Scroll. In it the commander of the anti-godly powers is also called Belial. However, there it is not just the heavenly hosts who defeat his troops, but the members of the community, 'the sons of light'. Their armies, the organization, weapons and tactics of which are described in detail, fight for forty years against those of Belial with varying success, until God annihilates the latter with his own hand.

So within the same Jewish community the end-event is 'filled in' in very different ways. Only one work from the rich literature of these centuries sketches out the picture of a future Messiah, which derives many features from 'messianic' texts of the Hebrew Old Testament. It is called the Psalms of Solomon because it contains eighteen psalm-like poems, each of which has the name of Solomon as author in the title. At the beginning of this collection there are clear allusions to the Roman general Pompey who after the conquest of Jerusalem in 63 BC entered the temple precincts with his troops and desecrated the sanctuary. The penultimate psalm, the seventeenth, which at the same time is the longest, and again the eighteenth, is about the coming ruler from the dynasty of David. He will give shape to God's rule over Israel and the world. The pagan occupants of the land will be expelled by him, as will all strangers and sinners. So he will reign over a sanctified nation as king, endowed with perfect righteousness and wisdom. The scattered Jews will return to their land, which will be inhabited in accordance with the system of the old tribal territories. Jerusalem and the temple will again be hallowed. All the peoples of the world will obey this king and thus God will be glorified by all humankind. It is impossible to tell from the book within which Jewish group it was written; perhaps it was compiled from earlier collections. Nor is it clear how far it circulated outside these circles.

The conclusion to be drawn form all this is obvious. The literature of the time makes it impossible for us to go on claiming, as was often done earlier, that in Jesus' time *the* Jews were expecting *the* Messiah. All that is certain is that all pious people looked with longing towards the great day on which God would establish his kingdom.

# 3   Jesus from Nazareth

On the last page of the collection of prophetic books in the old Bible stood this word of God: 'Behold, I will send you Elijah the prophet before the great and terrible day of the Lord comes...' John the Baptist seemed to be the fulfilment of this old promise. In his garb and life-style he recalled the legendary Elijah and he preached like a prophet that the great day of judgment was at hand. Only those who had been baptized by him as a sign of their conversion would be able to withstand that judgment. So John corresponded to an expectation which had been expressed some centuries earlier.

That could not be said of his disciple Jesus, from Nazareth. He spoke and acted in the certainty that this great day of God had already dawned, had dawned as a time of forgiveness and restoration, the beginning of the final 'salvation'. The Jewish scholar David Flusser has rightly said that Jesus is the only Jew known to us from antiquity who not only proclaimed that people were on the brink of the end-time but at the same time that the new day of salvation had already dawned. So this was a totally unexpected message, which caused amazement among the audience. For them that 'kingdom of God' had always been something in the future. But their enthusiasm caused offence and increasing disquiet among the leaders of the people. These leaders finally felt compelled to eliminate Jesus from the community permanently.

Anyone who wants to get some idea of Jesus' person and activity has to go to the four Gospels which form the beginning of the New Testament. These short books, almost booklets, can mislead an unprepared reader. The authors describe what happened from time to time, what Jesus did or said at a particular moment, where he went after that, and so on. In so doing they give the impression of offering an account, a report of facts, which other bystanders could equally observe, But the Gospel stories are not 'historical' in this way. They have another character, which is also determined by the circumstances in which they are written. The Greek name for gospel, *euangelion*, already to some degree indicates their nature. These books set out to give a report, a message (*angelion*), which is good (*eu*), which causes joy. It relates to the person of Jesus. When the evangelists relate what he said and did and suffered, they are not just concerned with an exceptional figure from the past who had already been dead and buried for some time. For as unprecedented as his message was the fact that after he was dead and buried he made contact again with his faithful followers by 'appearing' to them. This made these Jewish people believe that God had taken Jesus to himelf, that he lived in God and so willed to be with them in a new way, again the inspiring centre of the circle which he had formed around him during his lifetime. This circle soon extended to new believers, in Jerusalem and outside. For in this way more and more new groups, 'communities', arose in which stories and sayings about Jesus were handed on to new members.

This happened first of all by word of mouth. And as always happens when we recall memories, the form and content of what we say are always determined by our own situation at that moment. While these people were talking about what Jesus had done and said, another factor was what he meant to the narrators in their new situation. Probably teachers here and there in such communities had set something of the oral teaching down in writing. But where these writings have not been incorporated into our four Gospels, they are lost.

Many biblical scholars assume that 'Mark' was the first to create a consecutive narrative out of this oral and written material, and that he did this around 70, shortly before or shortly after the year in which Jerusalem and the temple were destroyed by the Romans. The unknown author of that Gospel, only later called Mark, therefore wrote his work around forty years after the events narrated in it.

This raises the question why someone did not earlier hit on the idea of preserving in writing for posterity the extremely important event associated with Jesus. One of the reasons is that the first generation of Jesus' followers lived in expectation that he would appear very soon to all the world in glory, as the Son of man, who would pronounce the definitive verdict on all humanity and thus put an end to what we call history. Why put something down in writing for a generation which was not to come? But this appearance of the glorified Christ did not take place, and those who had been with him during his days on earth and had been witnesses to his resurrection had almost all died. In place of the public triumph of their Master, Christians had to experience the opposite. In the year 64, under the emperor Nero, believers in him had been arrested, under suspicion of having caused the great fire which had devastated the city, and had been burned alive as the instigators of it. It is not certain whether Mark wrote his book in Rome, but it is clear that he wanted to acquaint his readers with the prospect of opposition, persecution and martyrdom ('martyr' derives from a Greek root meaning 'bear witness'). That has recently been demonstrated convincingly by Bas van Iersel in his exceptionally clear book about Mark. In it he shows how carefully the evangelist has constructed his story, and how each part of it, down to the smallest detail, has a function in the whole and seeks to take the reader a step further in his or her understanding of the mystery of Jesus. He also demonstrates the role played by 'the way' in the Gospel: Jesus often talks about the way that he himself has to go in obedience to his Father, and in all kinds of ways the reader of the Gospel is challenged and encouraged to follow him on this way.

This first written Gospel was composed by a very gifted Christian for his fellow-believers, perhaps those in a particular community. They probably soon made copies of the book for their other groups. For while many stories about Jesus and sayings about him were going the rounds in them, of course including the account of his crucifixion and resurrection, groups will never have seen the intrinsic connection of all this and therefore also the mystery of Jesus the Messiah as clearly in Mark's short book. Now this book might also fall into the hands of an outsider, a pagan. What would he think of this strange story? Some years ago an expert in what was written and read in the Roman empire at that time, a classical scholar, tried to answer this question. He had not been brought up on the Bible in his youth and he had had no religious teaching. At the request of a scholar friend he began to read the book during his vacations. Under the title *A Pagan Reads the Gospel of Mark* he described what this book must have looked like to an educated reader of the first century of our era. To begin with, such a reader would have had to get used to the unliterary Greek of the author, and also to all the different words and names which were clearly part of his 'group language', strongly influenced by the Jewish Bible. Here is some of this scholar's verdict:

My impression, hardly troubled by any preconceptions, was a strong one. It seemed to me that something vey important was being put forward here with a superior purpose and concentration throughout the book: from the *fortissimo* in the marvellous opening scene, through the development of a theme with inexhaustible significance, to the tragic end and a last comforting lightning flash. Only when the end approaches (from 11.28 onwards) does it become increasingly clear that what is presented here in unforgettable scenes and statements is the course of a predestined world drama. But from the beginning the style and content of the story arouse a feeling of otherness, a feeling that this is not a history like other histories, not a biography like other biographies, but a development of the actions, sayings and suffering of a higher being on his way through this anxious world of human beings and demons.

Fifteen to twenty years later two Christians, independently of one another, each decided to write a new Gospel. They were familiar with that of Mark, but possessed more written and oral traditions than he had included. Later these two authors were given the names Matthew and Luke, a usage which we still retain. Each in his own way supplemented the narrative of Mark with stories and above all utterances of Jesus: short sayings and parables. Moreover they gave this a framework; at the beginning they wrote stories about the birth of Jesus as a kind of prologue, and at the end they recounted appearances of the risen Jesus as an epilogue. They wrote in about the eighties of the first century, and therefore from a new situation: at that time a break had taken place between the Jews who regarded Jesus as the Messiah and the great majority of other Jews who could not share that belief. Further on in this book, in Chapter 6, I shall be describing that development in detail. Here I would say only that this situation of course also influenced the way in which they handed on the recollections of Jesus.

As far as the public ministry of Jesus was concerned, both evangelists kept to Mark's framework; after Jesus' baptism in the Jordan he works for some time in Galilee and then, around the feast of Passover, goes to Jerusalem where he drives the traders out of the Temple, is arrested and then is handed over as a rebel

60

to Pilate, who has him crucified. Thus during his public life Jesus makes one journey to Jerusalem, which is also the last.

After the three Gospels I have mentioned a fourth was written, which was associated with the name of John. In many respects it is very different from the first three. Here I can mention only the different order of events in it. According to John, right at the beginning of his public life Jesus goes from Galilee to Jerusalem at the Passover and there drives the merchants out of the temple. After returning to Galilee, he makes a number of further visits to Jerusalem at the time of liturgical feasts. There, in the temple, most of the discussions with 'the Jews' take place: Jesus speaks to them in exalted language about himself and his mission. In John, therefore, there are several journeys to Jerusalem and thus a public ministry of Jesus which lasts two or perhaps three years. There is another far-reaching difference. Shortly before the last Passover, in Bethany, a village near Jerusalem, Jesus summons from the grave the body of his friend Lazarus, which is already beginning to decompose. This, too, is difficult to reconcile with the narratives of Mark and the two authors who expanded his Gospel: they give other motives for the resolve to kill Jesus and nowhere do they make any mention of anyone in the circle around Jesus who is called Lazarus.

Those who are familiar with the forms of historiography which are to be found in the Old Testament will not be surprised at the divergence in John's narratives. Earlier Jewish narrators were not primarily concerned to communicate precisely what had happened in the past, but rather to say what was important for their hearers and readers now. In this respect they dealt very freely with the facts at their disposal; they omitted anything that did not fit their message and added new stories to it. So the history that was narrated was completely at the service of their proclamation of faith.

The earliest traditions about Jesus already tell us that he had raised people from the dead. It is possible that John also knew the story of a certain Lazarus who had been healed by Jesus. With his strong sense of dramatic contrasts he would then have shaped his message in this way: Jesus raises the dead man Lazarus to life and therefore men put him to death, the one who has become the resurrection and the life for all.

We might ask whether John put the event of the 'cleansing of the temple' right at the beginning of Jesus' public ministry to make

61

more room for what he wanted to tell his readers. When he was writing his Gospel, Jews who believed in Jesus had already been 'expelled from the synagogue'. Hence John and his community reflected above all on the person of Jesus and his unique bond with God, as Messiah, as Son, and above all as final 'revealer' of God. They also talked about that with other Jews who still doubted whether the expulsion from the synagogue had been legitimate. So these discussions were really about the question which was put to Jesus after his action in the temple, concerning the basis, the origin, the authority for his words and actions. By putting the 'cleansing of the temple' at the beginning of his Gospel, John could distribute these discussions with 'the Jews' about Jesus and his mission throughout his narrative, making Jesus speak regularly in person about his relationship with the Father, something that happens very rarely in the other three Gospels. But in that case he had to make Jesus go up to the temple several times.

Two facts are quite certain: that Jesus had himself baptized by John and that as a result of his appearance in Jerusalem he was crucified at the Passover. The only uncertainty is over the length of time between these two facts. No precise dating can be given. As I remarked earlier, only Luke felt the need to put the emergence of John the Baptist in a kind of historical framework: 'In the fifteenth year of the emperor Tiberius' – by our dating that is about 27-28. But Luke does not say how long John had been baptizing before Jesus came to him from Nazareth. He does comment later that Jesus was 'about thirty years old' when he began his preaching. There is no denying that here Luke was thinking of what his Greek Bible said about David in II Samuel 5. When David was anointed (verb *chrio*, hence Christ) king in Hebron by the tribes of Israel, he was 'a son of thirty years': Jesus lived about this long.

Little can be said with any certainty about Jesus' life during all these years. We can hardly derive any historical information from the prologues of Matthew and Luke which I have already mentioned. Their stories about the birth of Jesus have the character of confessions of faith in narrative form. That also applies to what Luke says about the twelve-year-old Jesus in the temple. This short narrative is clearly focussed on its climax: the first words of Jesus. To his parents who have been looking for him he says, 'Did you not know that I must be about my Father's business (or house)?' The reader must remember this saying in order to understand the sequel better. In Mark 6 we read something that Luke did not take over: Jesus, the son of Mary, was known in Nazareth as the carpenter, and his brothers were called James, Joses, Judas and Simon; he had sisters as well. Earlier in Mark's account Jesus' family went after him after it was suggested that his relatives regarded him as someone who had lost his mind, someone who was crazy.

In addition to the members of the family, at the end of his book Mark also mentions women from Galilee, who had gone with Jesus to Jerusalem. Nowhere in the Gospels is there any indication that Jesus himself had a wife. Did this not appear in the reminiscences because she had died young? That is assumed to have been what happened to Joseph the father of Jesus, who does not play any role in his public life. Or did Jesus remain unmarried? It transpires from the writings of the community by the Dead Sea that most of its members lived a celibate life. That was connected with their radical view of the purity which was demanded of priests. But it was very un-Jewish. The normal Jewish male regarded marriage as a command of the creator and at the same time as an obligation towards his people by which God had bound himself from eternity.

It was once suggested that Jesus was also regarded as exceptional because he was unmarried and that he was once taunted with being a 'eunuch'. That could be the background to the remarkable statement which is quoted in Matthew 19 after Jesus' discussion with the Pharisees over divorce. In his tranquil and at the same time mysterious way Jesus would then have reacted to the taunt. He referred to two kinds of eunuch: those who had been castrated and those who were born that way. Every Jew knew that the Law of Moses did not allow those who had been mutilated to have any access to the community of Israel. But, Jesus added, there is a third possibility: people could make themselves unfit for married life by total dedication to the kingdom of God.

These are conjectures. We can be more certain that Jesus grew up in a pious Jewish family. Then in the weekly meetings in the synagogue he took in the great traditions of his people and his family life was also governed by the old faith and the expectations that it aroused. Moreover, his natural tendency to pray occupies a major place in later recollections. It was also recalled in the

Greek-speaking communities that as an adult Jesus continued to address God with the familiar term 'Abba', one with which small children addressed their fathers. Perhaps Jesus was attracted in the synagogue above all by the readings from the second part of the book of Isaiah. These announced the coming of God as king, good news for Israel, 'a gospel'.

We may infer from all this that the Gospels give us little reliable historical information. This conclusion is not entirely justified. It has rightly been observed that the first three Gospels in particular tell us far more about the daily life of people in Palestine during the first century than any other historical source. And this is above all thanks to the sayings and parables of Jesus. He seems to have noticed everything. The everyday things which happen in the home: kindling a light, kneading dough, mending clothes, filling a wineskin, looking for a lost coin and going to bed between the children in a one-room dwelling. While all sorts of things are being bought and sold on the market, children are playing their games there. The farmers sow and reap and look after their livestock. The Gospels also talk of catching fish, of nets and boats. Every aspect of social life is mentioned: there are rich and poor, masters, workers and slaves, and people go to law before a judge. There is attention to the way in which the seed germinates and trees produce fruit. Moreover all kinds of animals appear on the scene, like dogs, foxes, doves, snakes, scorpions; and there is also the miraculous phenomenon of the flash of lightning which illuminates the whole earth from one end to the other.

### Foretastes of God's kingdom

Jesus once described the unprecedented nature of his message in his rapturous exclamation: 'Blessed are the eyes that see what you see! I tell you that many prophets and kings have asked to see what you see and did not see it, and to hear what you hear and did not hear it.' What they saw was Jesus' way of living and dealing with his fellow men and women, and what they heard was his proclamation of the coming kingdom of God that was already at work in him. Everything that Jesus did and said had to do with this, with the ultimate reality which he as it were 'represented': one could regard him, what he said and did, as a foretaste of the world as God originally meant it and would soon make it: a world made whole.

I shall now attempt to sketch out some aspects of Jesus' activity to show how they are interconnected. First there is the fact that he freed people from all kinds of torments, including that torment which people in his environment called possession: an evil spirit had 'taken possesion of' someone, had as it were made its home in that person, and this resulted in phenomena of disease, specifically leading to incomprehensible and repugnant behaviour. As I showed in the previous chapter, many Jews of this time regarded all kinds of evil and wickedness as the consequence of diabolical influences, anti-godly powers. These powers were regarded as 'personal', as demons. It was also believed that they were an organized army under the command of a chief, referred to as Satan, the devil, Beelzebul and so on. He too was a creation of God, but he had refused to obey God and had rebelled. He used his army to do harm to individuals and nations and so to corrupt God's good creation.

There are some stories about exorcisms by Jesus in the first three Gospels (but not in the fourth). Their first readers will have found nothing special in this fact alone. They were familiar with it. This can be seen from a casual piece of information given by Flavius Josephus. Where he describes the reign of Solomon in his *Jewish Antiquities*, he follows his custom of supplementing the biblical narrative with later legends about the wisdom of this ruler. God also gave Solomon skill in prescribing cures, which included methods of driving out evil spirits so effectively that they did not dare to return. Josephus comments that these methods still appeared to be effective. Then he describes something that he himself had experienced. In the presence of the emperor Vespasian and his staff his compatriot Eleazar drove a demon away as follows. He held under the nose of a possessed person a ring with a seal under which was a piece of a root that Solomon had prescribed. When the man smelt its scent, the demon left him through the nose and the man fell to the ground. After that Eleazar prohibited the demon from returning by pronouncing conjurations in the name of Solomon. To convince the onlookers that he really had this power, he put a pot with water nearby and commanded the demon to knock this down and so show that he had really left the man. Thereupon the pot overturned. It was striking to the first readers of the Gospels that in driving out demons Jesus made no use of magical formulae and conjurations.

For him a single word sufficed and immediately the demon obeyed, though sometimes under protest.

People who were critical of Jesus sometimes supposed that he was in league with the head devil, the leader of the evil powers, Beelzebul. This was a very vile calumny. Jesus quietly answered that this prince could not damage his own cause. Moreover, he said, 'pious people among you, your "sons", also drive out devils'. But 'if I by the power of God cast out devils, then the kingdom of God has come upon you'. Of course Jesus freed only a limited number of those who had been possessed from the tyranny of evil powers. But he saw that as a foretaste of the ultimate defeat of those powers, and that had apparently once been shown to him in a vision. Luke has preserved his exclamation: 'I saw Satan fall like lightning from heaven.'

Mark narrates that immediately after his baptism in the Jordan Jesus saw the heavens open and the Spirit descend on him like a dove. Then a voice from heaven said: 'You are my son, my beloved; in you I am well pleased.' Immediately after that the Spirit drove him into the wilderness. He spent forty days there being tested by Satan. With Matthew and Luke we find this testing by Satan developed into an impressive scene. The devil invites the hungry Jesus to make bread from stones. Then he takes him to the very top of the temple and invites him to throw himself down. And finally Satan suggests the possibility that Jesus can take possession of all the kingdoms of the world and their riches if he falls down before him. But Jesus keeps to his perfect dedication to God, as his beloved and obedient son.

Later on in the story, when it becomes clear that Jesus is risking his life in his decision to go to Jerusalem, Peter seeks to dissuade him. This provokes the fierce reaction from Jesus: 'Get away from me, Satan. You are not concerned about God's will.'

Several times in stories about the expulsion of devils it is said that the demons are afraid of Jesus. Evidently someone who lives so wholly from God, as his devoted 'son', is a threat to them and their world which is characterized by rebellion and hatred against God. Where Jesus speaks in the Gospel of John about his imminent death he says that at that moment 'the prince of this world' is condemned and 'cast out'. The underlying notion is clearly that Jesus' loving to the end has brought a power into this world which will ultimately be victorious over all evil powers.

In summary statements about Jesus' ministry the evangelists

often mention his exorcisms in the same breath as his healings of other diseases. But they also have many specific stories about these healings. Mark describes in his very first chapter, after his story of an exorcism in the synagogue of Capernaum, how Jesus healed Peter's mother-in-law of her fever (Luke writes that he 'rebuked' this fever) at the request of those in her house. He goes on to say that Jesus touched a leper and 'purified' him from his illness with a single word.

As motives for Jesus to heal a person we are sometimes told of a pressing request made by the sick person himself or herself or by relatives, and of how this then arouses his compassion. The presence of such an afflicted person in the synagogue on a sabbath seems to be a challenge to Jesus to use his healing power on that particular day. That is the case with the woman who was bent double, in Luke 13. Jesus lays his hands on her and then she can stand upright again. When he is justifying this healing action to those who disapprove of it, he says that the woman had already been 'bound by Satan' for eighteen years, and that she is a 'daughter of Abraham', as he describes her with an unusual honorific title.

A whole series of stories about 'supernatural' healings went the rounds at that time. Some of them are set at a famous sanctuary, some cluster round a recognized miracle worker. In a comparison with the Gospel narratives it is striking that Jesus often performs healings with a single word, even on a sick person who is somewhere else: in other words, he performs healings at a distance. It is sometimes said that he touches the sick person, for example by laying on hands. He also sometimes uses his spittle, with which he moistens the eyes of a blind man. Nowhere is there mention of his praying to God to heal the sick, though he does sometimes says to the person who has been healed: your faith, your trust, has made you better.

The evangelists did not preserve any sayings in which Jesus explicitly associates these healings with the coming kingdom of God. Probably that is fortuitous, and for Jesus they were just as much pointers to the 'whole' world which was coming into being. In it people would enjoy life to the full, together, in community with one another. It is striking that Jesus healed many sick people who as a result of their disease could not take part in ordinary social life or were even excluded from it. This last had long been the case with lepers, but the paralysed, cripples, the blind, the

67

deaf and the dumb were also hindered by their handicap in their contacts with fellow men and women.

### A society made whole

He liberated people from sickness and possession and thus from their isolation. This was a foretaste of a world made whole. But people could not become whole as long as their hearts remained divided. Hence some of Jesus' summonses seem to us to be very radical and not in accord with our picture of a gentle and loving healer. 'Radical' is derived from the Latin *radix*, root. If people want to take part in this coming world of God, then they must change their hearts, the root from which their thoughts and actions come. Matthew included some of these radical demands in his Sermon on the Mount, first in the form of comparisons with important commandments from the old law, which sought to protect society in Israel and were largely formulated in negative terms. Here are a few snatches from this sermon, in everyday language.

The old law says that you shall not murder. Anyone who murders makes himself guilty before God. But I, Jesus, say to you that anyone who is angry with his brother is already guilty before God. For it is there, in your heart, that there arises that longing for the other to disappear, and that can ultimately lead to murder. The old law prohibits adultery. But I say to you that to look covetously on another man's wife is already forbidden; for that is where adultery begins in your heart.

The law says that you may not swear false oaths, commit perjury. I tell you that you must not swear at all, in other words take God as a witness that you are telling the truth. Your yes and your no must be so unconditional that others can trust them completely. Then you do not have to bring God into things. The old law said 'an eye for an eye and a tooth for a tooth', and that was good. For a man is very inclined to recompense an evil done to him a hundredfold, saying: 'You'll really pay for this!' But I, Jesus, say to you that you must not resist those who do you evil: if anyone hits you on the right cheek, offer him the left.

According to Matthew the old law says that you must love your neighbour and hate your enemy. This last statement was never in the law, but at that time there were certainly pious Jews who felt that it ought to have been. Jesus says: love your enemies and pray for those who persecute you. In this way you will be children of your Father in heaven, who makes his sun shine on both the good and the bad and the rain fall on both the just and the unjust. As usual in the Bible, to love here means to give someone what he or she needs, to help the other person actively. The term therefore does not involve one's cherishing particular feelings for this other, finding him or her attractive; this is not something that anyone can command, even God.

You can only love in this way if you no longer have any concern or anxiety for your own welfare, your possessions, your good name, your status. This is what the Sermon on the Mount goes on to talk about. You can no longer seek security in your possessions if you really believe in God. For no one can serve two masters, God and 'mammon' (as possessions and property were then called). Here the term 'serve' has religious connotations, worship as the supreme good, that on which everything hinges.

Anyone who looks for security in God alone can live free from care, like the birds who do not sow and reap and do not build barns because God feeds then, and like the lilies of the field who do not spin and weave and are yet dressed more attractively than king Solomon. The reference is thus to unlimited trust in God. Matthew follows this summons with a prohibition which is extremely radical and also seems to be connected with the trust in God to which Jesus issued his invitation: Do not judge. Those who were really religious in this society had constantly to ask themselves whether they might have dealings with this person or that; they therefore had to judge his behaviour and in so doing, of course, themselves as well, by way of comparison. Here Jesus uses the vivid metaphor of one person having a speck in his eye and the other having a log in his. The pious spiritual leader who is concerned about someone else's mistakes and gets at him over them is offering to remove the speck from his eye while failing to note that he himself has a log in his own eye. At the same time, judging another person is a way of reassuring oneself. If you put a label on another person, assign him to a particular category, then you put this person in a world that you can control. Then he is no longer a threat. But anyone who looks for security only in God has nothing to fear from anyone and can be open to any fellow human being.

Anyone who has reflected on human society, whether on a small or a large scale, will concede that in fact things must be as Jesus commanded: people must deal in complete honesty with one another, consistently, without violence, thanks to perfect trust in God, made free for an unconditional love which no longer asks whether the other in fact deserves it. But is that possible? Are people capable of it? It may seem like a utopia, something that can never really happen in our world, but only in a land which does not exist: utopia means 'nowhere land'.

Jesus does not give the impression of having had any illusions. In his Sermon on the Mount Matthew also reports Jesus' exhortation that we must pray undaunted, ask God for whatever we need. In doing so he makes this comparison: 'Which of you, if his son asks him for bread, will give him a stone? Or if he asks for a fish, will give him a serpent? If you then, who are evil, know how to give good gifts to your children, how much more will your Father who is in heaven give good things to those who ask him!' Jesus actually says, 'You who are evil'. That is in comparison with God, who is the only one who can be called good. And these evil people are nevertheless by nature good to their children.

That only God is good reminds us of the story in Mark 10: a well-to-do man asks Jesus, 'Good master, what must I do to have a share in eternal life?' (that is another term for what Jesus calls the kingdom of God). He is told: 'Do not call me good. No one is good but God alone.' The man then insists that he has kept all the commandments from his youth up and is evidently so sympathetic that Jesus begins to feel for him and invites him to join his disciples. To do that he must sell all that he has and give his money to the poor. The man hesitates to do that, and goes away sorrowful: that is a step he cannot take.

Yes, Jesus goes on to say in conversation with his disciples, it is easier for a camel to go through the eye of a needle than for a rich man to enter the kingdom of God. And when they exclaim that in that case no one really has a chance, Jesus replies: 'For human beings that is impossible, but with God everything is possible.'

As often in Gospel narratives, here various aspects of Jesus' way of dealing with people come to light. First there is his protest when someone calls him 'good'. Evidently he does not want any attention to be paid to himself, let alone anything that looks like veneration. Then there is his attitude towards the man who has observed God's commandments so faithfully (Jesus 'loved him', Mark writes). When the man goes away sorrowful because he has so many possessions, Jesus does not trouble to call him back: he

70

respects his inability to take the last step. Then there is the powerful, comic comparison of the camel going through the eye of a needle, followed by Jesus' expression of trust in the possibilities of God. Before looking at these aspects more closely, I need first to say something about following Jesus.

When Jesus proposes that the rich man should follow him, he probably means (though this is not said in so many words) that he should join the group which formed around him and which went with him through the country. Following Jesus in this way indeed required those who did so to leave behind all that they had. The nucleus of this group consisted of 'the Twelve'.

That was the ancient number of the tribal ancestors from which the people of Israel had emerged. In this way Jesus clearly meant to express his awareness that he had been sent to all Jews, to call all Israel to share in the kingdom.

It is evident from the Gospel narratives that Jesus restricted himself to purely Jewish cities and villages. Sepphoris was a few miles from Nazareth. This city had been rebuilt by Herod Antipas, of course in Hellenistic style. It became his residence until the completion of the resplendent new city on the seashore which he called Tiberias after his patron in Rome, the emperor Tiberius. Jesus seems not to have visited these 'Gentile' cities, although many Jews lived there. We are certainly told twice that Jesus healed someone who was not a Jew, the daughter of a Gentile woman who was possessed of a devil and the servant of a Roman officer, but here the emphasis is on the exceptional nature of these healings.

So this new society is not a utopia but a tangible group of Jews among whom that 'ideal' began to take shape. They went through Jewish territory with Jesus, and the tradition has it that he sent out the Twelve two by two, endowed with his authority, to reach as many Jews as possible.

That was only a small beginning. However, as is evident from the story of the rich man, 'with God everything is possible': Jesus lived by an unshakeable trust in God. To convey that to others he was fond of referring to the miracle of growth in what we call 'nature'. The believing Jew did not use this term: he saw God's power of life at work in plants. From the mustard seed, much smaller than a pinhead, God made a shrub grow that was as tall as a tree. A farmer sows, and without his doing anything the seed germinates and brings forth a stalk and an ear and the grain in it.

71

Jesus also once compared the kingdom of God to a bit of yeast which a housewife put (the text says 'hid') in a large mass of dough and this pervaded the whole mass. The comparison must have seemed very striking to his audience. It was not new, but it was generally used in a negative way: the contagion of evil is as irresistible as the yeast which permeates all the dough. Paul was later to order the Corinthians to expel an immoral man from the community because 'a bit of yeast is enough to leaven the whole dough'. Quite contrary to custom Jesus uses the pervasiveness of the yeast to depict what God has now begun on a small scale – almost in a 'hidden' way – and will certainly bring to a conclusion: his kingdom which will renew the world.

So Jesus is quietly confident that more and more Jews will join the nucleus and be converted to a completely new way of dealing with one another, as though in a kind of family. Jesus himself once suggested that image when he was told that his mother and brothers and sisters were outside and wanted to speak with him. He was sitting in a house surrounded by his disciples. Thereupon he said: 'You here are my mother and brothers and sisters, you and all those who do the will of my Father in heaven.' Did he then see himself as the centre of this family?

On another occasion he described how 'alternative' this new form of society would be: 'You know that those who are supposed to rule over the Gentiles lord it over them, and their great men exercise authority over them. But it shall not be so among you; but whoever would be great among you must be your servant, and whoever would be first among you must be slave of all.'

In this society, in accordance with the will of the Father, Jesus wanted to bring together or 'assemble', as an old prophetic term had it, all Jews. This term related to the dispersion at that time of the Jews over many countries, and to their God who would bring them together again, assemble them, in his land. Jesus was probably thinking of the internal divisions of his people, with all those groups in conflict with one another and all those outcast, all like stray sheep without a shepherd. One of his short sayings runs: 'He who does not gather with me scatters'. He also uses this term once in a lament addressed to the 'lady' Jerusalem, in which he compares himself to a mother bird: 'How often would I have gathered your children together as a hen gathers her brood under her wings, and you would not!' There was some resistance to his proclamation. That is understandable. For to be able to belong to this new society one had to think and live in a very different way, be converted. Alongside the apt parables and piquant imagery the evangelists also record very urgent appeals, sometimes warnings and threats. If the comparisons with the growth of the seed and the working of the yeast in the dough suggested a slow but unstoppable process, other words of Jesus about the coming kingdom indicate a sudden event, an unexpected occurrence, which has the character of a judgment, the Greek for which is *krisis*. 'Truly, I say to you, there are some standing here who will not taste death before they see the kingdom of God come with power.' So Jesus' own generation would experience this. No one, not even Jesus, knew precisely when it would happen. The day and hour are known only to the Father. It might happen in a few years, but equally well in the following week. Hence Jesus' exhortations not to put off conversion. More than once he recalled the well-known story of the flood: while Noah was building his ark, people went on leading their ordinary lives, as though no disaster were hanging over their heads.

However, he also issued summonses to conversion in stories which alluded to circumstances familiar to his audience. So he once told a story about a steward who was accused before his master, a great landlord, of not adminstering his master's money properly. This was a not improbable situation in that society. The man was given notice. Then he went to his master's debtors and suggested that they should falsify the bills of debt. One should put fifty in place of the hundred jars of oil that he owed. Another should put eighty in place of the hundred measures of wheat. Jesus did not say in any way that this action was immoral. He was only concerned that this man did something: because he had been told that he was to be dismissed he was in a critical situation and immediately took precautions. This story is handed down only by Luke, as the beginning of his chapter 16. It ends with this sentence: 'The lord commended the dishonest steward for his prudence'. If 'the lord' refers to the steward's employer, then this comment is the end of Jesus' story. But the 'lord' came also refer to Jesus himself, in which case the sentence was added by the first disciples who related it: Our lord Jesus commended this steward because he had been so skilful! Later disciples clearly had difficulty with this. For the sequel to Luke's text contains some attempts to attach positive conclusions to this shocking story.

Following on from this, I should say something more about this striking feature of Jesus' proclamation: his brief stories, usually called parables. Like his brief sayings, sometimes making vivid comparisons, these were meant to liberate his audience from their familiar patterns of thought and expectation and in this way to open their hearts to the new dimension that was beginning with him. The story about the steward that I have just recalled must have shocked the audience. Perhaps its moral was that one could learn something even from 'bad people'. For one of the things for which Jesus was criticized was that he had dealings with such people as the 'friend of publicans and sinners'.

According to Luke 18 Jesus also once told a story about a judge who did not fear God and did not respect any man (certainly not those who could not pay, the audience would have been thinking). A widow in that city kept urging him: 'Give me justice in the face of those who have done me injustice!' To begin with, the judge took no notice. But the widow kept on so much that he finally gave in. He said to himself: 'Although I do not fear God and take no notice of any man, because this widow is such a burden to me I shall give her justice; otherwise she will finally "hit me in the face".' This may be a reference to physical violence; it can also mean to blacken, bring into disrepute. At all events the audience was clearly to understand what the unjust judge was saying to himself. Luke introduces the story as encouragement to believers in situations of oppression to continue to pray to God unceasingly, as the widow continued to badger the judge until he gave in.

The story in Matthew 13 about a treasure which lay buried in a field is apparently an innocent one. The labourer working there came upon the treasure and covered it up again. That too was not exceptional, like an unjust judge. It often happened in areas which had constantly been ravaged by war: people sometimes had to flee in haste and buried their treasures in the ground. Many of them never returned. Hence such discoveries. Hence, too, laws which prescribed what had to be done. According to both Roman and Jewish legislation the person who discovered such a treasure had to share it with the landowner. So what the person in Jesus' story did was illegal. But clearly that point was not important to Jesus. What was important was the immediate reaction: to get the treasure the man unhesitatingly sold all that he had and did so 'joyfully'. It looks as if the treasure had taken possession of the finder. Perhaps we may have some indication here of Jesus' own joy for the gift of being so entirely absorbed with the coming kingdom of God that he sometimes referred to it as a wedding, a feast of love.

An unexpected feast seems to be the chief motive in Jesus' story of the 'prodigal son' which Luke includes in his chapter 15. In this story too Jesus begins from a situation which could come about in the world with which he and his audience were familiar. The younger of two sons asks his father to give him immediately the share of his possessions that was due to him. That was possible according to the existing law of inheritance. And it probably was often the case that a young man wanted to get away from the restrictions of his parents' house in order to build up a life of his own somewhere else. He certainly knew what he risked by doing this: from then on he had no further claims on his father.

The son in Jesus' story emigrated to a distant country. Because of his own extravagance and other circumstances he ended up there in the utmost distress. When he was almost dying of hunger he thought of the hired labourers who worked for his father. It was possible that his father would employ him as such a labourer. So he went home with this spark of hope. On the way he repeated the request that he would put to his father.

When he was approaching the house, something happened that he had not thought possible. It seems that his father had been on the look-out for him. For he saw his son coming from a distance and, moved by compassion, ran up to him and flung his arms around his neck. The young man did not even get the opportunity to finish the speech he had prepared, for the father dressed up the starving beggar to be the guest of honour at a feast which was then celebrated. What seemed impossible had really happened, as a result of the incomprehensible love of this father.

But the story is not over yet. Jesus now describes the protest of the older son who did not want to take part in this feast. He was harsh and brutal to the father who came to urge him to come. He had always been dutiful and had never got anything extra for it. And now here was a festival for 'that son of yours who has wasted your property with riotous living...' The father addresses him lovingly as 'my child' and tries to persuade him to join in the festival. Jesus does not tell us whether he succeeded. His audience had to draw that conclusion for themselves.

The reaction of the older son once again stresses the totally new perspective that is opened up by the father's love. According to him his younger brother should really have been punished for his misdeeds. He really did not deserve such a reception. Where are we, if the principle of 'reward according to merit' does not apply? Surely the whole of society is based on that! The father urges the son nevertheless to come to join in the festivities. Perhaps at that point a new world begins to open even for him, this new world in which other criteria apply.

Luke includes this story in the context of Jesus' reply to a critical comment made by Pharisees and scribes: 'This man receives sinners and eats with them!' First Jesus describes the joy of a man and a woman who after much searching had found what they had lost: a sheep from the flock and a coin from a purse. Both end up with the 'moral' that in the same way there is joy in heaven over a sinner who repents. In this way Luke suggests that the third story, about the 'lost' son, must also be understood similarly. He makes the father twice give the reason for this festal joy: his younger son 'was dead and is alive again, was lost and now found'. These seem to be two modest supplements to Jesus' story which make its application easier: the son who has run away stands for the sinner, and the father who receives him so lovingly stands for God. Jesus himself usually leaves it to his audience to attach significance to the story he has told.

Jesus did this clearly in his story about 'the workers in the vineyard' which has been preserved in Matthew 20 and ends with a question. That story, too, begins from a familiar situation. The ripe grapes had to be harvested in time. Those who are experts on viniculture in Palestine at that time tell us that for example the threat of a heavy rainstorm sometimes made it necessary to pick the bunches very quickly, sometimes within a day. The owner of a vineyard gets up at 6 a.m. to hire grape pickers in the market place (the labour exchange) and agrees that their wage shall be a denarius a day (denarius means a ten-coin, the normal wage for a day's work). At 9 a.m. he goes back to the market and hires more workers there, with the promise that they can count on a fair wage. He does the same thing again at noon and at 3 p.m., but without saying anything about wages. Finally, at 5 p.m. he still finds workers whom he hires. Here the narrator is on very improbable ground. But he has indicated clearly how long this day's work lasted and has also aroused expectations about the payment.

Then he brings a new figure on the scene: the steward who is responsible for wages and who has to begin with the workers who came last. He gives each of them a denarius. Those who worked the whole day receive that sum too.

In a third scene the owner then appears, as the object of the protest of those who came first and had expected a much higher wage. To their spokesman he says: 'Friend, I do you no wrong. Did you not agree with me for a denarius! Take what is due to you and go!' But this is not his last word. He continues: 'I mean to give to those who came last the same as you. May I not do what I like with what is my own? Or is your eye evil because I am good?'

Jesus' audience will doubtless have sympathized with the indignation of those who had worked all through the long hot day. What the owner did did not fit the usual pattern: wages had to correspond to the work done. He broke that pattern. But he did not put anyone at a disadvantage. He only did good, and did so in such a way that no one suffered damage except himself. Perhaps he considered that the others had also stood in the market hoping for work, for they too needed their daily wages to support their family. But Jesus does not say that. It is, however, clear that he opens up a new possibility with the story; a world in which other standards prevail than those which are customary.

Unexpected things also happen in his story about the 'good Samaritan'. It takes place on the road that runs from Jerusalem to Jericho, which lies more than 3000 feet lower. It goes through the inhospitable wilderness where nothing grows except in the rainy season and where robbers are on the prowl as well as wild beasts. So the first sentence describes a familiar reality. 'A man was going down from Jerusalem to Jericho. And he fell among robbers, who stripped him and beat him, and departed, leaving him half dead.' Unless he gets help soon, this man will die. And true enough, help does comes along, and what help! 'Now by chance a priest was going down that road; and when he saw him he passed by on the other side.' How inhuman, the Jewish hearer would have thought; you would have expected differently from a priest. 'So likewise a Levite, when he came to the place and saw him, passed by on the other side.' The minister of lower rank behaved just as heartlessly.

The dying man can hardly expect anythting of the next passer-by. He is a Samaritan, and this name indicates that he belongs to a group of apostates. They had separated themselves from the one true temple in Jerusalem, and constructed a religion of their own. Jews had no dealings with them and sometimes used their name as a taunt when they argued among one another and wanted to call someone a godless villain. 'But a Samaritan, as he journeyed, came to where he was, and when he saw him, he had compassion, and went to him and bound up his wounds, pouring on oil and wine; then he set him on his own beast and brought him to an inn, and took care of him. And the next day he took out two denarii and gave them to the innkeeper, saying, "Take care of him, and whatever more you spend, I will repay you when I come back."'

In Luke's time this story was told to give believers an evocative example of love of neighbour. That is evident from the context in Luke 10; a lawyer asks Jesus what is meant by the neighbour whom according to the Torah one has to love as oneself. Jesus replied with this story: one has to love like this Samaritan. But that was probably not the original meaning. In that case Jesus would have done better to present his Jewish audience with a layman who did help the wounded man after the priest and the levite had passed him by. The wounded man could have been a Samaritan, and then the Jew would have been an example of love of one's enemy that Jesus preached.

But Jesus' story was meant to strike home because it was unexpected. First comes the heartlessness of the two ministers, professional religious, who lived by their calling. Their refusal to help is described in Greek with only two words: having-seen he-went-by-on-the-other-side. Even more unexpected is the Samaritan who does have a heart: having seen, he was deeply moved by compassion, mercy – and then Jesus uses a great many words to describe his help in detail; it continues even after the Samaritan has gone. Here the emphasis comes to lie on the act of love from a totally unexpected quarter, a new reality in a world in which violence and heartlessness and stereotyped relationships dominate society.

These were some examples of challenging or, perhaps better, inviting, stories of Jesus. In recent years biblical scholars have studied these texts in the first three Gospels a great deal. First of all they have done so in order to trace their original wording amidst the adaptations which later disciples made to them and sometimes incorporated into them for the benefit of instruction in the faith in their own time. Secondly they have been studied in order to analyse these statements and narratives of Jesus as a particular use of language. Both in Jewish circles and in other cultures pithy comparisons were used in the formulation of wisdom: comic, shocking or mysterious, in a short sentence or a story, and always easy to remember. Comparison of these with sayings of Jesus not only makes clearer what he wanted to achieve with this use of language but also shows that he was a master of this kind of communication. He used it in order to show through his words something of the kingdom of God, which since his appearance was no longer purely in the future but was already at work in the here and now; he now confronted his audience withthe decision whether to 'gain' their life or to 'lose' it.

## Who was he?

There was somethings contradictory about Jesus' behaviour. On the one hand it was very presumptuous: the eternal destiny of his audience would depend on their reaction to what he preached. No prophet before him had made such a radical claim. On the other hand he showed an almost exaggerated modesty. As Mark related, he was offended even when someone addressed him as 'good master'. People had to look carefully and listen to what he did and said, but not occupy themselves with his person.

Both Matthew and Luke relate what John the Baptist asked Jesus from his prison: 'Are you he who should come or do we look for another?' The messengers did not get an answer in the style of, 'Tell him that I am he.' No, they had to go to John and tell him what they could see and hear: the blind see, the lame walk, lepers are cleansed and the good news is proclaimed.

Jesus' audience, the people of his generation, 'this generation', would experience the great day of judgment and the manifestation of God's kingdom. He once recalled two well-known stories from the scriptures. The wisdom of Solomon was so famous that the Queen of Sheba, in the south of Arabia, made the long journey to Jerusalem to hear Solomon. The prophet Jonah was sent by God to the capital of Assyria, the inhabitants of which were promptly converted. Jesus says: 'The queen of the South will arise at the judgment with the men of this generation and condemn them; for she came from the ends of the earth to hear the wisdom of

Solomon, and behold, something greater than Solomon is here. The men of Nineveh will arise at the judgment with this generation and condemn it, for they repented at the preaching of Jonah, and behold, something greater than Jonah is here.' That 'here' seems to divert attention from his person and direct it towards his preaching, both the way in which he communicated wisdom and his call to conversion. At the same time he offended his Jewish audience with the prospect that they would be condemned by non-Jews.

According to the evangelists he often spoke about the 'son of the man', an expression which sounded as strange in their Greek as it does in our language. This strangeness is to some degree diminished by our usual rendering 'the son of man'. It is striking that none of the four Gospels ever has the term used by anyone else, in the style of, 'What do you think of this, son of man?' Or, in a conversation with him, 'Say, Peter, I have encountered the son of man of whom you speak so often'. All *eighty* times the term occurs in the four Gospels it is used exclusively by Jesus. It looks as if the evangelists had come to an agreement on that. But that cannot be the case. The only explanation is that this use of the term by Jesus had already become obvious in the earliest traditions that they knew.

It is certainly the case that sometimes one of the authors uses the term instead of 'I'. Where Mark relates that Jesus asked his disciples, 'Who do men say that I am?', Matthew changes this to, 'Who do people say that the son of man is?' But there seems no doubt that Jesus sometimes referred to himself in this way, in the third person. The question is, why did he do this and what did he mean by it?

According to some scholars the strange 'the son of the man' is the literal rendering of an Aramaic expression which simply meant a human being, a man, someone. They suppose that Jesus sometimes used this term to divert attention from his person. One of their examples is a remark about John the Baptist. Jesus recognized John as someone who had been sent by God, as he also knew himself to have been sent. There were certainly differences between them in life-style and in message. Those who rejected Jesus appealed to them to avoid the real issue, the demand that God made on them through this messenger of his. Such unwillingness was not appropriate for grown men. Jesus says this (here 'son of man' is translated 'someone'):

80

To what then shall I compare the men of this generation, and what are they like? They are like children sitting in the market place and calling to one another: We piped to you and you did not dance. We sang laments to you and you did not weep. For John the Baptist has come eating no bread and drinking no wine; and you say he has a demon. Then comes someone eating and drinking; and you say, 'Behold a glutton and a drunkard!'

If 'the son of the man' here in fact means someone, a man, then Jesus seems to indicate by it that in the last resort what is at issue is not John the Baptist and himself, but how those with negative attitudes react to any messenger of God: they seek such excuses. There is no bitterness or hostility in this remark, but rather a touch of sadness about the way in which people make fools of themselves. Playfully introduced by the comparison with peevish children who refuse to join in a game, these words of Jesus present a challenge to look the truth in the face.

As another example in which 'the son of man' can be used in this more general way, scholars refer to the famous comment: 'The foxes have holes and the birds have nests, but the son of man has nowhere to lay his head.' If 'someone' is meant here, the meaning would be more general: a person can be so totally dedicated to the proclamation of the kingdom of God that he no longer has any place for himself. In that case Jesus would leave this possibility open for others than himself, which could represent a challenging sign to his disciples.

But other scholars doubt whether the Aramaic expression which is presupposed here could have had the general significance 'a man, someone' in the milieu of Jesus. Moreover this would apply to only some of the many texts about the son of man. Then the question remains: how did Jesus come to apply this term to himself? Were there models for this in scripture? Reference has been made to the use of son of Adam, i.e. son of man, in the book of Ezekiel. The prophet is always addressed by God in this way, as many as ninety times! In the first chapter Ezekiel describes the vision in which he saw the heavenly beings which surround God, and afterwards a figure who looked like a man and emanated an indescribable glow, sitting on something that seemed to be a throne. Overwhelmed by this sight the prophet fell to the ground and then heard a voice say to him: 'Son of man, stand upright, and I shall speak to you.' He was then given the task of going to the Israelites and prepared in detail for the fact that the people was rebellious: it was not ready to listen, for 'it has a hard countenance and a heart of stone: it is a rebellious people'. This is a hard task for anyone who has been given a glimpse of God's glory and has to speak in God's name, but at the same time has remained an ordinary weak man, a son of Adam.

It is more usual to refer to the mysterious figure which Daniel saw in his first vision. The four beast-like monsters who emerge from the sea represent the inhuman rulers of the world powers. They are annihilated, and then eternal rule over all nations is entrusted to 'one like to a son of man', but at the same time this appears to be the symbol of 'the people of the saints' who had to suffer so much in their struggle against the powers of evil. Of that people, too, it is said that it will receive royal power, just like the one who appeared as a son of man. So the image could arise of a son of man who had to endure humiliation and suffering and at the same time was destined to exercise the highest conceivable authority for ever.

In fact according to the first three evangelists Jesus used the term 'son of man' in these two apparently contrasted meanings. On the one hand he did so with reference to his power or authority, sometimes in relation to that which he already had, for example to forgive sins or to determine what could be done on the sabbath. Often the evangelists have him use the term when he is talking about 'the last things': then the son of man will appear in glory and pronounce his judgment on humankind, as judge in the name of God. On the other hand, according to the evangelists Jesus talks about the son of man when he is describing his imminent suffering or the death that he must undergo, to which he sometimes adds his resurrection.

From what I have said in this all too general survey of the many 'son of man' texts, you may have noticed where the difficulty really lies. As I said at the beginning of this chapter, the evangelists drew on oral and written traditions; each of them compiled, or perhaps better, composed, his own account from them, emphasizing the themes which he thought important and which he wanted to impress on his readers. Anyone who is familiar with this will be as ready to say that an evangelist makes Jesus use the term in a particular way as that Jesus himself used it in that way.

Although questions remain about Jesus' use of 'the son of man', there can be no reasonable doubt about some characteristics of his behaviour which come to the fore in all recollections. On closer inspection they seem to be intimately connected. One striking feature was the way in which he conversed with God and spoke about him. Like all believing Jews Jesus prayed a great deal. But his prayers seem more spontaneous and less bound by rules and formulae. His disciples continued to remember that he addressed God as Abba, a kind of diminutive of the usual Aramaic word for father. Small children called 'Abba' after their fathers. It is possible that other pious Jews used the term in their personal prayer, but that certainly did not happen when they were praying together in the synagogue. Jesus used it publicly and taught his disciples to address God in this confident way. They evidently did so, for when at a later date Greek was the dominant language in their communities, they still retained the Aramaic word. For Paul this communal cry in prayer of Abba, Father, was a sign that those who prayed could rightly feel themselves to be children of God.

Jesus' firm trust in God, which I have already mentioned in this outline, seems rooted in his prayer to the Father. For a Jew, in practice belief in God coincided with trust and hope in him. Many prayers in the book of psalms bear witness to that. In the deepest distress those who pray remain confident that God will bring salvation, to the individual or to the people. Jesus trusted that God would complete what had been begun in his own person, although that beginning might seem insignificant and weak, and come up against resistance.

That trust in God seemed also to lead to the sense of freedom on the basis of which Jesus was not afraid of violating sacred laws and customs. In his environment anyone who was truly pious had to avoid the company of 'sinners' and abstain from anything that could make him 'impure'. But God had made himself known to Israel as the one who stands up for those who are despised and oppressed, and constantly had this preference confirmed by lawgivers and prophets. In the spirit of that ancient faith Jesus, too, felt himself compelled to bring the message of the coming kingdom of God particularly to the marginal figures, those despised and excluded by the pious.

In so doing he gave the impression of having an inner freedom which put him in a position to encounter anyone openly, free from any prejudice, without anxiety or shame. He also treated the women he encountered in the same way. Such freedom was striking in his environment. But any form of discrimination was evidently alien to him. He even paid attention to children. This complete openness to everyone seems to be connected with his sense of God as Father. In the coming kingdom people would deal with one another as children of this father.

So these are a few characteristics of Jesus' behaviour. Anyone who tries to sketch this kind of picture of him on the basis of the first three Gospels sometimes comes up against the objection: is it really necessary to portray Jesus as having been so unique? The answer to this question is given by David Flusser: we know of no other Jew from antiquity who proclaimed that the coming time of salvation had already dawned. That is the reason why people could not place him. Other Jews performed healings, but not as a foretaste of the coming kingdom. There were many teachers who expounded God's will in all kinds of situations. As professionals they appealed to the Torah and the equally authoritative oral exposition of it. Jesus simply expressed his own thoughts and never referred to any authority. Nor was he a prophet in the old style, for he never spoke in the name of God. In that respect he seems to have been like John the Baptist, whom many people regarded as a prophet. But what he announced was still completely in the future, though it was very near.

Thus to the people with whom he had to do he was 'unique', not to be put in any known category. His concern with what he called the kingdom of God could indeed suggest that he would reign in it in God's name, as did David and his successors, the anointed of Yahweh. In the circumstances of this time such a reign was inconceivable unless the Roman rulers had previously been expelled. But Jesus vigorously rejected the thought that he was destined to be the Lord's anointed, Messiah, in this sense. Such considerations involving national politics were alien to him. He had taught his disciples to pray for the coming of the kingdom of God. This wish was also the first and most prominent in Jewish prayers of that time. But it was usually followed by urgent petitions for the liberation of Israel and the restoration of the 'throne of David' in Jerusalem. No saying of Jesus has been preserved in which these perspectives are expressed.

Jesus even rejected the thought of ruling over others. In his comment about 'rank' in the kingdom of God which I have already quoted, Jesus says that those who want to be first in it will have to be the servants of all. Mark and Matthew relate what he went on to say: for 'the son of man did not come to be ministered to but to minister and to give his life a ransom for many'. Luke describes the sequel like this: 'For who is greater, the one who reclines at table or the one who serves? Is not the one who reclines at table? But I am in your midst as the servant.' Perhaps Luke gave the saying this form because he quotes it in his story about the last supper of Jesus with his disciples. According to John 13, Jesus then matched his words with his deeds: he washed his disciples' feet, a service which according to rabbinic texts even a slave might not undertake if he was of Jewish descent.

The term 'service' seems best suited to denote the work of Jesus. He had left behind all that he had. He could no longer call anywhere his own. He lived on what others gave him. He certainly had 'spiritual' possessions, like the charisma of freeing people from sickness and demons and his gifts as a poet (an English expert on the Aramaic that Jesus spoke wrote a book on *The Poetry of Our Lord*). But he put all this completely at the service of his proclamation. Still, his dedication to God's cause would only become complete and irrevocable when he had also given his life for it, the life that he could still call his own as a man of flesh and blood.

### His end in Jerusalem

According to Mark's framework Jesus first worked for some time in Galilee and then went to Jerusalem, where he was put to death. At the end of his chapter 9 Luke marked this journey with a sentence which is loaded with terms from the Greek Bible: 'When the days drew near for him to be received up, he set his face to go to Jerualem.' That 'receiving up' could refer to his death and at the same time to his being received up into heaven. 'Setting his face' seems to be taken from the book of Ezekiel and here denotes the resolution with which Jesus went to meet his prophetic fate.

Jesus does not arrive in Jerusalem until ten chapters later: Luke has used the fact of this journey to hand down 'on the way' all kinds of traditions about Jesus which he had found in other sources than Mark. One of them is in his chapter 13:

Then some Pharisees came to Jesus and said to him, 'Go away from here, for Herod wants to kill you.' And he said to them: 'Go and tell that old fox, "Behold I cast out demons and perform cures today and tomorrow, and the third day I finish my course."'

The warning by the Pharisees will seem strange to many Christians. But it is not improbable. The negative image of this Jewish group is above all based on the Gospel of Matthew, the first of the four and the one most read in the churches. It will emerge in due course (in chapter 6 of this book) why the evangelist depicted the Pharisees as enemies of Jesus. The reasons that he had for this did not apply to Luke. So in his work he could include recollections in which Pharisees showed interest in Jesus and, for example, invited him to their table. We know from other sources that they often had differences of opinion, even on important points relating to the practice of their faith. That may also have been the case with their verdict on Jesus. Perhaps some of them were amazed at the freedom with which he treated all kinds of customs, a freedom which was obviously connected with his candid piety. Their difficulty was perhaps that he promised God's forgiveness all too easily to people who had not yet shown any sign of real conversion. That could lead to laxity and in the long run undermine the morality of the people.

Herod Antipas's plan can hardly surprise us, given the reasons for which he had John the Baptist executed. Jesus, too, had a great influence on his audience. He went through the country with a growing group of Galileans and above all, unlike John the Baptist, he constantly spoke with enthusiasm about the kingdom of God that was on the way. To the ears of Jews well disposed towards Rome this apparently religious language expressed a concern for resistance to the occupying forces. Therefore Jesus was much more dangerous than John the Baptist. The anxious Pharisees were naturally thinking of territories outside Galilee where Herod had no jurisdiction, and not of Judaea. For there Jesus' life was in much more danger; however, he continued with his plan. Luke follows up the words which I have quoted with a remark which takes up the mysterious 'on the third day'. It runs: 'Nevertheless I must go on my way today and tomorrow and the day following, for it cannot be that a prophet should perish away from Jerusalem.'

It was almost Passover when he reached the capital via Jericho. For practising Jews that festival – *pesach* in Hebrew – is the greatest festival of the year. It was already so in Jesus' day, but at that time the temple was still standing. The festival could only really be celebrated properly there in Jerusalem. For at the festal meal in the family circle a lamb had to be eaten, the passover lamb, and according to the Law only lambs which had been slaughtered in the temple could be used for that. For that reason, around Passover Jerusalem was packed with pilgrims from all parts of the country and even from far away. There was unbounded joy among the crowds, of which thousands must have camped around the city. It has been reckoned that at this period Jerusalem numbered 25-30,000 inhabitants and that at passover time between 85,000 and 125,000 pilgrims were added to that number.

At that time the Roman garrison was also considerably strengthened. For Passover was essentially a feast of liberation, a celebration of the exodus from the oppressive power of the Pharaoh. Now the majority of the people was under the yoke of Roman occupation, no less pagan than that of the Pharaoh and, even worse, dominating the very land of Israel's God. One inspired Jew who gave himself out to be the king of Israel called by God could set the crowds celebrating Passover on fire and unleash a rebellion which could only be put down in blood by a number of legions. So there were many soldiers to guard cope with any possible rebels, and the Roman governor was also present. He normally resided in the luxurious coastal city of Caesarea: at Passover he came in person to take command in Jerusalem.

Some days before the last Passover in which he was to take part, Jesus came from Galilee via Jericho to Jerusalem with his group of twelve, accompanied by the men and women who had attached themselves to him. Mark relates that he ordered two of his disciples to go into a neighbouring village to fetch the foal which he knew to be tied there and on which no one had yet ridden. He sat on it and, surrounded by a jubilant crowd which cried out Hosanna with a verse from Psalm 118, he rode into the city.

That is what we learn from the story of the entry into Jerusalem in Mark 11 which Matthew and Luke took over from him with some variants. They also follow Mark in the further course of events. Having arrived in the temple, Jesus drives out the traders there. Then follow a number of discussions with the Jewish leaders in the temple and finally a great speech in which Jesus forecasts the devastation of Jerusalem and the end of the world. After that, in Mark 14, the passion narrative proper begins on the Thursday evening. The entry seems to have taken place on the first day of this week, our Sunday. Hence the name Palm Sunday for the day on which Christians commemorate this entry into Jerusalem at the beginning of 'Holy Week'.

The name Palm Sunday brings us to the Gospel of John. The three other Gospels do not mention palm branches in connection with the entry, and rightly so: no palm trees grew in the neighbourhood of Jerusalem. Only John mentions them, in his shorter version of the story, which moreover has another function in his Gospel. There it in fact appears in chapter 12, which forms the conclusion of the first part of his book, about the public life of Jesus. He devotes the following five chapters to the intimate gathering of Jesus and his disciples at their last supper, and his many words of farewell. Only after that does John's passion narrative begin with the arrest of Jesus in an orchard alongside the brook Kedron. As I have already observed, according to John the 'cleansing of the temple' had taken place a year or more earlier, at the beginning of Jesus' public ministry. For the three other Gospels it seems to have been this action of Jesus in the temple which led to the decision to arrest him and have him killed. Historically this seems more probable. Certainty is no longer attainable. The narratives of the last decisive events are strongly influenced by the faith in the person of Jesus which was only given to the disciples after his death.

Much of that belief has already been incorporated into Mark's account of the entry. On that basis people attributed to Jesus supernatural knowledge by means of which he knew of the foal that stood tied up in the village. As Messiah-king he had the right to ask for an animal to ride on, but he also observed the old rule that what had been borrowed had to be given back after it had been used. It would not be fitting that someone else, perhaps an unjust or an impure person, should have ridden on the foal before Jesus, and the narrators evidently assumed that the animal would be immediately ready to carry this its first rider.

The excited people supplemented the cry of Hosanna from Ps.118 with words in which they welcomed Jesus as a ruler from the house of David, as Messiah. The later Easter faith also played a part in this exuberant homage. For it is extremely improbable that such a demonstration would have escaped the watchful eye of the Romans. It is not mentioned in the charges that were made against Jesus. Therefore it is sometimes supposed that this whole story of the entry into Jerusalem grew out of the Easter faith. It is said to have been derived from the text of the prophet Zechariah,

88

part of which was quoted by Matthew at length and by John in part: daughter of Zion, 'behold your king comes meekly and riding on an ass'.

What seems more likely is the suggestion that there was indeed a historical nucleus, even if the question remains just what it was. Some people suppose that as he approached Jerusalem Jesus mounted an ass and in so doing went against a venerable custom. Pilgrims who could afford a mount dismounted when the holy city came into view: they had to enter this city on foot. Jesus is supposed to have done the opposite and begun to sit on an ass because of his strong feeling that he had been sent by God, and was vested with an authority that he would now exercise at the centre of God's people. That would have been a 'prophetic' gesture, very significant and perhaps also understood to be such by the small group of disciples. But Jesus himself did not put this significance into words.

Jesus also made a similar prophetic gesture when he entered the temple and there drove out those who bought and sold, at the same time overturning the tables of the moneychangers and the stalls of those who were selling doves. This action by Jesus was unprecedented and very challenging. It went against the age-old and sacred course of affairs at the centre of Jewish religion. There 'dwelt' the God of Israel, in that dark place which only the High Priest could enter and then only once a year, on the Great Day of Atonement. Around this dwelling the mighty acts of God were celebrated each day with singing and musical instruments, both the creation and the special benefits shown to Israel; and above all, there every day communion with him was experienced in sacrificial worship in accordance with the precepts of the Torah, especially those in the book of Leviticus.

Jews from all over the world went there to offer burnt offerings, peace offerings and sin offerings. For this, sacrificial animals were needed. Those who lived in or around Jerusalem could bring these themselves. But those who came from a long way away had to buy them in Jerusalem. Rich people could buy oxen and calves, less rich people sheep and goats, while the poor had to make do with doves. Hence the livestock dealers and sellers of doves. But there were also moneychangers, for these animals could not be purchased with coinage on which there was an image of a pagan ruler. These coins had to be changed into an older kind of money. This coinage was also used to pay the annual temple tax which every Jew was obliged to pay, no matter where in the world he lived, and he had to use it whenever he offered a sacrifice.

The Jerusalem temple has been called the national bank of Israel. Enormous quantities of money and bars of gold were kept in its treasure chambers, capital with which trade was also carried on: in addition there was also income from the lands which the temple owned in Palestine. All these finances were administered by members of the temple hierarchy, priests, many of whom were members of the richest families in the land.

The Roman rulers recognized the key position of the temple and its priesthood. It was also in their interests that this priestly grip on economic and political administration should be preserved. Hence at the time of the great feasts with their enormous influx of pilgrims the extra reinforcement of the garrison that has already been mentioned. In the citadel Antonia at the north-west corner of the great temple complex, there was always at least one cohort, a detachment of 600 men. There was also a Jewish temple police under the orders of the hierarchy. But if there was any disturbance which escaped the notice of this police force, the Roman soldiers could immediately hurl themselves on the trouble-makers from the citadel. They sometimes also patrolled on the roofs of the colonnades which surrounded the courts.

For these reason one cannot assume that the action of Jesus which is usually referred to as the cleansing of the temple was on a large scale. Had it been the soldiers would have intervened immediately. Perhaps it was no more than a small incident at one of the gates which gave access to the extensive 'Court of the Gentiles'. It must have been reported to the authorities. Mark relates that after it they asked Jesus the question. 'What authority do you have to do this? What is it based on?' Jesus asked a question in reply: 'Did the baptism of John come from God or from men?' They could not reply to that. If they said 'From God', they would have had to explain why they had not recognized John as a messenger from God. If they said it was human work then they would incur the hostility of the people, since they regarded John as a prophet.

According to the Fourth Evangelist, after the cleansing of the temple 'the Jews' asked for a sign that would legitimate him. His answer was: 'Destroy this temple and in three days I shall raise it up again.' The evangelist explains that Jesus was talking about 'the temple of his body', but he adds that his disciples 'remembered' that only later, after Easter.

It is striking that an almost identical remark, about the destruction of the temple and its replacement after three days with a new one, also appears in Mark and Matthew, but not in connection with Jesus' action. They record the saying as having been reported by witnesses at the time of the nocturnal interrogation by the Supreme Council; and the next day there were scoffers who reminded Jesus of the saying when he was hanging on the cross.

There is little doubt that the activity of Jesus in Jerusalem considerably disturbed the Jewish authorities. He was popular among the Galileans, who were well known for their anti-Roman feelings. Moreover his criticism of how things were going could also make its mark on ordinary people in Judaea, who were not very fond of the rich priestly families: the latter were more concerned with money than with God and therefore they had an understanding with the Roman authorities. According to the Fourth Gospel the members of the Supreme Council expressed their disquiet like this: What are we to do? If they all run after this man, the Romans will destroy our holy city and our people. The high priest Caiaphas then remarked: It is better that one man should die than that the whole people should perish. Hence the decision to do away with Jesus, and as quickly as possible.

The problem was how to lay hands on him without starting an enormous row, with all the terrifying consequences. The solution came from an unexpected quarter. One of Jesus' twelve closest companions reported that he was ready to indicate the place outside the city where Jesus was to go to spend the night with his small group on the Thursday evening. This man was called Judas. To distinguish him from numerous other Jews of the same name (derived from Judah, the tribal ancestor), he had the surname Iscariot. The meaning and origin of this surname are obscure, as is the reason that led Judas to hand his master over to the authorities in this way.

Deeply rooted in the earliest tradition is the story that earlier on this Thursday evening somewhere in the city Jesus held a meal with the Twelve and at it did and said something so full of significance that it could never be forgotten. As a Jewish householder he said a blessing when he took bread. He broke it into pieces and shared it out. In place of a detailed explanation he simply said, 'This is my body.' They could hear and see it being broken, and he did not have to say that this was happening for them: to give someone some of the most basic food, bread, means wanting to nourish his or her life. The one who had shown himself to be such a master at inventing parables which were as unexpected as they were apt here made two things clear simultaneously: that his body would soon be broken and that suffering to the point of death would be for the benefit of the life of this twelve, representatives of the renewed people of God.

Later he poured wine into a cup. When he handed it round to the others after a blessing, for them to drink it, he said, 'This is my blood.' Again his remark was as short as it was significant. Wine was called the 'blood of the grape' and was regarded as a divine gift, intended to 'gladden the heart of man'. But at the same time the shedding of blood suggested to a Jew the sacrificial worship in the temple in which Israel's community with God was expressed and experienced, 'the covenant'. According to the well-known story in Exodus 24, that covenant was concluded when Moses poured out the blood of sacrificial animals, half on the altar, a symbol for God, and half on the people that committed itself to live as he wanted it to. The sacrifices in the temple were aimed at expressing and maintaining this communion; some of them were seen as an opportunity to return to God which God offered to those who had gone outside the community as a result of their own guilt, 'sin offerings'.

But at the same time every believing Jew knew that in the last resort God was not concerned with those sacrifices but with the human heart. The suppliant of Psalm 40 was not the only one to assert that God did not want all these kinds of burnt- and sin-offerings, but inner dedication: 'to fulfil your will is my delight and your law is in my innermost parts'. And Jeremiah 31 is not the only text to look forward to a 'new covenant'. In it each member of God's people would take that word of the psalmist to heart. Then there would no longer be any need for instruction in the Torah because young and old would know what God wanted of them from within.

Perhaps Jesus himself expressed what was implied in the identification of his blood with the wine that he gave them to drink. The tradition gives two somewhat different versions: 'This is my blood of the covenant which is shed for many (with the addition 'for the forgiveness of sins')' or: 'This cup is the new covenant in my blood that is shed for you.'

After the meal Jesus went out of the city with his group, to a garden or orchard which was called Gethsemane. According to Mark there he told some of his closest companions that he was sorrowful to death. Later they related how in a lonely prayer to his Father he had reconciled himself to the death that awaited him. On information supplied by Judas a detachment of Jewish police arrested him and led him to the house of the high priest, at which members of the Supreme Council were present. There it was resolved to hand Jesus over to Pilate. We can no longer determine from the Gospel narratives what reasons were given for this, since the Gospels differ from one another. That is understandable, as none of Jesus' disciples was present at that council and the filling in of what must have happened was strongly influenced after Easter by belief in Jesus as Messiah and Son of God. We may assume that it had been a difficult decision for members of the council. The Romans had allowed the subjected Jews their own jurisdiction. It was quite something to hand over one of their own people to a Roman magistrate. Moreover, the Jewish judges felt themselves bound to the Torah, and this provided for the death penalty for certain crimes like sabbath-breaking, apostasy and blasphemy. And someone who gave himself out to be a prophet and misled the people had to be executed; executed, moreover, in the presence of all the people, and thus preferably at one of the three festivals at which everyone who could, made a pilgrimage to Jerusalem. But scholars differ over the precise application of these ancient laws and therefore over the question when someone was guilty of such a capital offence.

Probably the council had confirmed that Jesus had 'messianic' pretensions. This was not punishable under the law, but was sufficient reason to hand him over to Pilate as an enemy of the state, a rebel. The procurator sometimes kept some resistance fighters in prison in order to have them crucified at a festival when there were many Jews in Jerusalem, to make it clear to them that any attempt at rebellion against Rome would be punished mercilessly. So Jesus, with two others, underwent the death that awaited rebels.

An American Jew has recently written a fascinating book under the title *What Crucified Jesus?* Note that this title refers to 'what', not 'who'. The author, Ellis Rivkin, is Professor of Jewish History in Cincinnati. Above all on the basis of information from Flavius

Josephus, he describes the political situation at the time of Pilate and Caiaphas, and of Herod Antipas in Galilee. A charismatic who drew crowds could count on being executed. For excited crowds threatened the law and order that the Romans and their helpers wanted to maintain at any price. That is why the charismatic John the Baptist was murdered. Jesus is said by Rivkin to have been a charismatic of charismatics. In him the miraculous power of Elijah was combined with the visionary gift of Isaiah and the didactic persuasiveness of a Pharisaic sage. But he had also entered into the suffering of the poor, the humiliation of those who had been written off, the despair of the sinners, and he had received all who approached him with friendship, compassion and unconditional love. Therefore his closest followers knew that he could not be dead after he had been crucified. In one of the main chapters of his book Rivkin discusses the question whether the difference between the charismatic John and the supercharismatic Jesus could not lie in the fact that the life of the former ended in death and the death of the latter ended with Life. At all events, Rivkin makes it clear that there is only one correct answer to the question who put Jesus on the cross: it was the imperial system of Rome.

# 4 Easter, Pentecost and Afterwards

Jesus had been put to death on a cross. That was the most shameful and cruellest form of execution known at that time. For some Jews it also had a religious significance. According to the law of Deuteronomy 21 the body of anyone on whom the death sentence had been carried out had to be put on display on a stake for the rest of the day. However, before nightfall the body had to be buried, for a hanged man was 'accursed': to have him hanging on the stake all night would defile the land given by God. When crucifixion was introduced as a form of execution, the law of Deuteronomy came to be adapted to include those who had been fixed to a cross. Consequently, according to that saying in the Torah, Jesus had to be regarded as accursed.

We can hardly conceive what his death meant to 'the Twelve' and Jesus' other close companions. His converse with God had been so natural and he had shown so clearly that the final kingdom of God was already beginning in him, in the healing power which emanated from him, in his restless quest for those who were lost, all those many people who according to the norms of the time had been written off, rejected, shut out by God, without a future. With his whole person Jesus had insisted that the God of Israel was now unconditionally offering his 'salvation', to all Jews without distinction, but particularly to those who according to the pious were unworthy, did not deserve it. Now he himself had become one of the rejected, outcast from the community of Israel, accursed. That put a line through all that he had said and done and also through the expectations that he had aroused: first of all among those who had left everything to be with him in order to proclaim the coming kingdom.

He had certainly spoken about the approaching end of his life in cryptic terms, and at the last supper had shown in a telling gesture that his death was to be lifegiving, for them and for everyone. But that did not prevent them, according to Mark's account, from all taking flight as early as the time of Jesus' nocturnal arrest. Only Peter, 'the rock', dared to follow the detachment to the courtyard of the high priest's dwelling. But when he was addressed by one of the serving girls he said in terror that he was nothing to do with the one who had been arrested.

Some weeks later the same people proclaimed with great enthusiasm in Jerusalem that God had raised the crucified Jesus from the dead and taken him to himself. For, they said, he has appeared to us and given us the Holy Spirit, as you see and hear. This is what we are told in the 'Pentecost narrative' in the second part of Luke's work, later entitled the 'Acts of the Apostles'.

One may ask when and where the crucified Jesus appeared to his closest followers. For the evangelists themselves raise this question. Mark relates how some women went to the tomb of Jesus on Easter morning and there were bidden by a youth in white garments to tell the disciples and Peter to go to Galilee: there they would see Jesus. Thereupon the women fled in terror and dismay, and according to the sentence with which Mark ends his Gospel: 'they said nothing to anyone, for they were afraid'.

Matthew wrote a sequel to this. In his work the women went off to do this bidding. Then Jesus came to meet then and told them what the angel had said: his brothers were to go to Galilee; they would see him there. This they did, and on the appointed mountain Jesus commanded 'the eleven' to make all peoples his disciples and to baptize them in the name of the Father and of the Son and of the Holy Spirit. Then he parted from them with the last sentence of Matthew's Gospel: 'Lo, I am with you to the end of the world.'

According to these two evangelists Jesus appeared to his disciples in Galilee, i.e. some time after his death. But not according to Luke. Luke had omitted the clause in which Mark said that the disciples took flight after the arrest of Jesus. In his account of Jesus' death on the cross he had said that 'all his acquaintances stood watching from afar'. On the evening of the first Easter day Jesus appears in Jerusalem to the eleven and those who had been with him, having earlier made himself known to the two who were on the road to Emmaus. Finally he orders them to remain in the city until they have received the Holy Spirit which he has promised. After that, obviously still on the same day, he accompanies them to Bethany, where he 'departed from them and was taken up into heaven'.

The Fourth Evangelist also puts the appearances on the first

Easter day in Jerusalem. Early in the morning Jesus appears to Mary Magdalene in the garden by the tomb and after that he comes to his disciples in a closed room, a visit which he repeats a week later when Thomas is with them. That is what we are told in chapter 20, but the narrative of chapter 21 transports us to Galilee, to the sea shore: Peter and six other disciples are there fishing without catching anything when suddenly they see someone standing on the shore, who asks for something to eat and then tells them that they must cast their net on the right of the boat. After they have taken his advice and made an enormous catch, they recognize the man as Jesus.

This account in John 21 thus follows the tradition given in Mark and Matthew: Jesus only appears some time after the first Easter day, in Galilee. This tradition presupposes that after the execution of their master, Peter and the others had returned to their homes and resumed their former occupation. That is meant to confirm how disturbed and disappointed they had been after this failure in Jerusalem and also to show how deeply the 'appearance' of Jesus must have affected them. First Peter and then the others were suddenly overwhelmed by the certainty that God had not abandoned their master in death, but had raised him up and taken him into the divine life. Thus God stood behind all that Jesus had said and done. He had made it possible to see and hear the kingdom of God, the future world made whole, in his proclamation and healings. Now it suddenly emerged that this new world of God had really come into being in Jesus himself. He had been the first human being to enter into this inconceivable fullness of life and came to meet them from there! He had often said that the kingdom of God was on the way in what he said and did, but also that they had to pray for the coming of the kingdom. So there was also a future element in it. But they also remembered his saying that the kingdom would soon come in power and majesty: 'some of you standing here will see it.' This manifestation would of course take place in Jerusalem. There, on Zion, therefore, Jesus would soon reveal himself to Israel as the heavenly Son of Man to whom the final judgment had been entrusted. Indeed that might happen as early as Pentecost, the feast that was celebrated seven weeks after Passover and for which many Jews came to the temple.

Be this as it may, Peter and the others returned to Jerusalem. There they met acquaintances of Jesus who had remained there after his death, and also the women who had found the tomb empty on the first day of the week and told how they had seen angels appearing. We may imagine how all these people exchanged their experiences in an atmosphere of tense expectation. They reminded one another of what Jesus had once said to the Twelve: they would sit on twelve thrones when the tribes of Israel were judged. Hence the decision to choose someone else to fill the empty place left by Judas, someone who had also been with Jesus from the beginning: the lot fell on Matthias. So the number of twelve had been completed again when the whole group, assembled in prayer, was suddenly overwhelmed by a kind of communal ecstasy which expressed itself in a strange kind of speaking and singing, as though everyone was drunk.

In this way one can connect the Pentecost account with the ancient fact that Jesus first appeared to his disciples in Galilee. That does not mean that Luke's account is historical in the modern sense of that word. That concept had not yet come into being. Moreover, Luke wrote his two-volume work in the eighties, i.e. more than half a century after the death of Jesus and the appearances. And above all, the second part of his work, Acts, comes under the genre of 'biblical history writing'. That means that in the foreground is the view of faith that Luke wants to hand on to his readers. In his 'second book' he sets out to describe how the new movement, supported and guided by the Spirit of God, extends from Jerualem, first into Judaea and Samaria, then into Syria, Asia Minor and Greece, and finally how the great preacher Paul brought the message to Rome, the centre of the world at that time.

According to Luke, the descent or outpouring of the Holy Spirit on the disciples was the beginning of this movement. It would later come to be called the birth of 'the church'. This was the same Spirit which according to Luke's first book had stood at the beginning of Jesus' life; the Spirit had begotten Jesus in his mother's womb, and also at the beginning of his public ministry: when he was praying after his baptism in the Jordan the Spirit came upon him in a way which all could see, in the form of a dove.

As I said earlier, the writers of biblical history could combine confidence in facts which had been handed down to them with a great freedom in dealing with them. The reader who is interested in history can confirm this from the Gospel of Luke by considering the way in which he took over large chunks of Mark's Gospel without acknowledgment and adapted these passages to his own style and purposes. Unfortunately we do not have such a parallel account of the first beginnings of the church in Jerusalem. Only as a result of a close analysis of Luke's style and vocabulary in Acts does it emerge that in some passages he used 'documents', accounts which were already in existence and therefore differ from the passages in which he was free to write in his own fashion.

So Luke's account of the miracle at Pentecost suggests that he incorporated a variety of traditions in it. First he describes a phenomenon which is familiar to us above all from Paul's letters: people who are seized by the Holy Spirit begin to make incomprehensible sounds and utter disjointed words. The Greek word *glossa* means both tongue and language, rather like the French *langue*. The 'tongues as of fire' which descended on each of those present led them to begin to speak in tongues or languages, at all events in incomprehensible sounds. Luke then makes that more precise: 'other tongues'. Jews from all over the world who had settled in Jerusalem heard this enthusiastic speech in the language (now *dialektos*) of their former homeland. They themselves said that they had heard the proclamation of the mighty acts of God 'in our own tongues' (now *glossai* again). So they could understand the sounds as language. But then those who spoke were nevertheless taken to be drunks. It is also clear that Luke inserted a list of peoples and lands, apparently to give his readers, at the moment of the birth of the church, an idea of its universal significance. But he stresses that these are inhabitants of Jerusalem, Jews from all over the world who had come to live there. It is to them that Peter then addresses his long speech, in which he expounds the meaning of what has happened: Jesus the crucified one has been raised by God and has poured out his holy Spirit on his disciples, as this was prophesied for a later time by the propeht Joel. Luke makes this more specific by adding 'in these last days'.

### The risen Jesus and the Spirit

Luke is the only New Testament author to connect the outpouring of the Spirit with the 'fiftieth' day after Easter, Greek *pentekoste*, from which our Pentecost is derived. Whereas at the end of his Gospel he reports that Jesus was taken up in to heaven on the first Easter day, in Acts he reports that Jesus continued to appear to his apostles for forty days to give them instructions about the kingdom of God and only definitively ascended into heaven after that. Christianity took over Luke's datings for the celebrations of Ascension and Pentecost. But it did this only in the fifth century of our era. Before that time the one Paschal mystery was celebrated, in which these two aspects were incorporated: Jesus' ascension to the Father and the gift of the Spirit.

Here the description in John 20 was followed; these events took place on the first Easter day. Mary Magdalene, to whom Jesus first appears, may not hold him. She has to go to the disciples and say on behalf of Jesus: 'I am ascending to my Father and your Father, to my God and your God.' On the evening of this same first day of the week Jesus comes into the room in which the disciples are meeting behind closed doors. After his greeting of peace, which has a liturgical ring, he shows the wounds in his hands and his side. After that he says, 'Peace be with you. As the Father has sent me, so I send you.' Thereupon he breathes on them and says: 'Receive the Holy Spirit...' Thus John expresses in his own way the experience of those to whom the crucified Jesus showed himself alive: they were filled with the Spirit.

This 'breathing' of Jesus is not surprising. For the word 'Spirit' in our biblical translations first of all denotes a stream of air: wind and breath. These really are mysterious phenomena. There can be a sudden gust of air on a windless day. This invisible power sets everything in motion and can sometimes be so strong that it uproots trees and blows houses down. Just as mysterious is the breath in animals and human beings, an invisible stream of air on which life depends: when breath ceases, life departs and people and animals decay to dust.

For the ancient Israelites, wind and breath were connected with Yahweh. The Israelites used these words for phenomena in which they saw Yahweh at work. Before kings ruled over Israel, 'judges' arose who freed the people from oppressors. These were ordinary people who suddenly felt driven to attack the enemy, either alone, in heroic actions, or at the head of an army of compatriots which they had assembled in their enthusiasm. It was then said that the Spirit (wind, breath) of Yahweh had come upon them, entered into them or even had clothed them like a garment. According to these stories the spirit of God is a power which drives individuals from their familiar patterns and possibilities and instigates them to unexpected and sometimes superhuman action.

Thanks to this Spirit, breath, of Yahweh there is movement and life in what we call 'nature'. This is described brilliantly in Psalm 104. Towards the end the poet refers to the possibility that God may even turn away from all these living beings; in that case they will die and revert to dead matter. But, 'you send your spirit and they are created, and you renew the face of the earth'.

The vision of Ezekiel 37 is very impressive. Those who have been deported from Judah have complained that as a people they are dead, stone dead: 'Our bones are dried up, our hope is gone, all is up with us.' Then the spirit of Yahweh takes the prophet to a very wide valley which is full of dead bones. There he has to command the bones to hear the words of Yahweh. He then says to the bones: 'I will cause Spirit to enter into you and you shall live. And I will lay sinews upon you, and will cause flesh to come upon you, and cover you with skin, and put breath in you, and you shall live.' Ezekiel does this, and then the bones are joined together and sinews come upon the flesh and they are covered with skin. Then he has to say to the Spirit: 'Thus says Yahweh the Lord: come from the four corners of the wind, Spirit, and breathe into these fallen bones, that they live again.' Then the Spirit enters into them and the prophet sees them become alive and stand up: a numberless multitude.

This passage is so difficult to translate because the word 'spirit' really means wind (or breath). The prophet has to say, literally: 'Come from the four winds, o wind, and blow into these dead and they shall live.' But it is quite clear that as in the psalm that I have quoted, the Spirit of God can restore dead people to life.

There are a great many other texts which show in what contexts believing Jews spoke of the Spirit of God or the Holy Spirit. But from those I have quoted it should already have become clear why the first disciples of Jesus use this expression so often. The appearances showed that God had raised the crucified Jesus from the dead or, in biblical terms, had breathed new life into him with his creative breath. This was new in the full sense of the word. For that life was no longer capable of death. So he was not raised from the tomb as Lazarus was later said to have been raised from the tomb; that good man later had to suffer the painful process of dying once again. Jesus had been taken up into the life of God's own world, in which death has no power. Another term for this world was the kingdom of God, the term which Jesus himself used so often. That kingdom had now been realized in him, for ever.

One of the new expressions which came into being in the first period after Pentecost was the description of Jesus as 'the firstborn from the dead'. If God was to put an end to all the powers of evil which dominate the world, the dead should rise to take part in this new world. That was the expectation of many Jews. The resurrection of Jesus signified that the decisive turning point had begun. In this first person to be raised the process had been set in motion and thus the end of this evil world had drawn near.

This insight overwhelmed the first disciples. For them this expectation, too, was a work of the Holy Spirit. The breath of God had blown away all the patterns of thought and action which had been instilled into them, all the unbelief, doubt and anxiety. They felt themselves driven by powers which they had never experienced before. That also happened to those who received their message joyfully. When Paul reminds the Galatians of their reaction to his preaching he speaks of the Spirit which they then received, the Spirit which brought about all kinds of miraculous phenomena among them. The author of the Letter to the Hebrews describes what had happened to these people in his own way, in the framework of a warning: 'They have been enlightened; they have tasted the heavenly gift, and have become partakers of the Holy Spirit, and have tasted the goodness of the word of God and the powers of the age to come.'

Transfigured by this Spirit, the closest followers of Jesus now gained another perspective on what they once had seen and heard of him. His death had not invalidated all this, as they had feared in the first days; on the contrary, only now could they see its real meaning. In that new light of the Spirit they now began to read the ancient scriptures in a different way from before. The next chapter of this book will be all about that. But first we must discuss another topic.

## A division of spirits within Israel

As Luke relates in his Pentecost narrative, Jews were living in Jerusalem who had come from the Diaspora. That is understand-able, because for all those who lived scattered over the cities of the Roman empire Jerusalem was and remained the holy place in which God 'dwelt', the centre of their interest and devotion. Hence any Jewish community, no matter where it was in the world, made an annual contribution to the temple, a contribution in keeping with the number of its male members. This financial contribution also kept the memory of Jerusalem alive. So we can understand how particularly pious Jews who could afford to do so moved to Jerusalem in order to live close to God's abode and to die there.

We can see from the story about Stephen in Acts 6 that Jewish immigrants from the Greek-speaking Diaspora had 'synagogues' of their own. Evidently they could not master the vernacular, Aramaic, and formed groups in which the biblical texts were read aloud and expounded in Greek and the liturgical prayers were also sung in that language. At the same time they could meet their former fellow-countrymen there. Luke mentions such a synagogue of 'freemen': these were perhaps descendants of Jews who had been taken to Rome as prisoners in 63 BC by Pompey, sold on the slave market there and later set free. Luke goes on to mention synagogues of Jews from Cyrene (roughly present-day Libya) and from Alexandria, and also people from Cilicia and the province of Asia.

We may suppose that these immigrants reacted in different ways to what they heard and saw in Jerusalem and especially in the temple. To go to the extremes: some were above all happy with the privilege of being able to live so close to God. They were fully occupied in sharing in the many forms of worship which evoked a festal sense of community, a shared bond with God, the God of the fathers, of Moses and the exodus, but also the God whose universal rule, now sung about in all kinds of psalms, would one day be made manifest. For many people this was also a situation in which they could be more obedient to the regulations of the Torah, in other words could be better Jews, than had been possible in the pagan surroundings in which they had once lived.

At the other extreme one can imagine Jews who felt disappointed. Familiar with the openness which was so characteristic of the Hellenistic cities, they were not at all attracted by the faith in Jerusalem, which seemed to them narrow-minded and constricted. Moreover, having for generations become accustomed to the idea that the offering of animal sacrifice derived its real value from the disposition of the person making the sacrifice, his concern for justice and love of neighbour, they felt antipathy to all this slaughter and the noisy commerce surrounding it. It was also their impression that in these many sacrifices the main concern was to observe the regulations exactly.

There is no doubting that the group of followers of Jesus who had experienced 'Pentecost' soon made contact with Greek-speaking Jews. There were already Greek speakers among the Twelve. Their story of Jesus of Nazareth, his execution and resurrection from the dead, told in an enthusiastic manener, was probably heard with interest by 'critical' immigrants. The openness of Jesus, his appearance in the temple which cost him his life, and his rehabilitation by God made a strong appeal to them. Among the other group, the most orthodox Jews, it could initially have provoked only resistance and disbelief: it was downright nonsensical and blasphemous to say that God had taken to himself a man who had not treated the Torah very seriously and was critical of temple worship, and therefore had rightly been rooted out of Israel.

From the beginning of Luke's story about Stephen it seems that there were very soon two groups in the first community in Jerusalem: Greek-speaking disciples and Aramaic-speaking disciples. In the document which Luke clearly had at his disposal these were called the Hellenists and the Hebrews respectively. The story begins with the somewhat surprising information that the Hellenists complained to the Hebrews that their widows were being neglected in the daily distribution of food. This point of difference may well be connected with the fact that immigrants from the Diaspora in Jerusalem had fewer family members and friends in Jerusalem than the Hebrews, who had lived there for generations. As a social group, widows were at a disadvantage; so it could come about that widows among the immigrants were much more dependent on the charity of the disciples of Jesus.

The story further presupposes that the group of Greek-speaking disciples was very numerous. For it had been possible to choose a kind of administrative body of seven men, in accordance with a traditional Jewish model. Luke found in his source the list of their names, all thoroughly Greek: Stephen, Philip, Prochorus, Nicanor, Timon, Parmenas and Nicolaus. Only the last of these is a 'proselyte', a pagan who had become a Jew. The six others are born Jews. Luke does not tell us whether those who had been chosen, all of whom had to be 'filled with the Spirit and with wisdom', also devoted themselves to material matters, 'serving tables'. On the contrary, the sequel to his story is concerned above all with the first two, Stephen and Philip, as 'inspired' preachers.

Stephen, who was clearly a charismatic, attracted attention and got into discussion with other Greek-speakng Jews, who evidently belonged to the orthodox trend among the immigrants and rejected the message of the disciples. However, these conversation partners can do nothing in the face of Stephen's conviction and go so far as to bring him before the Supreme Council. There they produce false witnesses against him who claim: 'This man never ceases to speak words against this holy place and the law; for we have heard him say that Jesus of Nazareth will destroy this place, and will change the customs which Moses delivered to us.'

Thereupon Stephen replies with a long speech in which he recalls the history of Israel from the call of Abraham. When he gets to Moses he stresses that Moses, whom God himself had sent to be a liberator and leader of his people, had been rejected by that people: 'Our fathers would not listen to him.' Finally he says of these fathers that they brought the tabernacle of Yahweh from the wilderness to the promised land and that it was Solomon who built a house for God. But, Stephen goes on, as the prophet says: God cannot dwell in a house made by human hands. Then he abruptly ends his argument with sharp accusations against his audience in terms which are all derived from the Old Testament: they are stubborn, uncircumcised in heart and ears, and they resist the Holy Spirit. After that he no longer speaks of 'our' fathers but of 'your' fathers: he no longer feels bound to those who had killed Jesus.

After this Stephen is stoned, an action to which a certain Saul consents, someone who was obviously an orthodox Jew. He also takes part in the persecution of the disciples which then breaks out and which for many of them is the occasion to leave Jerusalem and proclaim their message in Judaea and Samaria. Luke seems to see these persecuted disciples as the Greek-speaking disciples, for he then adds that 'the apostles' remained in the capital, as if this time they were left in peace.

Philip first proclaims the Gospel in Samaria, where it receives a warm welcome, and after that to an Ethiopian who is on his way home from a pilgrimage to Jerusalem. As we have seen, in the eyes of Jews Samaritans were outcast, even worse than pagans. The Ethiopian was a eunuch: again as we have seen, according to the regulation in Deuteronomy 23 for that reason he could not be admitted to the community of the people of God. Does this suggest that the disciples, in the footsteps of Jesus, turned to the outcasts?

## Division in the Western Diaspora as well

In Acts 9 Luke tells the well-known story of Paul's conversion near Damascus. He does not relate how Paul was thrown off his horse; that detail derives from a famous painting. However, Luke can only give an account of the missionary journeys which Paul went on to undertake after he has told us how Peter, the leader of 'the apostles', was converted. This story begins with Cornelius, a Roman officer, who lived in the 'imperial' city of Caesarea on the coast. This 'god-fearing' pagan is visited at mid-day by an angel who tells him to summon a certain Simon Peter from the port of Joppa (later to become Jaffa), thirty miles to the south. The next day, around noon, while Cornelius' men are approaching Joppa, Peter is praying on the roof of the house in which he is staying. He falls into ecstasy and sees something like an enormous sheet which is lowered from heaven by the four corners just beside him. In it swarm all kinds of animals: quadrupeds, reptiles and even birds. A voice commands him to slaughter one of these animals and to eat it. As a Jew who is faithful to the law Peter indignantly refuses: he has never eaten anything unclean! Thereupon the heavenly voice replies: 'Do not regard as unclean what God has declared to be clean.' This happens twice more and throws Peter into confusion. Then the men from Caesarea come and accompany him and his companions to Cornelius' house. Cornelius has already summoned his family and friends. In the meanwhile Peter has realized what all this is about, for after the greeting he says to the gathering:

> You yourselves know how unlawful it is for a Jew to associate with or to visit any one of another nation; but God has shown me that I should not call any man common or unclean.

Peter has now understood that God 'has no respect of persons', as the old translation has it. This means that God does not prefer any one person to another: he has no favourites; he loves everyone equally.

Then Peter talks about Jesus of Nazareth, and the good that he did, how he was murdered and how after his death he appeared to his followers. These, including Peter, are now fulfilling God's command to bear witness to him. While Peter is still speaking, the Holy Spirit descends on all the audience and they begin to speak in tongues or languages, to the surprise of Peter's companions:

The believers from among the circumcised who came with Peter were amazed because the gift of the Holy Spirit had been poured out even on the Gentiles. For they heard them speaking in tongues and extolling God.

Luke finds this event, something like a second Pentecost, but this time experienced by non-Jews, so decisive that in chapter 11 he repeats the story all over again, now as told by Peter himself. It is his answer to the accusations made against him by the believers from among the circumcised on his return to Jerusalem: 'You entered a house of the uncircumcised and ate with them.'

As Luke saw things, in this way Peter was liberated by God from the constricting obligation of always keeping his distance from non-Jews, which stood in the way of his task as witness to Jesus the Messiah. In the next, twelfth, chapter Luke describes how Peter is liberated from a real prison in a miraculous way. He had been put there on the orders of Herod Agrippa. This grandson of Herod the Great reigned as king of Judaea between 41 and 44. Flavius Josephus also tells us that Agrippa, who at that time was trying to live in accordance with Jewish customs, did his best to gain the favour of his subjects. So it is probable that he had one of the Twelve, James the brother of John, put to death, a fact which Luke reports without going into further details. Luke puts in this context the story about Peter which, in view of the local details, was evidently going the rounds in the Jerusalem community: he was freed from this heavily guarded prison by an angel. Luke mentions in passing that this happened during 'the days of unleavened bread', i.e. the passover. This is perhaps a hint to the reader to think of Jesus' liberation from the tomb, after which he too was recognized by a woman because of his voice.

After this, in chapters 13 and 14, Luke describes the missionary journey which Barnabas and Saul undertook from Antioch at the command of the Holy Spirit. First they go to Cyrus, where the Roman consul Sergius Paulus becomes a believer. From that moment on Luke no longer uses the Jewish name Saul but the Latin name Paul, which Saul had probably had since his youth. From Cyprus the preachers cross over to Asia Minor, where they reach the city of Antioch in Pisidia. There on the sabbath they go to the synagogue, where they are invited to say an encouraging word. Paul accepts and embarks on a long speech. It is clear that here Luke wants to give his readers a kind of model: this is the way in which Paul used to preach the gospel in the synagogues of the cities which he was to visit on his later journeys.

The manner in which Luke describes the reactions of his audience here in Antioch also seems intended to be an example: this is what usually happened. First there is interest among the Jews and the godfearers. But when a large crowd gathers to listen to the preaching, the mood of the Jews changes and they abuse Paul and Barnabas. However, many non-Jews become believers:

> Then the Jews incited the godfearing women of high standing and the leading men of the city, and stirred up persecution against Paul and Barnabas, and drove them out of their district.

The term "godfearers' is used by the Jews to denote those whom we would term sympathizers. In many cities of the Roman empire there were thoughtful pagans who felt attracted by the Jewish belief in one God, the one origin of all. For the Jews this was not just a theoretical outlook, as it was for the philosophers and the intellectuals. Among the Jews that faith determined everyday life, and that was evident to outsiders, for example in their lofty morality. Their family life was exemplary, and their way of celebrating the sabbath and other festivals together in the synagogue and at home was attractive, a pleasant contrast to non-Jewish practice in that area. However, usually they did not progress beyond such an interest, even where the godfearers were able to take part in particular services in the synagogue. For a godfearer could become a member of the Jewish people as a proselyte, but for men that involved the obligation to be circumcised, to live in accordance with the precepts of the law, and thus to break completely with one's own social background.

For women things were different. In his work on *Jewish Antiquities* Josephus describes an attack on Jews in Damascus and observes that almost all the women of this city were adherents of the Jewish religion. We know from him and from other authors of this time that in Rome, too, women from the highest circles of society showed an active interest in the Jews and their worship.

Among such godfearers the proclamation of Jesus as Messiah suddenly opened up new perspectives. Now they could also worship the God of Israel in practice and live in accordance wih his will, by entering the community of Jesus the Messiah, a new people of God, to which anyone could belong no matter what his or her background might have been. When such people joined the

108

new community this meant a substantial loss for the synagogue, not only of sympathizers but also of material resources. For the well-to-do among them had not been stingy with their financial contributions to the Jewish community. This will also have contributed to the hostile attitude of many Jews. But sometimes Jews were convinced by Paul's preaching. That happened, for example, in Corinth, according to Luke's account in Acts 18. There no less a person than Crispus, 'the ruler of the synagogue', was baptized with all his household. Such a leader was a central figure entrusted with supervising liturgical services but also responsible for the building, so that a wealthy Jew was usually chosen for this position.

At the beginning of his first letter to the Corinthians Paul mentions that Crispus was among those whom he himself had baptized. This is a remarkable confirmation of Luke's account. For although he had much documentation about Paul's activity he does not say a single word about his letters. This means that either he knew nothing about this correspondence or he had heard about it but did not find this information important enough to mention.

Two short quotations from these letters may clarify further the picture that I have sketched so far. In the polemic with his opponents in his second letter to the Corinthians Paul feels compelled to take refuge in the style of rhetoric common at the time, like ironical comparisons between himself and his critics. Then he sums up all the tribulations and dangers that he has endured. They include the comment, 'Five times I received from the Jews the forty-less-one.' This was the punishment inflicted in the synagogues on those who transgressed particular command-ments. The law prescribes in Deuteronomy 25 that such a person should not be given more than forty strokes. So as not to transgress that commandment by miscounting, thirty-nine strokes were administered. According to Jewish accounts of this punishment the culprit was bound in such a way that he received these strokes partly on his chest and partly on his back. It was a very painful and also humiliating punishment. Paul had to endure it five times, doubtless because his preaching was condemned as an attack on the Torah and the age-old tradition, in other words as blasphemy.

In I Corinthians Paul writes that Jews demand miracles and Greeks wisdom. But 'we proclaim a crucified Messiah, for the Jews a stumbling block and for the pagans folly'. Indeed. To sensible citizens this message must have seemed sheer nonsense: a charlatan from the land of the Jews, condemned to crucifixion by a Roman ruler, now proclaimed as Redeemer and Saviour of the world, a kind of new emperor Augustus! Jews could not but take offence at the claim that someone rightly cast out of Israel was the Lord's Anointed, the Messiah who at the end of time would establish the lordship of God... But there were always Jews who allowed themselves to be convinced by Paul's preaching, his fellow-workers and other apostles. They then formed the nucleus of the new community of Christ, of which former pagans were also regarded as full members. As the letter to the Ephesians puts it, they had formerly lived outside Israel, not knowing the promises of salvation, without hope and without God in this world. Now they who had been far from all this had come near in the Messiah Jesus and become 'co-inheritors of the promise'.

Thus the division among Jews which had begun with the preaching in Jerusalem at 'Pentecost' spread through the cities of the empire. We might ask how it came about that some Jews nevertheless dared to take this great step of leaving the familiar community of the synagogue and beginning to form a community which was open to people of a kind that they had formerly always avoided, the uncircumcised and the impure. According to the last pages of Acts Paul continued indefatigably in Rome to win Jews over to Jesus, and in so doing began from the law of Moses and the prophets. There too he argued from the holy scriptures. But could this argument be convincing for people who did not share Paul's starting point?

# 5  The Old Scriptures Read Anew

Paul's letters bring us closer to what happened after Jesus' death than the accounts of the evangelists. Paul sent his first letter to the Corinthians around the year 53, i.e. long before any of the Gospels that we know was written. In chapter 15 of this letter Paul discusses the resurrection of the dead, a difficult point for those to whom he was writing. He begins by reminding these Christians of the message that he had proclaimed to them when he had arrived in Corinth some years before and which he himself had received from others.

> For I delivered to you as of first importance what I also received,
> that Christ died for our sins in accordance with the scriptures,
> that he was buried,
> that he was raised on the third day in accordance with the scriptures,
> and that he appeared to Cephas and then to the twelve.

It is clear that Paul here is repeating literally the testimony that he had heard from the first group of disciples in Jerusalem. Their leader was Simon, who had been given the Aramaic nickname Cephas, rock; Greek-speaking disciples turned this into Peter. Paul usually continued to call him Cephas.

He must also have got from this group what he goes on to say after the confession that I have quoted, apart from the comment about those who are 'still alive' at the moment of his writing; he had enough contacts with Jerusalem to know that.

> Then he appeared to more than five hundred brothers at one time, most of whom are still alive, though some have fallen asleep. Then he appeared to James, then to all the apostles.

It is not strange that Paul mentions other 'apostles' here after referring to the Twelve. For it was only later, long after Paul, that this name came to be reserved for the twelve men whom Jesus had chosen from a wider group of disciples. This development

111

came about under the influence of the Gospels, especially that of Luke: he explicitly mentions that Jesus himself gave the Twelve the name 'apostles'.

After this story about others to whom the Lord appeared, Paul goes on to talk about himself. He is a special case, perhaps because he had not known Jesus personally, certainly because he had tried to destroy the 'community of God'. Perhaps that is why he calls himself one untimely born, not fully grown, hardly like a human being and not viable. When reading the following lines we should also remember that for these reasons some Corinthians did not regard Paul as a genuine apostle, whereas he felt that by his long and dangerous missionary journeys he had been able to bring the message to far more people than the disciples who had been with Jesus.

> Last of all, as to one untimely born, he appeared also to me. For I am the least of the apostles, unfit to be called an apostle, because I persecuted the church of God. But by the grace of God I am what I am, and his grace toward me was not in vain. On the contrary, I worked harder than any of them, though it was not I, but the grace of God which is with me. Whether then it was I or they, so we preach and so you believed.

This communal preaching claimed that the facts of Jesus dying for our sins and his resurrection on the third day had happened 'according to the scriptures', in accordance with what had been announced beforehand in the sacred scriptures. This insight was also among the bewildering things that had happened to the disciples. The execution of Jesus had totally perplexed them, and the fact that after this he had appeared to them as being alive had been just as bewildering for them. Just as much a mark on their lives seems to have been made by the sudden insight that God had done all this in accordance with what he himself had revealed in the ancient scriptrues. So they began to understand them in a new way, namely as one great prophecy of what God would do in 'the last days' which had now dawned.

Paul expresses this insight in passing when he warns the believers in Corinth. That they are all baptized and participate in the Lord's supper is still no guarantee of their future salvation. For the Israelites in the wilderness too had also been saved by God, from Egypt, and were fed by him, but many of them perished in the wilderness because they had sinned and as a result did not reach their final goal. Paul then says; 'What happened to them had deep significance and it was written as a warning for us, on whom the end of the ages has come.' And again in passing, in his letter to the Romans he observes after a sentence from Psalm 69 which he applies to Jesus: 'Everything that was written beforehand was written for our instruction...' When Paul dictated that, he was convinced that he himself, and those to whom he addressed his letter, would still live to see the end of historical time.

These convictions of Paul and his Christians are difficult for us to understand, living nineteen centuries later in a completely different culture. But it is possible to get some idea of them when we see the role that the Jewish Bible in fact fulfilled among the first generations of Christians. If I illustrate that by some examples, you will see how this interpretation of scripture fits into the framework of the culture of the time.

First of all there is the fact that the twenty-seven writings of the New Testament are 'larded' with quotations from the Old. This verb will not seem strange to anyone who thumbs through a modern edition of the Greek text: in it these quotations are printed in bold type. There are only a few pages without these bold lines on them. If this type had also been used for words and expressions taken from the Jewish Bible, then there would have been even more of it. For a good deal of the religious vocabulary of Christians derived from this Bible.

Furthermore, our 'New Testament' did not yet exist. As I have already pointed out, Luke was describing Paul's career in the eighties and at that time still knew nothing of his letters, or did not find them important enough for his account. In fact these letters were addressed to particular communities and written by Paul only as a makeshift, when it was impossible for him to visit them in person. They were kept by their recipients. Perhaps sometimes copies were made for neighbouring communities. But it was still to be many years before they were circulated further and finally collected, and even longer before they were regarded as authoritative in all the churches. Here is another example; Matthew and Luke knew the Gospel of Mark, and that was an authoritative text for them. But they evidently saw no difficulty in each making his own revised and enlarged version of it.

Finally, the earliest known list or 'canon' of authoritative writings for Christians dates from after the year 150, and corresponds only partially with the list of books in our New Testament, which was not accepted by the whole church until around 400.

So the Christians of the first century lived without the New Testament as we know it. Every week they recalled the life, death and resurrection of Jesus at the time of the eucharistic meal, on the basis of words and stories handed down orally. There were also recitations and songs at that time, sometimes hymns which had been composed by inspired members of the community. But the basic text was the Jewish Bible. A complete copy of it, containing the law, the prophets and the writings, cost a great deal of money. For that reason, too, it has been suggested that extracts were made, notebooks containing only those texts in which Christ and the salvation which had come with him were described most clearly; small collections with illuminating texts, 'testimonies', which were used in smaller communities and perhaps also served for the instruction of new members. This could explain why the same passages from the Old Testament occur so often in such different writings of the New Testament: they evidently formed part of the spiritual luggage which all Christians had acquired. That will also emerge from the following examples, chosen at random and, to use the popular phrase, no more than the tip of the iceberg.

### A biblical argument from 'Peter'

After Luke has narrated the miracle of Pentecost in Acts 2, he makes Peter give a long speech. Peter first showed that the enthusiasm of the disciples had been foretold by the prophet Joel. Then he goes on:

> Men of Israel, hear these words: Jesus of Nazareth, a man attested to you by God with mighty works and wonders and signs which God did through him in your midst, as you yourselves know – this Jesus, delivered up according to the definite plan and foreknowledge of God, you crucified and killed by the hands of lawless men. But God raised him up, having loosed the pangs of death, because it was not possible for him to be held by it. For David says concerning him,

> *I saw the Lord always before me,*
> for he is at my right hand that I may not be shaken;
> therefore my heart was glad, and my tongue rejoiced;
> moreover my flesh will dwell in hope.

For thou wilt not abandon my soul to Hades,
nor let thy Holy One see corruption.
Thou hast made known to me the ways of life;
thou wilt make me full of gladness with thy presence.

Brethren, I may say to you confidently of the patriarch David that he both died and was buried, and his tomb is with us to this day. Being therefore a prophet, and knowing that God had sworn with an oath to him *that he would set one of his descendants upon his throne*, he foresaw and spoke of the resurrection of the Christ, that he was *not abandoned to Hades*, nor did his *flesh see corruption.*

And now some comments on this profound text. David seems to be expressing his own feelings and expectations in the psalm. But that is not so, according to Peter. For he says to God: You will not abandon me, your faithful worshipper, to the kingdom of death, and will keep me from corruption, the dissolution of my body. Because David did die and his body was corrupted, he must have expressed this hope in the name of the great descendant that was promised to him, the Messiah.

In the Hebrew text 'David' says: You will not let your holy one see 'the tomb'. The Greek translator chose the term 'corruption, dissolution' to express this, perhaps because he expected a final resurrection of the dead, At all events, the force of Peter's argument depends on this Greek rendering of the text of the psalm. In passing, it might be pointed out that the sentence printed in italics about God's oath is a quotation from Psalm 132.

Peter goes on:

This Jesus God raised up, and of that we are all witnesses. Being therefore exalted at the right hand of God, and having received from the Father the promise of the Holy Spirit, he has poured out this which you see and hear. For David did not ascend into the heavens, but he himself says:

*The Lord said to my Lord,*
Sit at my right hand
till I make thy enemies a stool for thy feet.

Let all the house of Israel therefore know assuredly that God has made him both Lord and Christ, this Jesus whom you crucified.

Here Peter is quoting the first sentence of Psalm 110. In Hebrew it begins like this: 'Oracle of Yahweh to my Lord...' It emerges from what comes next that this relates to the rule of a king who resides in Jerusalem, on Mount Zion. Most biblical scholars assume that this psalm was intended for the solemn ceremony in which homage was paid to a new king of the dynasty of David, a descendant or son of his. At the enthronement a priest or temple prophet would have spoken this oracle to him: 'Go and sit at my right hand: I will help you to subject the enemies of my people, your enemies.'

The metaphor is clear: a seat at the right hand of a ruler is the highest conceivable place of honour. Anyone who is allowed to sit on it shares in his rule. Perhaps the situation in Jerusalem provided a specific occasion for using this image. There the 'house' of the king lay directly against the south side of the 'house' of Yahweh. At that time orientation was by the east, so the north was on the left side and the south on the right. In Hebrew there was one word for the concepts right, right hand and south. Furthermore the verb 'sit' also meant 'dwell'. The king of Jerusalem therefore dwelt or sat on the right hand of Yahweh who resided in this temple.

It is certain that in later centuries David was regarded as the poet of the psalm. It followed from this that he himself had referred to a descendant of his as 'my Lord', in other words, he himself had seen a 'son' of his as superior to him. Jesus had appeared to the disciples. He had therefore been taken up to God and from then on shared in his rule. Earlier David and his successors had borne the title 'anointed (of Yahweh)', *meshiach* in Hebrew, pronounced *messias* in Greek and translated with the term *Christos*. God had now given a new content to this title by making Jesus sit at his right hand: 'God has made him both Lord and Messiah.'

The first sentence of Psalm 110 is wholly or partially quoted in the widest variety of New Testament writings and is thus one of the first of all 'proof texts'. That is not the case with Psalm 16, which is used by Peter at the beginning of his argument. This text is not used by any other New Testament author. Only Luke himself has it quoted once again by Paul, in his 'inaugural' speech at Antioch, in combination with other proof texts. It would take us too long to discuss this as well. However, it is important to note the biblical quotation with which Luke ends his account of

Paul's preaching. It comes from the beginning of the short book of the prophet Habakkuk, where it refers to the sudden overwhelming show of power by the Babylonians. The Greek version of that prophetic saying bore witness to the incredible new thing that God had begun when he raised Jesus from the dead and at the same time contained a threat:

> Beware, therefore, lest there come upon you what is said in the prophets:
>
> *Behold, you scoffers, and wonder, and perish;*
> for I do a *deed* in your days,
> a deed you will never believe, if one declares it to you.

### The rule of the Son of man

The brief Psalm 8 begins and ends with a cry of amazement at the majesty of God who has created all things. After a sentence which I shall be discussing in due course, the poet writes:

> When I look at thy heavens, the work of thy fingers,
> the moon and the stars which thou hast established;
> what is man that thou art mindful of him,
> and the son of man that thou dost care for him?
> *Yet thou hast made him little less than heavenly beings,*
> and dost crown him with glory and honour.
> Thou hast given him dominion over the works of thy hands,
> thou hast put all things under his feet,
> all sheep and oxen,
> and also the beasts of the field.

One might say that this is a poem which is inspired by the creation narrative with which the Bible begins and by the place of man in it who, as image of God, is given rule over all animals. In the line printed in italics the term 'heavenly beings' renders a word which is also used for God or gods; this clearly refers to the heavenly beings who were thought to surround the divine throne. The Greek translator chose the term 'angels' for that. But even more importantly, he translated the expression 'little less' in such a way that the reader could also understand it in a temporal sense: *'you have made him for a short time less than the angels'*. Now if we remember that for the first Christians the term 'son of man' denoted the person of Jesus, we can understand how the passage was applied to him. He had indeed been humiliated for a short time and afterwards, as the risen one, crowned with glory and honour, for through God he had been made Messiah and Lord of all; thus God had placed all things under his feet.

The profound discourse which has been included in the New Testament under the title 'Letter to the Hebrews' uses a quotation from this psalm in chapter 2 in the following way:

For it was not to angels that God subjected the world to come, of which we are speaking. It has been testified somewhere,

*What is man that thou art mindful of him,*
or the son of man, that thou carest for him?
Thou didst make him for a little while lower than the angels,
thou hast crowned him with glory and honour,
putting everything in subjection under his feet.

Now in putting everything in subjection to man, he left nothing outside his control. As it is, we do not yet see everything in subjection to him. But we see Jesus, who for a little while was made lower than the angels, crowned with glory and honour because of the suffering of death, so that by the grace of God he might taste death for every one.

We do not know where and when the letter to the Hebrews was written nor precisely for what group of Christians this discussion or discourse was intended. Far less do we know who wrote it. It is certain that it cannot have been Paul. Now it is remarkable that in his first letter to the Corinthians, shortly after recalling the proclamation that he himself received, Paul uses a line from Psalm 8 in speaking about the resurrection of Christ. Christ is raised from the dead as the firstfruits of those who are asleep. After them the others will follow, and after that the end will come, namely when Christ hands over the kingdom to God the Father. Then he will have annihilated all rules, powers and authorities. Paul goes on:

For he must reign until he has put all his *enemies under his feet.* The last enemy to be destroyed is death. For God *has put all things in subjection under his feet.* But when it (scripture) says, All things are put in subjection under him, it is plain that he is excepted who put all things under him.

Finally Christ will subject himself to God, so that God will be all in all.

118

Clearly Paul cannot think about the power bestowed on Jesus without this line from Psalm 8 occurring to him. The same goes for the first of the two texts printed in italics, one of many instances in which that verse from Psalm 110 automatically occurs to a Christian.

There is one further sentence in Psalm 8 which is used in connection with Jesus. Before the passage quoted above the poet says:

> By the mouth of babes and infants,
> thou hast founded a bulwark because of thy foes,
> to still the enemy and the avenger.

That is a translation of the Hebrew text. It is not very clear how that can come about: strength or power or building a bulwark on what emerges from the mouth of the least of all. The Greek translator already had difficulty with it. He replaced the word 'bulwark' with 'praise, song of praise'. Perhaps he was thinking of a theme that is taken up in the Book of Chronicles: the power of the Jewish community, by which it can resist the most powerful enemies, lies in its unceasing praise of God.

Be this as it may, Matthew used the text translated in that way in connection with Jesus' entry into Jerusalem. Matthew evidently thought that children had taken part in the shouts of jubilation for the son of David. When Jesus has subsequently driven the traders out of the temple, the children appear again. For after these few lines about the 'cleansing of the temple' Matthew relates the following story:

> And the blind and the lame came to him (Jesus) in the temple, and he healed them. But when the chief priests and the scribes saw the wonderful things that he did, and the children crying out in the temple, 'Hosanna to the Son of David!' they were indignant; and they said to him, 'Do you hear what these are saying?' And Jesus said to them, 'Yes, have you never read, *"Out of the mouths of babes and sucklings thou hast brought perfect praise?"'* And leaving them, he went out of the city to Bethany and lodged there.

Yet more ancient scripture is incorporated into this passage. That Jesus healed the blind and the lame in the temple is related only by Matthew, as the one miracle that Jesus performed in Jerusalem. That too seems to be connected with his deep,

119

meditative knowledge of the scriptures. In II Samuel 5 we are told how David captured the city of Jerusalem, the fortress of Zion, and how in these circumstances the proverb arose: 'Blind and lame may not enter into the house.' The Greek translator added: (into the house) 'of the Lord'. By this he meant the temple, although it was not yet built at that time. According to the answer that Jesus gave to the disciples of John the Baptist, the healing of blind and lame people was one of the signs that the kingdom of God was already effective. Evidently Matthew saw the 'cleansing of the temple' by the true son of David also as a sign of this and therefore he introduced these healings into the story. The Greek word for the 'wonderful works' which the chief priests and scribes saw does not occur elsewhere in the New Testament, but it does occur many times in the Greek translation of the Old Testament, where it always stands for the wonderful works which God does for his people and which are celebrated by the Jews.

Finally, the Hosanna that the children cry out also comes from the ancient scriptures. It is the beginning of the cry of joy with which the crowds had escorted Jesus earlier on his entry into Jerusalem:

*Hosanna* to the Son of David!
*Blessed is he who comes in the name of the Lord!*
*Hosanna* in the highest.

The words printed in italics are one of the last verses of the long Psalm 118. This provided Jesus' disciples with yet another text in which they saw a clear expression of what God had done through him. The psalm seems to be a song which belonged to a kind of liturgy of thanksgiving, and was performed by various voices or choirs. Unfortunately instructions for the performance are not included in the text. However, it is clear that a spokesman is describing how he is attacked on all sides, even by whole peoples. But he continues to trust in God and with his help he smites his enemies. Yahweh shows his power and exalts this assaulted and humiliated figure. He can now say:

I shall not die but live
and bear witness to his mighty acts.

After that he seems to enter the temple. In his thanksgiving to God he describes the miraculous change in his fate in the following imagery, with which the bystanders evidently agree:

120

The stone that the builders rejected
has become the corner stone.
This is the work of Yahweh,
it is a miracle in our eyes.

In these lines the disciples after Easter saw a clear forecast of what God had done with the assaulted and profoundly humiliated Jesus. He had made the stone which had been cast aside and rejected into the cornerstone, the first and most important stone, which determined the form and extent of the new building. In his chapter 12 Mark makes Jesus himself quote the words about the stone after he has told the horrible story about the tenants of a vineyard who finally kill the owner's beloved son. Matthew and Luke follow him here. In Acts 4 Luke also makes Peter use the text, with a personal focus. Before all the Jewish authorities the spokesman of the apostles has to account for the healing of a lame man by the temple gate. He then proclaims that this man has been made whole through the name of Jesus whom they had crucified and whom God has raised from the dead:

> This is *the stone which was rejected by* you *builders, but which has become the head of the corner.*

### 'Reading in'?

There is another sentence in Psalm 18 which is quoted in the New Testament. But the examples above seem sufficient to give some idea of the way in which the Jewish disciples of Jesus read the ancient scriptures. When people note this for the first time, they often ask: Was that legitimate, to make all sorts of ancient texts say something that the writers had not intended? Is this not a matter of reading things in?

The answer is that it was indeed possible to do this then, in the Jewish milieu of that time. This practice was embedded in Hellenistic culture. Specifically when using ancient texts, which were regarded as 'inspired' and therefore authoritative, it was necessary to interpret them in such a way that they became meaningful in a contemporary situation. Among the ancient Greeks the works of poets like Hesiod and Homer were thought to be divine, to have been inspired by 'gods'. Homer had invoked the muse so often. Only a few centuries after him the great philosophers began to reflect on the nature of the divine, on the cosmos, on the place of man in it and the conditions for human society. Ideas about that later became the common property of educated people. They found it increasingly difficult to handle the old poetic works. It seemed impossible that the rough and sometimes quite pedestrian stories which were told in them about gods and goddesses were intended to be understood as they stood. The divine source of inspiration had of course concealed deep philosophical insights under that covering of gross forms, both the sensual and cruel adventures of the heroes and the verses in which they were described. For poetry is imagery, ambivalent, and therefore a lower form of communication than philosophical discussion with its clear concepts. So thoughtful Greeks arrived at a kind of exposition which was called 'allegorical': what stands in the text is an image, a symbol, of what is really meant. The image of an old man with a scythe in one hand and an hour-glass in the other was often used as a clear example of an allegory. What you see there is an image, a symbol of realities which are invisible: time and transitoriness.

Jews who lived in a Hellenistic milieu sometimes applied such allegorical exposition to their own holy scriptures. We can find a good example of this in the 'Letter of Aristeas'. This book was written in Alexandria in the second century BC by a Jew who wanted to commend the Greek translation of the Torah. By his work he put into circulation the story that I mentioned earlier in this book (pp.20f.). He presents himself as an educated pagan, and he relates how he had a conversation with the high priest in Jerusalem about certain regulations in the Torah. The high priest speaks of Moses as follows: 'In his wisdom the legislator, being endowed by God for the knowledge of universal truths, surrounded us with unbroken palisades and iron walls to prevent our mixing with any of the other peoples in any matter. Being thus kept pure in body and soul, preserved from false beliefs, and worshipping the only God omnipotent over all creation.' Then the high priest explains why the complicated regulations with which God has surrounded his true servants also include some about the eating of animals. In these laws (from Leviticus 11 and Deuteronomy 14) Moses was not really concerned with weasels and rats. He was really concerned with morality. To take one example: the birds that may be eaten are domesticated and clean because they feed on grain and plants, like doves, partridges and geese. The birds that are prohibited are birds of prey, who against all justice devour tame animals, even carry off sheep and goats, and indeed sometimes swoop down on human beings, dead and alive. By prohibiting the consumption of these Moses wanted to instil in us 'that we should be righteous and not do violence to anyone nor steal anything'.

The characteristics which Moses indicates, like cloven hoofs and chewing the cud, were also meant in a moral sense: he was concerned with avoiding bad company and with constant reflection on, rumination of, the mighty acts which God has done for his people. That is the argument of the high priest according to 'Aristeas'. His intentions seem clear; Jewish readers may infer from this that their way of living according to the Torah is not as irrational as outsiders tend to claim.

The scriptural exegesis of the great Jewish philosopher Philo of Alexandria (c.13 BC to AD 45) is much more profound than this. His interpretation began from the philosophical insights which he had gained through the study of different trends of thought, and these insights were not separated from his intense life of faith. For him the only ancient text which could be regarded as 'inspired' was of course the Torah, communicated by God to Moses, the greatest of all philosophers, and by the inspiration of this same God translated into Greek: it is from Philo that we have the story that each of the seventy-two translators completed his task in complete isolation and that their translations corresponded down to the smallest detail.

According to Philo, things are said in the Torah which cannot possible be true in a literal sense, for example in the account of paradise. For would it not be foolish to suppose that God planted vines or olive trees and apple trees? And how could one imagine that a woman or another human being can come forth from the side of a man?

Later on Moses wrote: 'Cain departed from the countenance of God.' That cannot have been meant literally. For the One who exists of Himself has no countenance. If he did, he would have to have a body, with entrails and external organs, along with the experiences and passions associated with them. Moreover, where could Cain go to get away from God? After all, God fills the whole universe! 'We can only conclude that none of these expressions is meant literally and that we must follow the course of the figurative exposition which is so dear to our philosophical spirits.' After this Philo treats the scriptural quotations which he uses in his customary way; he expounds them in connection with the circum-

123

stances of 'the soul'. This is not only the principle of virtue and sin, but also that element in human beings which can live in a relationship to God and in so doing can make further progress. What the Torah tells us about the patriarchs is really meant to describe the stages that the soul has to go through on its way to mystical union with God.

The Jews in Palestine who expressed themselves in Aramaic and Hebrew also expounded the scriptures in terms of the present, the situation in which they found themselves. The scribes had already done that for centuries with the regulations in the Torah. Towards the beginning of our era a number of rules came into use for expositors of the Bible to observe. They were attributed to the great scribe Hillel, a contemporary of Herod the Great. According to scholars they have some affinity with the principles of exposition which had been established by legal experts in the Hellenistic world.

The Jews, however, dealt much more freely with quotations from the scriptures. Somewhere between the years 160 and 140 a pious Jew wrote the book which is usually called Jubilees, and sometimes the 'Little Genesis'. This title is clearer. For the author gives his version of the narratives in the book of Genesis and the first part of Exodus, up to the events at Sinai. He does so in his own way: he is very interested in chronology. He divides the time from creation into periods of forty-nine years, seven times seven. According to the law of Leviticus 25 such a period is concluded with the fiftieth year, a 'year of jubilee'. On the basis of this division the author gives exact dates to all the events narrated in scripture. After Adam had lived seven years in paradise, 'in the second month on the seventeenth day the serpent approached Eve...'

According to the author the Torah had already been written on heavenly tablets before the creation, so it had been valid from the beginning of the world. Hence the angels, the first created beings, always celebrate the sabbath with joy, obedient to the most important commandment of the Torah. Once he has left paradise, every morning Adam offers a fragrant incense-offering, prepared in accordance with the precepts of Exodus 30. Abraham celebrated the Feast of Tabernacles in accordance with the precepts of the Torah, but as these were implemented in the author's day.

What he does not retell from the book of Genesis are the less attractive actions of the tribal ancestors of Israel, like the lies told by Abraham and Isaac about their wives, the ways in which Jacob deceived Laban and Jacob's fear of his brother Esau. He does recount some misdeeds of these patriarchs, but only to praise them. In his view Simeon and Levi acted commendably when they exterminated the population of Shechem; indeed on the basis of this action Levi and his tribe were chosen for the priesthood. The reason is that in the author's day Shechem, the name of the city, suggested the Samaritans, who were regarded by the Jews as apostates and were deeply hated. Therefore it was praiseworthy to murder the inhabitants of 'Shechem'. The book of Genesis describes how Jacob became reconciled to his brother Esau; according to our author Jacob killed his brother. For the Torah regards Esau as the tribal ancestor of the Edomites. Now in 587 this people had helped the Babylonians to besiege and plunder Jerusalem. Since then Edom had become a kind of code name for everything pagan and felt to be anti-Jewish. Therefore the author found it better to tell how Jacob (= Israel = Jews) had killed his brother Esau (= Edom = Gentiles) than follow the Torah in saying that he had become reconciled with him. In this way the sacred narratives were used in the service of the community of faith. In those years after 160 in fact the watchword of those faithful to the law was to reject radically any influence from Greek paganism; that was necessary to preserve their identity, the covenant with God. In biblical imagery: Jacob might not be reconciled with Esau in any way whatsoever. Far from it!

The book of Jubilees was popular reading, at all events among the Essenes who lived by the Dead Sea. For fragments have been found in their library, from which it appears that they had a number of copies of the book. More important for the subject of this chapter are the remains of their commentaries on texts from the prophets and the psalms. These show a close affinity to the biblical interpretation practised by the first Christians. The Essenes regarded themselves as children of the light who formed the community of the new covenant. As I said earlier in this book (pp.55f.), their eyes were firmly fixed on the fulfilment of the history to which all previous generations had looked forward and about which prophetic figures from the past had spoken in mysterious words. God had revealed these hidden meanings to the leader of the community. It would take us too long to discuss the fragments of their interpretations of the texts in detail. The most important thing to note is that in them every detail of the biblical text is related to the community itself and its destiny.

It should emerge from this how naturally the Jews read their sacred texts in terms of their own situation and their own faith and expectations, without being concerned with the question what the biblical authors might have meant by their words in their own day. The disciples of Jesus thus did what was customary in their environment. They saw clearly indicated in these scriptures their conviction that God had set in motion in Jesus the consummation of history and that they were involved in this as the community of Christ. They regarded the scriptures as one great prophecy of the 'last things'. So this answers the question which was raised at the end of the first chapter of this book: how did the evangelists come to see the 'fulfilment' of the scriptures in what happened with Jesus? After Easter and Pentecost it became increasingly clear that the majority of Jews could not share the belief of the disciples and therefore could not share their 'interpretation' of the scriptures. It was impossible for them to see Jesus as the Messiah and the Son of God and therefore he could not be referred to in the texts which the Christians cited as proofs. In this way there came into being that division of spirits which finally ended up in a complete and irrevocable break. The disciples also saw that painful event of the 'unbelief of the Jews' foretold in the ancient scriptures.

# 6   The New Scriptures: Anti-Jewish?

The events of the year AD 70 had a decisive influence on the controversy between the followers of Jesus and the other Jews. After a siege of four months the Romans captured Jerusalem and thus put an end to the 'Jewish War' which had begun with the revolt of 66. Only in a few remote fortresses could groups of resistance fighters carry on the struggle. But their bastion had been the capital and this was now literally razed to the ground.

According to Flavius Josephus all that was spared were the three famous towers of Herod's palace and part of the western city wall: the towers as an indication of how strong and beautiful the city had been and the piece of wall as protection for the army camp in which the garrison was to be housed. All other buildings were completely destroyed: future visitors were not to suppose that the place had ever been inhabited.

It is impossible to describe in a few pages what this meant for Jewish society, in Palestine and far abroad. All I can do in a few matter-of-fact sentences is to indicate what was important for the subject with which we are concerned. First of all the loss of the temple meant the end of the daily sacrifice in which the relationship between Israel and its God had been expressed for centuries. There he had also offered atonement for the transgressions and sins which Jews had committed either individually or collectively. At the same time the function of the high priest also disappeared. At the great feasts he had always represented the Jewish people before the face of God. The supervision of sacrificial worship and the priests and Levites who were involved in it had been entrusted to him. In the political sphere he managed the affairs of the people in consultation with the Roman governor, as president of the Supreme Council (Synedrion, pronounced Sanhedrin in Hebrew). This council was composed of high priests, elders and scribes. As the governing body it had controlled domestic politics and enjoyed wide-ranging authority in governing the Jewish people, including jurisdiction. All these institutions disappeared in the year 70 when Judaea became a Roman province and the Jewish inhabitants were reduced to the same sort of position as their fellow-Jews in other parts of the empire.

Many Jews regarded the destruction of the capital and the temple as a punishment from God, in the same way as their forefathers had regarded the disaster of 587 BC, when the Babylonian armies had destroyed Jerusalem. Then, too, it had been the misdeeds of the kings and people which had provoked this punishment from God, misdeeds like the rejection of the prophets whom God had sent to lead his people to repent and who in his name had threatened the destruction of city and temple.

This time only a small group of Jews connected the disaster with the rejection of Jesus of Nazareth whom they regarded as someone sent by God, the last of the prophets. For most other Jews this event was a compelling reason for doing the will of God henceforth with more zeal, and fulfilling more strictly than ever all the precepts of the Torah which did not relate to the temple. Who knows, God might then rebuild Jerusalem and come to dwell in a new temple there.

It goes almost without saying that the Pharisees took the lead in this new orientation. They had always been zealous for the observance of God's law in everyday life and at that time they also enjoyed the respect of many ordinary people along with the trust of the Romans. Moreover the other 'parties' had disappeared. There could no longer be any question of the Sadducees being influential. And the party of armed resistance, that of the Zealots, formerly admired by many people for their courage, had vanished. Its members had died in the struggle or perished in internecine quarrels. Although many of the destitute had joined the Zealots, impoverished Galileans who no longer saw any future for themselves, their zeal had been deeply religious: God was the only king over Israel and he could only assume actual rule when the Roman rulers had been driven out. Hence their armed revolt. But their struggle had proved fruitless and had ended in the downfall of the city and the temple, in other words in utter defeat. As before, the Pharisees continued to say that the kingdom of God only became real when more and more Jews gratefully subjected themselves daily to his laws, the Torah.

One of the leading Pharisees was called Johanan ben Zakkai. He soon became legendary. Thus it was later told how at the time of the siege of Jerusalem he was carried out of the city in a coffin to negotiate with the Roman general. According to a more reliable tradition he had tried to make contact with Vespasian earlier. His urgent request was that Vespasian should spare the wise men, the scribes, who were to take over the central role of the temple in the years to come. He also asked for consideration to be taken of the 'school' which already existed in the city of Jabneh (Jamnia in Greek). Johanan asked permission to develop this into a kind of academy, a centre for the study of the Torah. For the end of Jerusalem was in sight and Jewish society could only survive with a new religious centre. Both Vespasian and his son Titus had a favourable attitude to Jewish religion and gladly acceded to the request.

This 'academy' soon began to flourish greatly under the leadership of Johanan and after him under Gamaliel II. It was also recognized outside Judaea. Among the increasing number of scribes a council of seventy seems to have been formed, a kind of new Sanhedrin. Later it was also said that Jews, even from abroad, made pilgrimages three times a year to Jabneh, as they had once gone to the temple.

The concern of these Pharisaic leaders was primarily for clarity. Their studies were predominantly concerned with the Torah and the holy books of two other collections, the Prophets and the Writings, and above all with the best expositions of the Torah which had been given by former scribes. They did not waste any more time on Jewish works which had been composed in Greek, far less on the literature which had emerged from groups with 'apocalyptic' attitudes: their concern for what was to happen in the future, and their fantastic descriptions of this, could only distract attention from what was really important, the faithful fulfilment of God's will in life here and now.

This concern of the Pharisees for clarity and uniformity also led to the decision to add something to the Eighteen Benedictions. These were a series of eighteen blessings: praise of God along with ardent petitions for his mercy and help. This ancient prayer, a sublime expression of the beliefs and hopes of the Jews, had to be said three times a day by everyone, including women, children and slaves, and it was also a fixed part of the synagogue liturgy. A new strophe was introduced in Jabneh. It ran:

For the apostates let there be no hope.
And let the arrogant government be speedily uprooted in our days.
Let the Nazoreans and the heretics be destroyed in a moment.
And let them be blotted out of the book of Life and not be inscribed together with the righteous.
Blessed art thou, O Lord, who humblest the arrogant.

This insertion is understandable. The Jewish community could only survive if all its members conscientiously adopted Pharisaic forms of belief. Before the year 70 Jewish life had been extremely varied: at that time there was room for many different views and life-styles. But in the new situation, when the very existence of Judaism was at stake, dissidents could no longer be tolerated.

Among this group were the Jews who had joined the movement around Jesus and worshipped him as the Messiah of Israel: the Nazoreans. The new strophe in the old prayer made it impossible for them to continue to join in synagogue worship. They could no longer answer Amen to this blessing and certainly could not accept an invitation to lead the Eighteen Benedictions. In this way they were in effect banished from the synagogue.

### John : 'Your Father is the devil'

Exclusion from the synagogue also had social consequences. Those who had assented to the prayer about the 'heretics' of course no longer had anything to do with these dissidents. They no longer bought things from such people. Now was it any longer possible for a young man from this group to train for any trade. Administrators and officials were Jews from respectable families, many of whom had adopted the Jabneh programme and explicitly and proudly called themselves Pharisees.

The Jews who had followed Jesus Messiah thus had special difficulties. As dissidents they felt surrounded by a hostile outside world and could only survive if they formed a closed group characterized by strong mutual solidarity. It very much looks as though the Gospel according to John was composed in their circles and was written with an eye to them. Only in this Gospel is mention made of expulsion from the synagogue, and that happens three times. We find it first in the sublime narrative of chapter 9, about the man born blind who receives his sight. Jesus spat on the ground, anointed the man's eyes with the moist earth and told him to wash in the pool of Siloam. The man does this and regains his sight. Those to whom he tells his story then take him to the Pharisees, for the day on which he had been healed was the sabbath. These Pharisess do not agree among themselves: Jesus desecrated the sabbath and yet did something that only God can do. After that the author abruptly calls them 'the Jews'. They do not believe that the man was born blind and interrogate his parents. But they refer the interrogators to their son: he is old enough to answer for himself. The author gives the following reason for their action:

> His parents said this because they feared the Jews, for the Jews had already agreed that if any one should confess him to be Messiah, he was to be put out of the synagogue.

There follows a discussion between the Jews and the man who has been healed. He continues to maintain that someone who can open the eyes of a blind man must come from God. Thereupon he is 'thrown out': what his parents had been afraid of happens to their son. After that he meets Jesus and then comes to believe in the Son of man, the one who according to John 'descended from heaven'.

The story is constructed in a dramatic way. The one who was once blind first sees Jesus as a prophet, then as a man who comes from God and finally recognizes him as the heavenly Son of man. The leaders of the synagogue go in the opposite direction. Their doubt becomes repudiation, they refuse the evidence of the miracle and in so doing confirm their own blindness. The one thing that is not clear is whether for John 'the Jews' are completely identical with 'the Pharisees': Jesus addresses only some of them at the end of the story. This is also a good example of biblical history writing. The situation of the author and his readers determined his account of past events. It is rather like having two slides in the projector at once: a photograph taken recently superimposed on one taken long ago, with the more recent one much easier to see on the screen. The blind man who gains his sight and begins to see in Jesus a man who has come from God is at the same time the Jew of the author's day, who becomes a disciple of Jesus and consequently is expelled from the synagogue.

In chapter 12 John ends the first part of his work, which describes the public life of Jesus. Jesus had come up against the unbelief of the majority of Jews. After quoting the famous 'hardening of heart' text in Isaiah 6 John writes:

> Nevertheless many even of the authorities believed in him, but for fear of the Pharisees they did not confess it, lest they should be put out of the synagogue.

In the next five chapters, the second part of his work, the evangelist has Jesus speaking only to the small group of his closest followers with whom he has his last meal. In these 'farewell discourses', the expulsion from the synagogue is mentioned once again. The disciples will find that the world hates them as it has hated Jesus. The world in that case seems to coincide with 'the Jews' to whom Jesus has spoken and who have seen his miracles. By hating Jesus they have also hated his Father. Jesus goes on:

> I have said all this to you to keep you from falling away. They will put you out of the synagogues, indeed the hour is coming when whoever kills you will think he is offering service to God. And they will do this because they have not known the Father, nor me. But I have said these things to you, that when the hour comes you may remember that I told you of them.

The Johannine community knows that it is hated by this surrounding world of Jews. That is understandable. John has reflected more deeply than the other evangelists on the person of Jesus. These others are often concerned with the mysterious authority with which Jesus spoke and acted. The reader of Mark can to some degree guess what it is based on. On the very first page the evangelist relates how Jesus was baptized in the Jordan, how God addressed him there as his beloved Son and how at that time he saw the Holy Spirit descending on him. The reader of Mark therefore knows that, but none of the people with whom Jesus has to do in the subsequent story knows it. Matthew and Luke begin their Gospels with a prologue about the birth of Jesus and each describes in his own way how Jesus was conceived by the Holy Spirit in the womb of his mother. But they do not return to that later in their work.

In his biblical meditations on the person of Jesus John has arrived at the insight that Jesus was already with God before the creation of the world. It is often said in the scriptures that God made everything, called everything into existence, by speaking, by his word. It is also said that God came to help people in need by sending his word. Isaiah 55 describes how the word that goes forth from God's mouth is sent to the earth and only returns to him when it has done his bidding.

The profound prologue with which John introduces his story is about that word. That word has become 'flesh', i.e. become man, and has dwelt among us. Only this man knows God with an unimaginable intimacy.

After this prologue John does not revert to that Word which exists before all things. But he does increasingly stress that in a unique way Jesus is associated with God, as his own Son. He is therefore not a 'son' in the way in which all kinds of special people like anointed kings, truly righteous men and even Israelites can be called sons of God in the scriptures. No, the son Jesus is one with his Father. This confession seems to run directly counter to the fundamental conviction on which Judaism rested: 'Hear, Israel, the Lord our God is one.' So in John this point often forms the focus of the discussions that he makes Jesus have with 'the Jews'. We may read this as inspired by what had been going on in his own heart as a believing Jew.

John records these discussions within the framework of narratives. Hence they sometimes end with the intention of the Jews to put Jesus to death. In chapter 5 John narrates the healing of a lame man. Jesus requires him to take with him the mat on which he had been lying. Then this day proves to be a sabbath, so the Jews protest. Jesus points out that his Father too never stops working, never stops being active, and so does not interrupt this activity on a sabbath day. Therefore, John writes, 'the Jews sought all the more to kill him, because he not only broke the sabbath but also called God his Father, making himself equal with God'.

Jesus carries on the discussion in chapter 8 in the temple. In it he appeals to the Father who sent him and whose will he is doing. Jesus is saying and doing only what is commanded him by the Father. Then the person of Abraham, the tribal ancestor of the Jews, is drawn into the discussion. It ends with the solemn declaration of Jesus: 'Truly I say to you, before Abraham was, I am.' Then the Jews took up stones to stone him, but Jesus escaped and left the temple.

Jesus here puts himself on the level of the God of Israel, who had referred to himself as 'I am'. So he was already with God before the creation. This was a blasphemous assertion which merited immediate execution. This is in fact the way in which the

Jews reacted to Jesus' remark in chapter 10: 'I and the Father are one.' And when Pilate says that he does not find Jesus guilty, they say: 'We have a Law and according to that Law he must die, because he has given himself out to be Son of God (literally: has made himself Son of God).'

But there seem to have been thinking Jews who felt sympathetic to John and sought contact with him. On closer acquaintance he did not seem to be a dreamer or a charlatan, but a thinker of a high order. Although he spoke and wrote in Greek, he knew the holy scriptures through and through, even in their original language: he also knew how particular texts were expounded by the tradition. He was equally at home in the richness of the meanings which were attached to old customs, particularly at the feasts which were celebrated in the temple.

But Jews who were respected had to keep their sympathies and certainly their meetings secret. Matthew says that a Jew who saw to the burial of Jesus, Joseph of Arimathea, was a disciple of Jesus. John's account here has two special characteristics. First of all he adds something to this description: 'who was a disciple of Jesus but secretly, for fear of the Jews'. His second addition is Nicodemus, who comes to help Jesus and who is referred to by John as 'the one who once came to Jesus by night', i.e. secretly. Two days afterwards Jesus comes amidst the disciples as the risen one; they are sitting behind closed doors 'for fear of the Jews'.

There is one passage in John in which Jesus takes an extremely negative view of the Jews. Fortunately it is not read in church as often as the Easter story that I have just quoted. In it Jesus says to the Jews that God is not their father; the devil is. To do justice to John, when we read these assertions we must try to put ourselves in his position. For him and his community, the belief in Jesus as God's own Son had opened up so many new perspectives and had brought them so close together that the harsh rejection of that belief by the majority of Jews was becoming increasingly incomprehensible. Now John is familiar with a way of thinking which had become current among many Jews of his time and is sometimes termed 'dualistic': two principles stand over against each other, two powers are working against each other in the world and also in every human heart: good and evil. Outside Israel they are often thought of as gods fighting with each other. For Jews that was inconceivable. No power could carry out its own plans independently of God. Evil must have begun at some time by the rebellion of a creature against God, and that creature had gained an enormous following and influence. He was called Satan, the devil, and had brought death and misery to humankind. In so doing the devil had as it were limited the sphere of God, for life is characteristic of God's own world. One can also say that truth is characteristic of it, and both are characteristic of the Son whom God has sent into the world to reveal him, to make known the truth about him and therefore also to give life to this world. Now the rebellion of the majority of Jews against the Son could not be explained from lack of insight or unwillingness. The cause had to lie deeper. In Jesus and the Jews these two worlds stand over against each other. They are totally different in nature. Therefore the Jews do not understand Jesus' language. This comes from a world of which they have no understanding: they have another origin.

In chapter 8 the Jews refer to their descent from Abraham. According to Jesus they should also have imitated Abraham's behaviour, but they do not do that because they are trying to kill Jesus, and are doing so only beause he has spoken the truth that he had heard from God. Abraham did not do anything like that. So the Jews say that God is their Father. Jesus' reply runs:

> If God were your Father, you would love me, for I proceeded and came forth from God; I came not of my own accord, but he sent me. Why do you not understand what I say? It is because you cannot bear to hear my word.
>
> You are of your father the devil, and your will is to do your father's desires. He was a murderer from the beginning, and has nothing to do with the truth, because there is no truth in him. When he lies, he speaks according to his own nature, for he is a liar and the father of lies. But because I tell the truth, you do not believe me. Which of you convicts me of sin? If I tell the truth, why do you not believe me? He who is of God hears the words of God; the reason why you do not hear them is that you are not of God.

Here John gives the impression that he is thinking of a kind of predestination. At other places he says that those who believe in Jesus are born of God. We can argue from a number of texts that at the same time he had reflected a good deal on the reasons why someone accepts or rejects that belief. But that would take us too far here. Here we are concerned with texts in the New Testament which have an anti-Jewish tendency because they have become holy scripture which has served down the centuries to justify a negative attitude towards the Jews. The passage about the devil as the father of the Jews which I have just quoted is one of the most shocking of these.

### Matthew: 'His blood be on us and on our children'

The Gospel according to Matthew also reflects the situation of the eighties: Jewish disciples of Jesus are living apart from the great community of Jews which under the leadership of the Pharisees was becoming an increasingly more coherent whole. Matthew does not speak explicitly about expulsion from the synagogue. But he does speak often in his account about *'their* synagogues' in which Jesus gives instruction. In chapter 10 he tells how Jesus chose the Twelve and gave them instructions before he sent them out. One of these was: 'Beware of men; for they will deliver you up to the councils, and flog you in their synagogues.' That means separation from the Jewish community to which Jesus had belonged, separation in time but also in a geographical sense. There are indications that the Christian community to which Matthew belonged and for which he wrote lived in a city in Syria in which Greek was the main language.

One can rightly speak of a 'community' here. For Matthew is the only one of the four Gospels to use the word *ekklesia*, church or community, and he does so twice. First in chapter 16, in which Peter has recognized Jesus as the Messiah, the Son of the living God, whereupon Jesus promises that he will build his 'church' on him, the man of rock. The powers that Peter receives are then given later, in chapter 18, to the church as a whole, in an address by Jesus which is devoted entirely to the communal life of its members.

This community was open to converts from the Gentile world, but it is probable that most of the members were born Jews. They observed the Torah, but as it was interpreted by Jesus. There were also scribes, like Matthew himself, and other men who acted as leaders. People were also familiar with the phenomenon of charismatics, those who prophesied in the name of Jesus, drove out demons and performed miracles.

It is striking that Matthew always speaks in negative terms about the Pharisees and the scribes who followed their approach. We can see this from the way in which he renders particular passages in Mark. Here is one example. Mark has the offensive and really absurd accusation that Jesus drives out demons as the agent of Beelzebul, their supreme chief, made by scribes who had come from Jerusalem. Matthew twice attributes this comment to the Pharisees. From indications like this we can see how polemical his attitude is towards reorganized Judaism. This influences his account of the Pharisees with whom Jesus was dealing in his day.

His chapter 23 is an indication of this: in translations it is often entitled a diatribe against the scribes and Pharisees. This chapter precedes Jesus' discourse about the last things. Matthew found a reason in the Gospel of Mark for putting this 'diatribe' at this point: there Jesus ends his debates in the temple in chapter 12 with a warning against the scribes who wear fine clothing, seek the places of honour in the synagogue and at meals, and devour widow's houses while pretending to make long prayers: a stern judgment will be pronounced on these people. Matthew further found in the document which Luke also used a series of three prophetic 'woes' against the Pharisees and three others against the scribes. Luke used these in his chapter 11, but Matthew preferred to incorporate them into his great diatribe, and to extend the number of the 'woes' to seven.

Jesus first of all addresses the people and his disciples. He says that the scribes and the Pharisees sit on Moses' seat. Therefore his audience must do what they say, but not imitate their conduct, since that in no way matches their words. They lay heavy burdens on peoples' shoulders, but do not lift a finger to help. They are concerned only with human reputations; they seek out the places of honour at banquets and in the synagogues and greetings from men, and are fond of being called rabbi.

> But you are not to be called rabbi,
> for you have one teacher, and you are all brethren.
> And call no man your father on earth,
> for you have one Father, who is in heaven.
> Neither be called masters,
> for you have only one master, the Christ.
> He who is greatest among you shall be your servant;
> whoever exalts himself will be humbled,
> and whoever humbles himself will be exalted.

There are also leaders and scribes in Matthew's community. They too are human. So what the Pharisees are accused of here can also happen among them. That would go completely against the spirit of Jesus, who as the Christ is now the Lord of the community. Hence this urgent admonition. Matthew also shows great concern in his Gospel for the little ones in his community, the less gifted, those who have difficulties with their faith. Hence in chapter 18, which I have already mentioned, the instruction on life together in this community, he begins with the question who is the greatest in it. Jesus replies by using a small child as an example: such a child is vulnerable, has no power and cannot assert itself. That must be the behaviour of those who function as leaders.

After this, Jesus addresses to the scribes and Pharisees, whom he calls hypocrites, seven cries of woe, condemnations in prophetic style, his own version (at least in the last five of them) of words which we also find in Luke.

The seventh woe is as follows:

Woe to you scribes and Pharisees, hypocrites! for you build the tombs of the prophets and adorn the monuments of the righteous, saying, 'If we had lived in the days of our fathers, we would not have taken part with them in shedding the blood of the prophets.' Thus you witness against yourselves, that you are sons of those who murdered the prophets.
Fill up, then, the measure of your fathers.
You serpents, you brood of vipers,
how are you to escape being sentenced to hell?
Therefore I send you prophets and wise men and scribes, some of whom you will kill and crucify, and some you will scourge in your synagogues and persecute from town to town, that upon you may come all the righteous blood shed on earth, from the blood of innocent Abel to the blood of Zechariah the son of Barachiah, whom you murdered between the sanctuary and the altar. Truly, I say to you, all this will come upon this generation.

One passage in the text I have quoted raises questions. After the taunt 'brood of vipers', which Matthew also attributes to John the Baptist when he sees the Jewish leaders approaching, Jesus talks about the prophets, wise men and scribes whom he himself sends. In Luke 11 there is a shorter version of this woe, formulated in the following way:

138

Therefore the wisdom of God has said
I shall send to them prophets and apostles,
and they shall kill and persecute some of them.

Matthew formulates this in such a way that this wisdom of God seems to be present in Jesus himself: 'Therefore, behold, I send...' In other places in his book he also appears to identify Jesus with the divine wisdom. So in his milieu there was further reflection along the lines of Jewish thinkers like Jesus Sirach, who regarded the Torah as the wisdom of God become a book. For Matthew, Jesus has come to expound the real and deepest significance of the Torah and in so doing to bring the final revelation of God's will. Therefore in Matthew Jesus himself can speak as the divine wisdom in person. So it was she who sent from the group of Jesus' disciples prophets, wise men and scribes to their fellow Jews (in Luke, prophets and apostles). In saying 'I send' Matthew seems to mean to indicate that Jesus was still at work in them.

In the next line it is again the earthly Jesus who, shortly before his death, is addressing the Pharisees and thus using the future tense: 'And they shall kill and persecute some of them.' We owe all we know about the clashes between Jesus' disciples and the other Jews in the years after Easter to the stories told by Luke in the book of Acts. So here we think of people like Stephen and the apostle James, but it is quite possible that Matthew had other names in mind, disciples from this first period who had to pay for their prophetic witness and their arguments from scripture with death or torture.

All this innocent blood will descend on 'this generation'. There seems to be no doubt that this term is often used by Jesus himself to denote people who were with him and who through his preaching were challenged to make a decision for or against the kingdom of God that was embodied in Jesus. Matthew is writing this in the eighties, and he is convinced that all the blood that has been shed already descended on this generation, at the time of the terrors of the Jewish war and the massacre at the fall of Jerusalem, an event the proclamation of which he introduces after these woes spoken by Jesus.

This generation itself has a voice in Matthew's version of the passion narrative. It should be said in passing that for all his criticism of the Pharisees Matthew does not have any of them participating in the condemnation and execution of Jesus. For him too it was clear that on the Jewish side only priests were involved in this, under the leadership of the high priest. In this context only Matthew mentions his name, Caiaphas: not Mark and Luke. Matthew follows Mark's text, but in the scene with Barabbas he has made telling changes and added two passages: the detail about Pilate's wife and the end of the scene in which Pilate washes his hands and the people take the responsibility upon themselves. Whereas according to Mark Pilate talks mockingly about Jesus as 'the king of the Jews', in Matthew he talks about 'Jesus who is called Christ (Messiah)'. Mark writes that the chief priests incited the crowd to call for the release of Barabbas. In Matthew they 'persuaded' the crowd to do that and, he adds, then to put Jesus to death. The cry of the crowd, 'Crucify him', in Matthew becomes something like the well-considered pronouncement of a jury: 'Let him be crucified.'

Here is Matthew's account in a somewhat slavish translation: the changes from and additions to Mark are in italics:

Now at the feast the governor was accustomed to release for the crowd any one prisoner whom they wanted. And they had then a notorious prisoner called Barabbas. When they had gathered, Pilate said to them: 'Whom do you want me to release for you, *Barabbas or Jesus who is called Christ?* For he knew that it was out of envy that they had delivered him up.

*While he was sitting on the judgment seat, his wife sent (a messenger) saying: Have nothing to do with that righteous man, for I suffered much over him last night in a dream.*

But the chief priests *and elders* persuaded the crowds that they should ask for Barabbas *and put Jesus to death.* The governor answered and said to them: Which of the two do you want me to release to you? But they said: Barabbas. Pilate said to them? What then shall I do with *Jesus who is called Christ?* All said, '*He must be crucified.*' But he said: What evil then has he done? But they cried even louder, *He must be crucified.*

*When Pilate saw that he was gaining nothing, but that the noise was getting even greater, he took water and washed his hands in front of the crowd saying: I am innocent of this blood, you must see that yourselves. And the whole people answered and said: His blood (come) upon us and our children.*

Both the remark by Pilate and the response to it from the people had a clear significance for Jews. The Torah prescribes in

Deuteronomy 21 what has to be done when a dead person is encountered in open country. The rulers of the nearest city have to wash their hands over a slain heifer and declare: 'Our hands did not shed this blood, neither did our eyes see it shed. Yahweh, forgive thy people Israel, whom thou hast redeemed, and set not the guilt of innocent blood in the midst of thy people Israel.'

Pilate is thus shifting the responsibility for the death of the innocent Jesus from himself in a gesture which was clear to any Jew, and then the whole people takes the responsibility on itself with equally clear words. Matthew here stops using the word 'crowd', as he has done so far, and replaces it with 'people', the Greek *laos*, which for him usually denotes the people of Israel. 'The whole people' does not occur elsewhere in his Gospel.

There can also be no doubt about the significance of 'us and our children'. According to biblical terminology speakers use this phrase to refer to themselves and their family. So Matthew here lets 'this generation' speak, the generation of Jews whom Jesus addressed and who have rejected his proclamation. He is not thinking of distant descendants of the Jews, far less of the millions of Jews who at that moment were living in the Diaspora.

However, in this generation there was one group of Jews which did not reject Jesus. These were his disciples. Jesus had involved them in his proclamation of the kingdom of God. Matthew stresses that this message was addressed exclusively to Jews. He is the only one of the evangelists to relate that when Jesus sent out the Twelve he said to them: 'Do not go among the Gentiles and do not enter into a city of the Samaritans: you must go only to the lost sheep of the house of Israel.' These lost sheep of which the house of Israel consists – for that is the meaning of the expression – also appear in his chapter 15 where Matthew takes over and expands a story fom Mark. This is about a Gentile woman who beseeches Jesus to heal her daughter who is possessed. In it Matthew includes the following saying of Jesus: 'I am sent only to the lost sheep of the house of Israel.'

Only when the crucified Jesus has been raised from the dead does he alter his earlier commission. Through the women at the tomb he has summoned his disciples to the mountain in Galilee that he has appointed. The only thing that is said to his disciples by the risen Jesus in the Gospel of Matthew is written in his last command: 'Go and make disciples of all nations, baptizing them in the name of the Father and the Son and the Holy Spirit, and teach them to observe all that I have commanded you. And lo, I am with you always, to the end of the world.'

In his work Matthew has often hinted at this coming integration of Gentiles into the new community. He already does this in his prologue. When Jesus is born in Bethlehem Gentile wise men come from the east to pay homage to the newborn king of the Jews. King Herod and *all* Jerusalem are dismayed at this. *All* the chief priests and scribes tell him that according to the prophet the Messiah should be born in Bethlehem, but they do not go there to worship the child. However, the Gentile wise men do. In chapter 8 Matthew relates how Jesus is amazed at the belief of the Roman officer who has asked him to heal his servant: 'Not even in Israel have I found such faith.' Matthew adds a saying of Jesus which Luke has taken up in another context and which thus was part of an earlier document: 'I tell you that many shall come from the east and the west and recline at table with Abraham and Isaac and Jacob in the kingdom of heaven. But the sons of the kingdom shall be cast out into outer darkness; there will be weeping and gnashing of teeth.' The word 'son' here again has the usual meaning of 'belonging to': it denotes those for whom the kingdom of God had been destined.

We find the most important indication of this new community made up of Jews and Gentiles in Matthew's version of the story of the wicked husbandmen in chapter 21. The tenants of a vineyard refuse to give the vintage to the owner. They maltreat and kill those whom he sends and finally kill his beloved son. When Jesus asks the audience what the owner should do to the tenants, in Mark they reply: 'He will come and destroy the tenants, and give the vineyard to others.' Matthew puts the answer in sharper terms: 'He will put those wretches to a miserable death, and let out the vineyard to other tenants who will give him the fruits in their seasons.'

After the saying from Psalm 18, about the stone which is rejected and becomes the corner stone, quoted here by all three evangelists, Matthew is the only one to add: 'Therefore I tell you, the kingdom of God will be taken away from you and given to a nation producing the fruits of it.'

By nation (here *ethnos*) Matthew undoubtedly means the *ekklesia* for which he is writing his work and which he is warning at the same time. The grace has now been given to it which was assigned earlier to Israel, the privilege of being the kingdom, the sphere of God. But that is at the same time a task. Matthew stresses that here.

The parable of Jesus about a man who had a vineyard and expected good fruit from it immediately reminded every Jew of Isaiah 5: Israel is a vineyard which God has planted with care: the good grapes which he expects are 'justice and righteousness'. If Israel does not produce these fruits, then it no longer has any reason to exist and will be destroyed.

In the new Israel, too (that building of which the rejected Jesus has now become the corner stone as a result of his resurrection), the fruits are important: that is, the practice of the new righteousness about which Jesus speaks in the discourse in chapters 5-7 of Matthew which we call the 'Sermon on the Mount'. In it the new righteousness is described and at the end summed up in what is sometimes referred to as the golden rule: 'Whatever you wish that men would do to you, do so to them.' Then Jesus goes on to speak about fruits, this time the fruits of a tree. Once again that is a clear image for any Jew of a man and his actions. Anyone who does bad things is a tree which deserves to be chopped down and thrown on the fire, an image of the divine judgment which was also used by John the Baptist. This is followed by Jesus' declaration:

> Not everyone who says to me 'Lord, Lord,' shall enter the kingdom of heaven, but he who does the will of my Father who is in heaven.
>
> On that day many will say to me, 'Lord, Lord, did we not prophesy in your name, and cast out demons in your name, and do many mighty works in your name?' And then will I declare to them, 'I never knew you: depart from me, you evildoers.'

In the Bible the term 'know' denotes familiarity with what is known, community, affinity. In this sharp rebuke Jesus says that he does not feel any bond with those who for all their spectacular religiosity do not in fact support their fellow human beings and therefore do unrighteousness.

The passage I have quoted forms the end of the admonitions in the Sermon on the Mount, Jesus' first great discourse. It is certainly no coincidence that Matthew concludes the fifth and last discourse of Jesus (24-25) with the unforgettable description of the last judgment on all peoples, all individuals. Immediately after this Matthew begins the passion narrative: after two days, Jesus says, the Son of man will be delivered up and crucified.

That definitive judgment on the life of every human being will be pronounced by the same Son of man when he appears in glory, surrounded by angels. To him is entrusted the judgment which in the Old Testament is entrusted to God himself. The Son of man, Shepherd and King, will then decide who are the blessed of his Father who may enter his eternal kingdom and who are not. The only criterion for this is what a person has done for fellow human beings in need: the hungry, the thirsty, the strangers, the poor without clothes, the sick and those in prison. This group is summarized four times, as examples of all those who are in need and those who suffer, with whom the Son of man declares himself to be in solidarity, as the least of his brethren.

The disciples may indeed now form the *ekklesia*, the new people of God made up of Jews and Gentiles around the Son of man, and be full of gratitude for this grace. But even their eternal destiny will be determined by this one criterion!

### Paul on other Jews

Even in the earliest letter of Paul that we possess there is a comment on the Jews which has had a fatal influence. The letter is Paul's first letter to the Christians in Thessalonica, which he sent from Corinth in the year 51 to the great port which is now called Saloniki. He had brought his message there shortly beforehand: first of all, of course, presenting it in the synagogue, as Luke tells us in Acts 17. But it was above all among non-Jews that the proclamation made an impact, and they were the ones who joined together to form the new community. The Jews found this hard to take. According to Luke, out of jealousy 'the Jews' had stirred up the people of the city and even the rulers against the Christians. But it appears from the beginning of Paul's letter that the latter had held out bravely. Christians in neighbouring ciites told how Paul and his companions had been received there and also, as Paul goes on to say,

How you turned to God from idols, to serve a living and true God, and to wait for his Son from heaven, whom he raised from the dead, Jesus who delivers us from the wrath to come.

144

Having reminded his readers of the disinterested and dedicated manner which had characterized his preaching and his leadership, Paul embarks on a second thanksgiving which ends in a very negative verdict on the Jews:

> And we also thank God constantly for this, that when you received the word of God which you heard from us, you accepted it not as the word of men but as what it really is, the word of God, which is at work in you believers. For you, brethren, became imitators of the churches of God in Christ Jesus which are in Judaea; for you suffered the same things from your own countrymen as they did from the Jews, who killed the Lord Jesus and the prophets, and drove us out, and displease God and oppose all men by hindering us from speaking to the Gentiles that they may be saved – so as always to fill up the measure of their sins. But God's wrath has come upon them at last.

It seems from this passage that the newly founded community in Saloniki was being troubled by compatriots, other inhabitants of this city, Gentile fellow-citizens. As a result it had as it were followed the example of the communities in Judaea, who there had to endure attacks from their fellow-citizens, i.e. Jews.

Paul then puts the Jews of Judaea in a wider perspective: they have killed the Lord, Jesus, and also the prophets, and persecuted Paul and his fellow-workers. Nowhere else in his letters does Paul name the Jews as those who killed Jesus. Apparently it is only here that the Jewish theme of the murder of the prophets occurs to him. That is already intimated at the time of Ezra, in his penitential prayer in Nehemiah 9, in which among the sins of Israel is also mentioned the fact that 'Our fathers killed your prophets.' This recollection was still a vivid one in the time of Jesus. His lament over Jerusalem as the city which 'kills the prophets and stones those who are sent to it' is bound up with this and was in circulation among the disciples of Jesus at a very early stage.

In Saloniki and elsewhere Paul and his fellow workers were pestered by Jews 'who displease God and oppose all men by hindering us from speaking to the Gentiles that they may be saved'. For Paul, God's good pleasure consists in the fact that he wants all people to share in his ultimate salvation, and has especially commissioned Paul to proclaim this salvation to the

145

Gentiles. The Jews who try to prevent that are thus going against the clear purposes of God and thus are 'filling up the measure of their sins'. We have already encountered this Jewish notion in the seventh woe of Matthew against the Pharisees and scribes.

As for 'the wrath', in the text from this letter which I quoted earlier this was clearly a reference to the last judgment: 'Jesus who delivers us from the wrath to come.' This is the final dénouement of human history which Paul believes to be very near: he himself will live to see that event. But sometimes he talks about this wrath of God as though it were already visibly at work among those who lead evil lives. In that case this wickedness is an effect of the wrath of God, and this wrath is at the same time increased by it. This is a difficult argument for those of us who are not familiar with the apocalyptic thought of Jewish groups of this period.

These passages in Paul, too, were written about *particular* Jews in a *particular* situation. So they are not about the whole Jewish people of this time. And they are certainly not about future generations: in a little while there was to be no earthly future. So Paul could not have any sense of a future in which his encouraging letter to Saloniki became 'holy' scripture and in which the passage about the Jews would be used to provide 'theological' justification for feelings of abhorrence and hatred towards Jews.

Paul's letter to the Galatians has also provided material for this. In it he gives a very negative picture of Jewish faith and one which is offensive to Jews. That is to be attributed both to the occasion for this letter and to Paul's character and style of speaking.

He has proclaimed the gospel in Galatia. Many people there received this message with gratitude, with the result that several communities came into being. Nowhere does it appear that Paul had first gone to synagogues. Perhaps there were none in that distant interior with no large cities. The enthusiasm of the converts had been great. They had once lived in uncertainty and anxiety. Their life seemed dominated by the whim of supernatural powers and forces, the 'elements of the cosmos': planets, stars, heavenly bodies, which were regarded as being animate, as divine beings, spirits, angels, and were thought to determine not only what we call the 'laws of nature' but also human destinies. All kinds of religious rites were used to gain their favour, but they were not much help. Certainly less well-to-do people lived under the pressure of destiny: nothing could be done to change it.

146

Then the inspired preacher Paul appeared in their area. Perhaps he was only travelling through and was detained there through illness. Be this as it may, he could not but speak about the one God who transcends all powers and forces, real and conceivable, as Creator and Lord of all. He loves us human beings, including you Galatians, so much that he has sent his Son Jesus to free us from all that oppresses us and makes us anxious. God has raised him from the death on the cross which was inflicted on him. Now he is sending from heaven his Spirit into the hearts of those who want to belong to him. When that comes about, all sorts of things happen to you: you gain new perspectives, you encounter fellow men and women at a much deeper level, and with them you can live in joy and in freedom, together looking forward to the moment when he comes to judge the world and put an end to all evil.

After Paul had gone on, now and then he got reassuring reports from Galatia: the Christians there were doing well. But suddenly, like a clap of thunder from a clear sky, came a report which affected him deeply. Jewish Christians had come to Galatia who had made the young community very confused. These Christians were convinced that Jesus had come as Messiah for Israel: so anyone who wanted to respond to him had to become a member of his people. That meant being circumcised and submitting to the regulations of the Torah. They propagated this conviction with arguments against which the new converts had no defence. They appealed to Jerusalem, to the apostles there, who were led by Peter and who had received their commission from the Lord himself. Your man Paul, they said, never knew Jesus personally and moreover everyone knows how fiercely he persecuted the first disciples. He may have been converted to belief in Jesus the Messiah, but it is impossible that he should now proclaim this belief without indicating those conditions for incorporation into Israel. Of course this semi-proclamation is bringing him success and he is well aware of that! But things cannot really be like that. His converts cannot call themselves real Christians, i.e. the Messiah's people.

This report cut Paul to the quick. The idea that these Jewish Christians had their own convictions was out of the question for him. For what they were doing there was quite wrong, quite wrong! It went directly against what he saw as the clear purposes of God; moreover it was utterly mean to act in this way behind his back by robbing these new converts of their joy and taking away their freedom while at the same time undermining his authority and imputing base motives to him. What he would like to have done best was to go straight back to Galatia. But at this moment he had obligations to his communities in Macedonia and so could not go. Therefore he dictated a letter to let the Galatians at least hear his voice, though they could not detect from it the tone of his deep concern.

We must always keep this situation in mind when reading the letter. Apart from an 'admonitory section' (5.13-6.10) it is clear that every sentence, every line, every transition from scriptural argument to an appeal to feelings and experience is in the service of what Paul wants to achieve. The Galatians have to hold to the gospel as he preached it and as they have experienced its riches, and they must firmly reject what the Jewish Christians want to impose on them. The letter is really one continuous plea which, according to the rhetorical rules of that time, appeals to the spirit and heart of its recipients and uses every possible means to gain their assent. Therefore it is impossible to give a short summary of it. The comments which follow here are meant only to draw your attention to the omnipresence of Paul's aim.

Already the phrasing of the first lines, the 'address' with this stress on Paul's mission, and the blessing that sums up the work of salvation in a few words, are determined by the aim of the letter. It must have seemed shocking that the usual thanksgiving was omitted: there was nothing to give thanks for! There is only bewilderment at the 'apostasy' of the Christians, their going over to 'another gospel' which does not really deserve the name. Twice Paul pronounces a curse on those who preach it, who go on to say that he is doing this to gain popularity.

Then Paul begins with the story of his call. He knows what zeal for the Law means from experience, and none of the Twelve apostles can deny him that, nor that he received his gospel directly from God. 'Jerusalem' did not come into the picture. Three years later he went up to Jerusalem to make the acquaintance of Peter. Only fourteen years after that short visit did he return, but then for a crucial meeting. He went from Antioch, along with Barnabas. He also took his Greek fellow-worker Titus with him and Titus was not compelled to be circumcised. In parentheses Paul describes how previously 'false brethren', i.e. fellow Christians, had slipped in, insisting on the circumcision of Gentiles. They did that – pay

148

careful attention, Galatians! – 'to spy out our freedom which we have in Christ Jesus, that they might bring us into bondage; but to them we did not yield in submission even for a moment, that the truth of the gospel might be preserved for you.' The leaders in Jerusalem, James the brother of the Lord, Peter and John, recognized this truth: the 'gospel of the foreskin' was entrusted to Paul, which meant that Gentiles could be received without being committed to circumcision and the Law.

Probably Peter had great authority among the Jewish Christians who came to Galatia. At all events Paul goes on to describe how he opposed Peter publicly in Antioch. Peter had sat at table there with Gentile Christians and had not observed the Jewish food laws. I should point out in passing that this story can make it clear to us how excruciatingly difficult it must have been for Jewish Christians even to sit at table with the uncircumcised and no longer bother about whether all the food served was kosher or not. Even to pay no attention to a life-style which had determined the religious life of many generations and for which Jews had even undergone a martyr death was an almost impossible demand.

Peter had sat at table in Antioch with Gentile Christians and had not observed the food laws. But then 'James's people' appeared and for fear of them Peter withdrew from this table fellowship. To Paul's deep disappointment his friend Barnabas shared in this dishonesty, this hypocrisy. For that is how Paul regarded it. He made this behaviour a matter of principle: how can you live as a Gentile – and that is what you are doing when you sit at table with the uncircumcised – and then compel Gentile Christians to live in Jewish style – which is evidently what 'James's people' want, these people to whom you yielded and to whom you, dear Galatians, you threaten to yield? Then Paul relates his subsequent conversation with Peter. Those of us who are born Jews have begun to believe in Christ and in so doing confess that we have found salvation in him and that therefore before this time we were as guilty before God as the Gentiles. Forgiveness, grace, communion with God are given to us only in Christ. We recognize that we are no longer given these gifts of God by observing the Torah: so these laws no longer bind us.

How can you, Peter, how can I, Paul, born a Jew just as you were, begin to impose these laws on Gentiles who have also come to Christ? To put it pictorially: if I do this, am I not building up the system which I had formerly demolished? Am I not suggesting that demolishing it had been sinful? Rather, it is the case that by believing in Christ I died to the Law; so it no longer imposes any obligations on me. For that 'I' no longer exists; it has been replaced by another 'I' which is leading a completely new life. In Paul's own words:

It is no longer I who live
but Christ who lives in me:
and the life I now live in the flesh
I live by faith in the Son of God
who loved me and gave himself for me.

I spoke to you at that time quite clearly about this crucified figure, and at that time you realized what his death meant for you. You yourselves experienced that new life, all these workings of God's Spirit in you. Then you received the promise that had already been given to Abraham: 'in you shall all the nations be blessed'. That could not happen earlier because Israel was still living under the Law, and this Law pronounced a curse on those who 'transgressed' even one precept of it, in other words who went outside this hedge. Christ has freed us Jews from this curse, freed us by himself becoming a curse in our place,

that in Christ Jesus the blessing of Abraham might come upon the Gentiles, that we might receive the promise of the Spirit through faith.

To make this clearer Paul compares this promise to Abraham with a testament. This is not undone by a measure which is taken much later. The Torah came only 430 years afterwards and it only had the purpose of seeing that the Jews had a safety net. It was a kind of attendant, the sort of slave who used to look after young children and protect them from accidents. Now Christ has come, this separation is no longer necessary: the Jews can now abandon this safe shelter and join those Gentiles who also believe in Christ. In this new community all are baptized in Christ and that means that the traditional discrimination is at an end. A pious Jew had the privilege and the calling to live completely in accordance with the Torah, which was impossible or barely possible for a Gentile, a slave and a woman. In the community of the baptized, Paul says, there are no longer Jews and Gentiles, slaves and free, male and female: you are all one in Christ Jesus.

150

In this sense you are thus heirs to the promise which God made to Abraham.

The term 'heirs' leads Paul to the remarkable notion that the heir who has not yet come of age is no different from a slave. He too is subjected to tutors and guardians until the time that has been determined by his father. So too it was with us, Jews: before we came of age, as slaves we were subject to the powers of the cosmos, just like the Gentiles:

> But when the time had fully come
> God sent forth his Son,
> born of a woman, born under the Law,
> to redeem those who were under the Law,
> so that we might receive adoption as sons.
> And because you are sons
> God has sent the Spirit of his Son into our hearts crying 'Abba! Father!'
> So through God you are no longer a slave but a son,
> and if a son then an heir.

The striking thing here is the shift in the personal pronouns: first Paul speaks as a Jew about *we*, then about *you* Galatians, and then about the Spirit which is sent into *our* hearts which has consequences for every Galatian: *you*.

What Paul goes on to say is the conclusion from what has gone before, which amounts to this: if you take the Torah on yourself, then you might just as well remain Gentiles. For that is the same kind of slavery, compared with the new freedom which you have now received as children of God.

After Paul has recalled in measured words the way in which the Galatians had once received him and treated him, as an ambassador of God with whom they were extremely happy, he expresses his deep pain for what they are now doing to him.

Then he takes up the theme of slavery as opposed to freedom. Not without irony he refers the Galatians to a story which stands in the same Torah that so fascinates them. It is about Abraham's two sons, one born of his slave girl and one born of his freeborn wife. The former had a son in the usual way; the latter, Sarah, bore her son when that was humanly no longer possible, by a divine miracle. Now, Paul says, you must understand this 'allegorically': the slave girl Hagar stands for the covenant of Sinai which brings forth slaves. That is present-day Jerusalem which lies in slavery with her children, in other words present-day Judaism. Sarah stands for the new community which is now growing, and in the image of Isaac consists of children of the promise. The conclusion is that we are therefore not children of a slave girl but of the free woman. Therefore you Galatians must not allow yourselves to be circumcised and in so doing take upon yourself the obligation of observing the whole law. In that case you are separating yourself from Christ and forsaking this new bond with God which the Spirit has made.

His last conjuration then ends with a derisive comment on the Jewish Christians who want to impose circumcision: 'I wish those who unsettle you would castrate themselves.' This is clearly an allusion to the priests of a pagan cult in Galatia who castrated themselves in honour of their gods.

In the conclusion to his letter, written in his own hand, Paul once again states clearly the contrasts between the propagandists for circumcision and himself. They want to cut a good figure to outsiders and avoid persecution for the sake of the cross of Christ. They do not themselves observe the Torah that they seek to impose on others, and want to boast of the success of their circumcision action. Paul boasts only in the cross of Christ. It no longer matters whether one is circumcised or not; all that matters is the total renewal of those who are taken up into Christ. They form the Israel of God. For that new people of God Paul has fought and suffered: the scars which he has from this mark him out as one who is dedicated to Jesus.

This letter, too, became 'holy' scripture and was thus removed from the circumstances in which it had come into being. Christians may therefore remain grateful for the way in which in this letter Paul often formulates essential features of their faith, in unforgettable sentences. At the same time they must recognize that his ways of approaching the law and circumcision do not in any way correspond to the actual experience of believing Jews.

We can also find an angry outburst against Jewish Christians who propagate circumcision in Paul's letter to the Christians in Philippi. He was very fond of the community there. They had been the first in 'Europe' to accept the gospel. The letter which has been included in our Bible seems to be composed of a number of short missives. One of them begins in chapter 3 with a series of terms of abuse:

Look out for the dogs,
look out for the evil-workers,
look out for those who mutilate the flesh.
For we are the true circumcision, who worship God in spirit,
and glory in Christ Jesus and put no confidence in the flesh...

Then Paul goes on to relate in glowing terms how formerly he
had all those things of which a Jew could rightly be proud:
circumcision, pure descent, zeal for the Torah and so on. He had
completely written off all these things, indeed they had become
refuse to him since he had come to know Christ, who now fills
his life and is its content. He describes this in almost 'mystical
terms', rather like those he uses in Galatians 2. Here too his 'I' is
at the service of his teaching: he hopes that his dear Philippians
will also allow their lives to be ruled in this way by their
communion with Christ. Later on he returns to the 'false brethren',
whom he describes as follows:

The enemies of the cross of Christ.
Their end is destruction,
their god is the belly,
and they glory in their shame,
with minds set on earthly things.

It has been suggested that the words 'belly' and 'shame' here
are euphemisms for the sexual organs, especially the male organ,
which was circumcised. In that case Paul would be alluding here
to the role that this member played in fertility religions, which
had many adherents in the great cities of the Roman empire. In
that case Paul would be being as coarse as in his letter to
the Galatians: 'I wish those who unsettle you would castrate
themselves!'

Paul dictated his letter to the Romans in Corinth, in 57 or 58. At
that time he was on the point of going to Jerusalem. There he
wanted to hand over the proceeds of the collection to the leaders
of the Christian community in person. On his former visit he had
come to an agreement with them that he should ask his Gentile
Christians to provide financial support for the poor members of
the community in Jerusalem. When he had finished this task there
he wanted to go and proclaim the gospel in the west, in Spain, but
to travel there via Rome. He had never been to this capital of the

empire before. The gospel had in fact already been preached there years before by Christians from among the Jews. So there was at least one community. But Paul's disciples had also preached there and gained primarily Gentiles for Christ. So that caused tensions between the two groups. Of course there had been much discussion about Paul among these groups in Rome, and he had already been praised or vilified depending on the standpoint.

As I have said, he wanted to proclaim the gospel in Spain. So it was important for him to have a Christian community behind him as a base, rather as Antioch had functioned at the beginning of his apostolic life. And this community should not be wasting its energy with mutual disputes and quarrels, but stand behind him as one. Hence an extensive and well-considered letter to prepare for his visit to Rome.

In the first part, chapters 1-8, he deals with the same themes as in his letter to the Galatians, but at much greater length and in a more profound way. The Jews with their Torah are as guilty before God as the Gentiles. Only faith in Christ can bind Jews and Gentiles together in one community which consists of the true children of the believing Abraham and is no longer bound to circumcision and Torah. All this is aimed above all at the Jewish Christians in Rome. Now they can level the charge against Paul which had certainly already been hurled against him earlier. 'With your interest in the Gentiles you have written off your own people. Even worse, you have really also made God such an "apostate", someone just like you, who has drawn a line through his past. For the scriptures say on many occasions, quite clearly, that God has bound himself to Israel and promised that people that he will always remain the God of Israel. According to you, Paul, God has abandoned these promises and now his preference is for the Gentiles!'

Paul tries to disarm these accusations in chapters 9-11. He bears witness under oath and with great emotion how much he feels bound to his people and how he constantly prays for the 'salvation' of the majority of his fellow-Jews who continue to reject the gospel, 'the disobedient'. He then demonstrates with a great many texts from scripture that their 'hardening' was as much foreseen by God as the salvation of the Gentiles. But these are as it were grafted on to the noble olive tree of Israel. Christians from the Gentile world must be well aware of that. They may not vaunt themselves above their Jewish fellow-Christians: these have grown by nature from the noble tree.

Furthermore, in fact things have come about in such a way that the resistance of the majority of Jews to the gospel is the occasion for those who preached it to address themselves to the Gentiles. Now in the style of an apocalyptic visionary Paul reveals the mystery of the future: if these 'recalcitrant' Jews see how fortunate the Gentiles are with that new salvation in Christ they will 'become jealous' and will open themselves to it: 'So finally all Israel will be saved...'

After the usual admonitory section, in chapters 14 and 15 Paul goes more closely into the tensions among the Christians in Rome and tells them about his travel plans. We can see from this passage about the strong and the weak how difficult it must have been for Jewish Christians to have dealings with Gentile Christians, even – indeed precisely – in Rome. In this thoroughly Gentile city all kinds of difficulties arose for the conscientious over eating meat and drinking wine, bought on the market and perhaps the remains of pagan sacrifices. The sabbath and other Jewish festivals had also remained special days for them. Their fellow-Christians with their 'Pauline' training found all these scruples and preferences nonsensical: that Jewish past is over, you should be done with it! Paul admonishes them, the strong, to respect these sensibilities of the weak in the spirit of Christ. With these admonitions he hopes to ensure that in Rome he will encounter a community which can stand unanimously behind him when he travels to Spain. But even now he is counting on its unanimous prayer for him with a view to what he is going to experience in Jerusalem.

There he will be confronted with two groups of fellow-Jews. First of all there are the religious leaders there, who hate him as an apostate, a traitor, and will certainly try to do away with him, whether with the co-operation of the Roman governor or not. Then there is the commmunity of Jewish Christians led by James the brother of the Lord. This community, whom Paul usually refers to as 'the saints', may perhaps hesitate over receiving the massive contribution for their poor. After all, it comes from the uncircumcised, the impure. Moreover this gesture from the hated Paul might call the attention of the already hostile Jewish authorities to them.

Before he asks for the prayers of the Roman Christians, Paul has first already described the aim of the collection in this way.

The communities who have contributed money for the benefit of the saints in Jerusalem were right to do that: 'for they are also in debt to them, for if the Gentiles have come to share in their spiritual blessings, they ought also to be of service to them in material blessings.' Following his argument in 9-11 Paul in this way recognizes the superiority of 'Jerusalem' and gives the Jewish Christians in Rome one more reason for accepting their 'Pauline' fellow believers in love. In this way they can make a unanimous response to the urgent request with which Paul concludes chapter 15:

> I appeal to you, brethren, by our Lord Jesus Christ and by the love of the Spirit, to strive together with me in your prayers to God on my behalf, that I may be delivered from the unbelievers in Judaea and that my service for Jerusalem may be acceptable to the saints, so that by God's will I may come to you with joy and be refreshed in your company. The God of peace be with you all. Amen.

We do not know whether Paul's letter had the effect that he intended. There is too little information about the Christians in Rome at that time. But one thing that is certain is that the prayer to which Paul so urgently summoned them found no response: he was arrested in Jerusalem and two years later taken as a prisoner to Rome. We know that from Luke's account in the book of Acts, which he wrote a mere thirty years later. At that time there was no longer any prospect of what Paul had still hoped for: that the 'hardening' of the majority of the Jews would only be temporary.

### Luke: the Gentiles will listen

We are used to talking about 'The Gospel of Luke' and the 'Acts of the Apostles'. Originally these were two parts of a single work. If Luke himself gave this book a title it has not been preserved. A modern reader could imagine the title being 'How Israel grew into a World Church', with the subtitle: 'The ongoing history of the people of God'.

Luke would probably have rejected that suggestion, since he was deeply convinced that history was and is directed by God, or rather by his Holy Spirit: his dynamic presence in our world. According to Luke, in any case, that would have to come out in the title of his two-volume work.

It is also possible that Luke did not intend to have a title because he had described the aim of his work clearly in the dedication to Theophilus. This consists of a long and solemn sentence completely in line with the literary taste of that time. Immediately after that Luke begins his story of the births of John the Baptist and Jesus, entirely in the style of the ancient biblical histories as he knows them from the Greek translation of the holy scriptures. The figures in the first chapters are all pious Jews who faithfully fulfil the law and look forward to the redemption of Israel. The sequence of stories breathes an atmosphere of joy and fulfilled expectation, further reinforced by the songs of praise which Luke puts in the mouths of Zachariah, Mary, the angels above the shepherds in the fields, and Simeon. But there is one passage which foretells disaster. After the aged Simeon has taken the child in his arms, he praises God for being allowed to see the salvation that he has looked for over a long and expectant life. With terms taken from Isaiah 42 and 49 he thanks God for that salvation 'which you have prepared for all people: a light to lighten the Gentiles and a glory for your people Israel'. After that he pronounces a blessing on the child's parents and then says to his mother Mary:

> Behold, this child is set for the fall and rising of many in Israel, and for a sign that is spoken against (and a sword will pierce through your own soul also) that thoughts out of many hearts may be revealed.

Here Luke has in mind what he is to describe subsequently, and especially in the second part of his work. It was above all the proclamation of the crucified Jesus whom God made Messiah and Lord that brought about a division in Israel. Most Jews rejected this message and came to grief. In the style of the ancient historians of Israel Luke now has this course of events already foretold by the aged Simeon, on whom the Holy Spirit rested. This division within the Jewish people may also be referred to by the sword that pierces Mary. Here she represents the people; she stands here for the woman Israel.

Where Mark, followed by Matthew, sees the appearance of John the Baptist foretold in the words of Isaiah 40 about the voice of one crying in the wilderness, 'Prepare the way of the Lord; make his paths straight', Luke cites even more of the text, obviously because he wants to include the clause 'and all flesh (all humanity) shall see the salvation of God'. For that is the aim of the history which is introduced by John the Baptist.

157

Mark describes the appearance of Jesus in the synagogue of his home town in his chapter 6. Luke develops that occurrence into a scene which he puts at the beginning of Jesus' activities in Galilee, immediately after his confrontation with the devil. In the synagogue, Jesus reads out a passage from the book of Isaiah in which the prophet says: 'The Spirit of the Lord is upon me because he has anointed me to bring good news to the poor. He has sent me to proclaim liberation to the captives and sight to the blind, to liberate the oppressed, to proclaim an acceptable year of the Lord.' Then he applies this prophecy to himself, apparently in a way which makes those present very excited. But then the mood suddenly changes. Jesus goes on to suggest that a prophet is not popular in his own city, or according to a different translation does not favour his own city. Then he says:

'But in truth, I tell you, there were many widows in Israel in the days of Elijah, when the heaven was shut up three years and six months, when there came a great famine over all the land; and Elijah was sent to none of them but only to Zarephath, in the land of Sidon, to a woman who was a widow. And there were many lepers in Israel in the time of the prophet Elisha; and none of them was cleansed, but only Naaman the Syrian.'

When they heard this, all in the synagogue were filled with wrath. And they rose up and put him out of the city, and led him to the brow of the hill on which their city was built, that they might throw him down headlong. But passing through the midst of them he went away.

In this story too Luke is preparing for what is to happen later. Following the line of these two great predecessors the prophet Jesus will bring God's salvation to people who do not deserve it, to outsiders. For that reason his own people will kill him, but their plan will not succeed.

After this, Luke roughly follows Mark's account until in chapter 9 with solemn words he introduces the new section of his book, the so-called 'travel narrative', which I mentioned earlier (85).

Luke picks up the thread of Mark again in the account of the entry into Jerusalem. After that he alone has the following passage:

And when he drew near and saw the city he wept over it, saying, 'Would that even today you knew the things that make for peace! But now they are hid from your eyes. For the days shall come upon you, when your enemies will cast up a bank about you and surround you, and hem you in on every side, and dash you to the ground, you and your children within you, and they will not leave one stone upon another in you, because you did not know the time of your visitation.'

The last sentence is again real biblical language. When in his chapter 7 Luke described how Jesus raised the dead son of a widow, he made the eyewitnesses glorify God and say, 'A great prophet has come among us', and also, 'God has visited his people.' And before that the aged Zachariah began his song of praise with the words 'Blessed be the Lord, the God of Israel, for he has visited and redeemed his people.' Jerusalem has not recognized that the coming of Jesus was a 'visitation', a grace given by God for her. Therefore she has brought judgment upon herself.

In the sequel to his story about the last days of Jesus Luke explicitly brings out this theme twice more. He does so first where he renders the apocalyptic discourse of Jesus from Mark 13 in terms which are less enigmatic for his readers. In Mark Jesus interprets the coming downfall of Jerusalem like this: 'When you see the abomination of desolation standing where it may not stand – the reader must pay attention here – then those who are in Judaea must flee to the hills...' This remarkable expression comes from the book of Daniel and is a sort of cryptogram for the altar to Zeus which Antiochus IV had erected in the temple. Luke makes Jesus say here in words which are clear to anyone:

But when you see Jerusalem surrounded by armies, then know that its desolation has come near. Then let those who are in Judaea flee to the mountains...

So here there is no devastation in the sense of a desecration of the temple, but a real devastation of the whole city. Mark adds to the specification of the time and the warning some further sentences which also indicate in apocalyptic style what is going to happen next. Luke alters almost the whole passage, and translates it into a more prophetic style. With an expression taken from the Torah Jesus says that now the days of retribution have dawned in which the scriptures are being fulfilled. Wrath is coming upon this people and the ultimate fate of Jerusalem is indicated by an expression taken from the prophet Zechariah:

For these are days of vengeance, to fulfil all that is written. Alas for those who are with child and for those who give suck in those days. For great distress shall be upon the land and wrath upon this people; they will fall by the edge of the sword, and be led captive among all nations; and Jerusalem will be trodden down by the Gentiles, until the times of the Gentiles are fulfilled.

Perhaps Luke took over the sentence about the pregnant women and the breast-feeding mothers from Mark because he already had in mind what he wanted to add to Mark's passion narrative. When Jesus had approached the city some days earlier, he had burst into tears about its fate, because he foresaw its destruction. When Jesus again leaves the city for the place of his execution, while Simon of Cyrene is carrying his cross after him, only Luke narrates how Jesus is accompanied by lamenting women and what he says to them, again in prophetic style and vocabulary:

Daughters of Jerusalem, do not weep for me, but weep for yourselves and for your children. For behold, the days are coming when they will say, 'Blessed are the barren, and the wombs that never bore, and the breasts that never gave suck.' Then will they begin to say to the mountains, Fall on us, and to the hills, Cover us.' For if they do this when the wood is green, what will happen when it is dry?

So for the third time Jesus speaks in prophetic terms about the downfall of Jerusalem. The Jewish leaders have not recognized God's gracious 'visitation' as such and therefore have called down his judgment on Jerusalem. That is the way in which Luke and his fellow-Christians interpret the events of 70, when the Romans destroyed the capital and the centre of the Jewish people.

To their minds, another development was connected with this. Not only Jesus himself had been rejected, but also those who proclaimed him as God's last offer of salvation. They did not find a hearing among most Jews. For them that was a reason to turn to non-Jews and to proclaim the new salvation to them. Luke also stresses this theme. He has it stated three times by Paul, the third time in the conclusion to his two-volume work.

In the story of Paul's appearance in Antioch which I have already mentioned earlier (Acts 13, cf. pp.107f.), Luke relates how the Jews were very envious and responded to Paul's explanations with taunts. Then he writes:

And Paul and Barnabas spoke out boldly saying, 'It was necessary that the word of God should be spoken first to you. Since you thrust it from you, and judge yourselves unworthy of eternal life, behold, we turn to the Gentiles. For so the Lord has commanded, saying,

*I have set you to be a light for the Gentiles,*
that you may bring salvation to the uttermost parts of the earth.'

In chapter 18 Luke relates that Paul could devote himself wholly to preaching in Corinth when his helpers had arrived there.

He testified to the Jews that the Christ was Jesus. And when they opposed and reviled him, he shook out his garments and said to them, 'Your blood be upon your heads! I am innocent. From now on I will go to the Gentiles.'

That is a statement of principle. Subsequently in Luke's account Paul always goes first to the synagogue. But here Luke is preparing the reader for the impressive scene with which he is to conclude his work.

After an adventurous voyage, Paul, still a prisoner, arrives in Rome. Christians from this city come to meet him, but these 'brothers' immediately disappear from the scene. For Paul is concerned with the Jews. He is allowed to rent his own lodgings in Rome, though still in fetters and always with a soldier to watch over him. To these lodgings he invites the leaders of the Jewish community. He tells them how he was arrested in Jerusalem and handed over to the Romans. They wanted to release him, but because the Jews were opposed to this he could hardly do other than appeal to the emperor. He has nothing against his people and therefore wants a conversation with them: 'It is because of the hope of Israel that I am bound with this chain.' The Jews prove to be ready for a conversation. They have had no bad news about Paul, but they have heard that the trend or party which he represents is spoken against everywhere. Luke then continues his story about these Jews:

When they had appointed a day for him, they came to him at his lodging in great numbers. And he expounded the matter to them from morning till evening, testifying to the kingdom of God and trying to convince them about Jesus both from the law of Moses and from the prophets. And some were convinced by what he said, while others disbelieved. So, as they disagreed among themselves, they departed, after Paul had made one statement: 'The Holy Spirit was right in saying to your fathers through Isaiah the prophet:

"Go to this people, and say,
You shall indeed hear but never understand,
and you shall indeed see but never perceive.
For this people's heart has grown dull,
and their ears are heavy of hearing,
and their eyes they have closed;
lest they should perceive with their eyes,
and hear with the ears,
and understand with their heart,
and turn for me to heal them.

Let it be known to you then that this salvation of God has been sent to the Gentiles; they will listen."'

And he lived there two whole years at his own expense, and welcomed all who came to him, preaching the kingdom of God and teaching about the Lord Jesus Christ quite openly and unhindered.

Readers have constantly been amazed at this sudden end to the book. The last half of Acts was entirely about Paul and seemed to be a piece of biography. Why then does Luke not tell us what happened to him after those two years? Did Paul's case then come to the imperial judgment seat? Was he condemned? If he was acquitted, what did he do after that and how did he die? It has been supposed that Luke himself did not know this when he finished his narrative: he was working on it during Paul's captivity. When he finished it after two years he sent the manuscript to Theophilus who was to bear the costs of its publication. Another hypothesis is that Luke had wanted to write a third book but did not get round to it; or he did write it, but then it was lost. Such hypotheses are unnecessary if we begin with Luke's plans for his two-volume work. There are plenty of indications that he wrote it in the eighties. Many Christian communities at this time consisted of former Gentiles and their children. They were a new phenomenon in the society of the time, quite different from the Jewish communities, the 'synagogues'. The members of the synagogues knew very well who they were. They were descended from the most ancient people in the world, chosen by the Creator to be his special possession among all the nations. Many centuries before the Greek writers and philosophers appeared on the scene Moses had described the history of humankind from creation and he had also laid down the rules by which God's people was to live. Moreover they had a centuries-old tradition of exposition of these Holy Scriptures and especially of the adaptation of the rules of behaviour to constantly changing cicumstances. So the Jews felt themselves to be deeply rooted in the past, and this contributed considerably to their inner certainty and their joy in life.

The Christians had gathered around Jesus, the Son of God who had lived not so long ago in Palestine, had been executed on a cross and had been raised to life by God. They had entrusted themselves to this God when they had joined the community of Christians. They came from very different backgrounds. They did not have those common roots in the past which bound the Jews so closely together.

The contrast became perhaps even stronger as a result of developments after the year 70: new reflection on the essence of being a Jew, directed by the Pharisees in Jamnia, along with the exclusion of dissidents like the Nazoreans. This renewal certainly penetrated to the cities of the Diaspora and there too increased the tensions between Jews and Christians. Perhaps among the latter the enthusiasm of the first beginnings had to some degree abated and it became more difficult for them to endure vexations and outside pressures. Perhaps in discussions with the Jews there was little resistance to their self-confident attitude. It was far too silly, this notion that someone who had been lawfully crucified could be the Messiah of Israel. And what an illusion to suppose that non-Jews could get privileges which God had given only to his people!

Anyone who tries to imagine the doubt and disillusionment of these Christians will understand better why Luke wrote his two-volume work as he did. His readers were never to forget how Jesus was born in a pious Jewish milieu, in the heart of believing Israel, and how he collected many disciples around him: in addition to the Twelve, there were seventy-two others who successfully proclaimed the message of the kingdom of God. Sometimes thousands of Jews had streamed to hear Jesus and then almost trampled one another under foot. Certainly the people left him in the lurch when he stood before Pilate, but they did not join in with their leaders when they mocked Jesus on the cross. And when he died, people went home beating their breasts in sorrow. At Pentecost the Holy Spirit descended on a group of about a hundred and twenty people. That same day, around three thousand people joined them and subsequently more came to be added every day. Only after the stoning of Stephen does it become clear that this large group of disciples came up against increasing opposition from the other Jews.

But no power in the world can prevent the spread of the message. Before his ascension Jesus had given his disciples a promise which at the same time contained a commission: 'You shall receive power from the Holy Spirit which is come upon you to be my witnesses in Jerusalem, throughout Judaea and Samaria and to the uttermost ends of the earth.' The Holy Spirit is really the hero of Luke's second volume. That is also the reason why it is such an encouraging book. Luke shows this power of God at work in those who proclaim the gospel and also in the many Christian communities which are mentioned. For all the opposition and difficulties it is a privilege to be allowed to live in such a community in which the salvation, grace and power of God are experienced in such an unmistakable way.

In his dedication to Theophilus Luke had promised to give an account of the things 'which have been fulfilled among us', i.e. among the community of Christians. It is of course God who has brought these things 'to fulfilment' there. With this significant expression Luke means not only things which have happened and been confirmed by witnesses but also that in it God has fulfilled his age-old promise of salvation. Certainly Christians still look forward to the eschatological fulfilment at the end of time, but now they already live in a time of 'fulfilment'.

When Paul proclaims this message of salvation in Rome, Jesus' commission has been completed. For Rome is the centre of the inhabited world, the centre from which roads go out to the ends of the earth. What happens to Paul after this is no longer important: the important thing was for the message to reach all peoples. It also emerges from other details in the concluding lines of Acts quoted above that they are meant as a conclusion to Luke's two-volume work. Paul bears witness to 'the kingdom of God' to the Jews in Rome. With this expression Luke refers his readers to the preaching of Jesus in the first part of his work.

Paul also tries to convince the Jews 'from the Law of Moses and the prophets'. That reminds the readers of one of the main themes of the book: the community which has gathered around the Messiah Jesus did not really come into being yesterday. Its credentials are those of the Jews, since Jesus the Messiah was proclaimed in their holy Scriptures. And in them it was also possible to read that God would give his salvation to all people.

Unfortunately this purpose of God was not recognized by most Jews. But this too had been foretold by the prophet Isaiah. His remark about the 'hardening' of Israel is quoted by Matthew in his chapter 13 about the parables: Jesus explains the meaning of the parables only to his disciples and not to people outside that circle. John uses it where in chapter 12 he concludes his story about the public ministry of Jesus. Luke kept this text for the end of his book. Because he does this the saying of Isaiah remains in the reader's mind after he or she has closed the book.

At the same time, Luke does not exclude the conversion of individual Jews. He writes: 'some were convinced by what he said' and 'they departed without agreeing among themselves'. Moreover for those two years Paul receives in his lodgings all who come to him: these could also have included Jews. But a mass acceptance of Jesus, of the kind that Paul still hoped for, seems to lie outside Luke's purview. The break between the two communities of faith seems to have become definitive for him.

## Reflections

A Christian can only regret that such 'anti-Jewish' texts came into being and began to circulate within the movement of Jesus which preached love, especially love towards enemies. But these expressions are understandable. That was recently stressed in an ecumenical journal by the Jewish biblical scholar Jon Levenson, who teaches the Hebrew Bible in Chicago. It is a universal phenomenon, he writes, that we are seldom generous towards rivals. When we take their place we try to show that they do not deserve it and that they are worse than we are. The first Christians believed that they now formed the real people of God, having taken the place of the Jews who had forfeited that privilege through their rejection of the Messiah Jesus. A further reason for blackening the Jewish religion as much as possible was the attraction it could still exert on doubters and would-be converts (the reader might think here of the Galatians and the hesitant Jews in the Fourth Gospel).

Then Levenson recalls that a similar attitude also occurs in the Hebrew Bible. In it the adherents of other religions are often mocked: pagans first make a god of stone and wood and gold and then begin to fall down and worship it. A text like that in Isaiah 44 is a parody, really unfair. No Babylonian would have recognized himself in it. But anyone who has steeped himself or herself in prayers from this ancient culture and has read texts about the power and mercy of a God like Marduk can understand why this religion could be seductive for Jews.

Another example is the way in which the population of Canaan is depicted. Israel did not take the place of another religion as Christianity did later, but appropriated the land of the Canaanites. It began to define that as Israel's 'promised land'. The Israelites sought their justification for this in the moral corruption of its inhabitants. For this reason they had to be exterminated completely.

As a particularly atrocious example of this, Levenson takes the texts about the Amalekites. These had to be exterminated root and branch. In Exodus 17 God swears that he will always continue to fight against them. The first king of Israel, Saul, was rejected because in a fight against the Amalekites he had spared the life of their king: the angry prophet Samuel then hacked the king to pieces with his own hands. The greatest enemy of the Jews in the Bible, Haman in the book of Esther, is a descendant of this king Agag. This hatred against Amalek long continued to have an influence: a rabbinic regulation from about 100 states that converts can be accepted from all peoples, except for those who are descended from Amalek. These texts, Levinson says, appear in writings which are declared to be holy. But there are no longer peoples against whom they can be used: the modern world no longer has religions like ancient Babylonian religion, and even the Canaanites belong to the distant past. He does, however, comment in a footnote that in Israel he heard these anti-Canaanite texts quoted in a radio broadcast as evidence that God wanted the Palestinian Arabs out of the country. That was in 1981, in the election campaign of a right-wing party.

But the people that is depicted in such a negative way in the New Testament does still exist. Those texts, read time and again as words of God, have kept alive and nurtured the hatred of Jews in Christian societies, with the abhorrent consequences in our century.

Levenson remarks that inter-faith understanding is in many respects a child of historical criticism. Anyone who champions inter-faith understanding must reflect that such a conversation has little chance of success without a historical approach to biblical texts.

That is Levenson's argument. A thinking Christian cannot but approve of his last remark. But unfortunately the circulation of Bibles goes on, as zealous as it is thoughtless. Recently there was an excited report that the Bible can now be obtained in four new languages. One of them is Moldavian. If there are anti-Jewish feelings among Christians in this Soviet republic, then they have now been given justification: after all, Jesus himself said that the Jews are descended from the devil! There are no notes to this text, nor is there an introduction to the Fourth Gospel. For the 'word of God' must be given in its pure form to the Moldavians, without human additions.

In a book about the interpretation of the Old Testament the English biblical scholar John Barton touches on the subject of the canon, i.e. the list of books which a community of believers regards as holy, inspired by God and therefore authoritative. On this he remarks: 'Perhaps, after all, it is better not to have a canon; perhaps Christianity should have resisted the temptation to become in any sense a religion of the book in any sense of the word; perhaps the canon is even a curse.' One does not expect such a lament from a scholar who is also a priest of his church and a minister of the Word. But anyone who is aware of what disasters an uncritical use of the theory of divine inspiration has had and still has will understand him. In the Netherlands Dr Joanna Klink recently expressed her feelings on the same issue. She is a Protestant minister and well known for her books about teaching the Bible to children. In her book *Naar de tred van kinderen* (1983) she shows how much harm can be done to children if they are given biblical stories to learn just as they are at an early age. 'One must not dump débris on a budding plant.' Her book is an ardent plea for a revision of the way in which we talk about the Bible as being inspired by God, as being the Word of God. I hope that this chapter, too, will contribute to such a revision.

# 7 Jesus. A 'Fulfilment' Nevertheless

The New Testament authors considered that what had happened with Jesus of Nazareth had been clearly foretold in the ancient scriptures. Therefore everything 'had to' follow the course that it did, according to plan: the plan which God had revealed long beforehand to his prophets.

It is impossible for us to take over that vision. It is too tightly bound up with a form of biblical interpretation which can no longer be ours. For the New Testament authors the ancient texts had come directly from God. God had inspired the writers, breathed into them what they had to write. We automatically raise historical questions: what did the author mean when he wrote this text? What did he want to communicate to his readers? In what situation did it happen? Why did people continue to copy his text and finally incorporate it into a greater whole?

Only towards the end of the last century did Christians begin to read the ancient Bible in the light of these questions. As they did so, amazing riches came to light, the extremely varied statements of people who experienced their existence in relation to God. This was an existence in groups, first as separate tribes, then as a nation and later as the Jewish people scattered over the world, with its centre in Jerusalem and using not only Hebrew but also Greek to bear witness to what they had experienced in their deaslings with God. They also did that as individuals, and in all kinds of circumstances and moods, grateful and rebellious, in trust and in despair, aware of their links with the past and at the same time looking forward to a new future.

In this rich hoard of witnesses of faith one can point to some aspects or lines which come together in Jesus. Perhaps it is better to say that some essential aspects of this rich Jewish experience of faith were concentrated in him and in what he evoked in other people. In this sense one can rightly speak of a 'fulfilment'. What I mean by this can perhaps be made clearer by a few examples.

In chapter 7 of the book of Jeremiah we are given the words with which the prophet proclaimed the destruction of the temple in Jerusalem. He accuses his audience of wrongly wanting to dwell safely in the capital, because the temple of Yahweh is there. Yahweh lives there himself and he will continue to dwell there with his people for ever and ever. Prophets had confessed that and it was constantly celebrated in the liturgy: the holiest place in the world was also the safest! Had God not endorsed that confidence himself, just a century earlier, when the powerful army of the Assyrians surrounded the city with the aim of capturing it and destroying it? At that time God himself had caused confusion in that army so that it had to withdraw without doing any damage to the city. So here was the safest place in the world. But according to Jeremiah that was a false, deceitful slogan.

> Behold, you trust in deceptive words to no avail. Will you steal, murder, commit adultery, swear falsely, burn incense to Baal, and go after other gods that you have not known, and then come and stand before me in this house, which is called by my name, and say, 'We are safe!'

Then God compares the temple with a robbers' den: in such a place criminals seek a safe refuge before going out plundering again. So God will do with this holy place what he had done centuries before with Shiloh, the city in the hill-country north of Jerusalem where for the first time the ark of the covenant had been housed in a building, a temple. This was destroyed with the city by the Philistines, a disaster which made a deep impression on the memory of Israel. In chapter 26 of the book Jeremiah's friend and helper Baruch describes how those present reacted to these words of the prophet:

> And when Jeremiah had finished speaking all that Yahweh had commanded him to speak to all the people, then the priests and the prophets and all the people laid hold of him, saying, 'You shall die! How dare you prophesy in the name of Yahweh, saying, "This house shall be like Shiloh, and this city shall be desolate. without inhabitant?"' And all the people gathered about Jeremiah in the house of Yahweh.
> When the princes of Judah heard these things, they came up from the palace to the temple and took their seat in the entry

of the new gate. Then the priests and prophets said to the princes and to all the people. 'This man deserves the sentence of death, because he has prophesied against this city, as you have heard with your own ears.'

Then Jeremiah spoke to all the princes and all the people, saying, 'Yahweh sent me to prophesy against his house and this city all the words you have heard. Now therefore amend your ways and your doings, and obey the voice of Yahweh your God, and Yahweh will repent of the evil which he has pronounced against you. But as for me, behold I am in your hands. Do with me as seems good and right to you. Only know for certain that if you put me to death, you will bring innocent blood upon yourselves and upon this city and its inhabitants, for in truth Yahweh sent me to you to speak all these words in your ears.'

Some Christians who hear or read this story for the first time immediately think of Jesus. He too had proclaimed the destruction of the temple and as a result was arrested and condemned to death. What happened to Jeremiah thus points to him. A foretelling? Or perhaps better a prefiguration? But we do better to leave this question aside. For Baruch has more to say. His story has a prelude and also a sequel. After Jeremiah's declaration that he is innocent Baruch continues like this:

Then the princes and all the people said to the priests and prophets, 'This man does not deserve the sentence of death, for he has spoken to us in the name of Yahweh our God.' And certain of the elders of the land arose and spoke to all the assembled people saying, 'Micah of Moresheth prophesied in the days of Hezekiah king of Judah, and said to all the people of Judah:

"Thus says Yahweh of hosts,
Zion shall be ploughed as a field,
Jerusalem shall become a heap of ruins,
and the mountain of the temple a wooded height."

Did Hezekiah king of Judah and all Judah put him to death? Did he not fear Yahweh and entreat his favour, and did not Yahweh repent of the evil with which he had threatened them? But we are about to bring great evil upon ourselves.'

After this Baruch goes on to relate something else that must have happened some years after the incident with Jeremiah. For that took place in the first year of the reign of king Jehoiakim, and therefore what comes next must have happened some time later. Baruch relates:

> There was another man who prophesied in the name of Yahweh: Uriah the son of Shemaiah from Kiriath-jearim. He prophesied against this city and against this land in words like those of Jeremiah. And when King Jehoiakim, with all his warriors and all the princes, heard his words, the king sought to put him to death, but when Uriah heard of it, he was afraid and fled and escaped to Egypt. Then Jehoiakim sent to Egypt certain men, Elnathan the son of Achbor and others with him, and they fetched Uriah from Egypt and brought him to king Jehoiakim who slew him with the sword and cast his dead body into the burial place of the common people.

So Micah was not murdered when he had proclaimed the downfall of the city and temple, but Uriah, who also did that, was. And according to the conclusion of Baruch's narrative, that this did not happen to Jeremiah was really only thanks to his influential friend Ahikam, a son of Saphan: he finally saw to it that Jeremiah did not fall into the hands of the mob which wanted to kill him.

As to the prelude to Baruch's story, by chance, the remark by the prophet Micah which is cited by the princes has been preserved in the biblical book of Micah. At the end of chapter 3 in that book there is this announcement that Zion will be ploughed over as a field and that Jerusalem will become a heap of ruins. Before that, there is a summary of the reasons why God will do this. Justice is held in contempt and law is perverted. Crimes are committed, the innocent are murdered, the leaders of the people are corrupt, even the priests and the prophets, and despite all this they appeal to the presence of God in the temple:

> Is not Yahweh in our midst?
> No evil will come to us.

Micah's contemporary Isaiah and their predecessors Amos and Hosea also fiercely criticized worship which did not go along with justice and righteousness in society. They had a strong awareness of Yahweh as he had been experienced in former centuries. He had made his nature known by freeing Hebrew slaves from Egypt and in that way had made them his own people. He had come to perform this action because of the cries of distress of the oppressed that had penetrated to him. He had shown himself to them as one who delivered them from distress and therefore no member of his people might cause distress to another. Anyone who belonged to Yahweh had to respect the fundamental rights of others: the right to life, freedom, marriage, good name and possessions as these were formulated in the Ten Commandments.

One can observe that this 'morality' was nothing new in the ancient world. It is true that the basic laws of a proper human society had already been formulated much earlier in the cultures of Mesopotamia and Egypt, formulated by wise men and lawgivers. The distinctive feature of Israel seems to lie in the fact that its one God Yahweh wanted to be served only in this way. The wish faded into the background when the monarchy was instituted in Israel, on the usual ancient Near Eastern pattern, in other words with a temple, a priesthood and a grand liturgy with sacrifices and songs. Along with this an upper class developed in society: priests, military officials and tax collectors on the one hand and an increasing number of impoverished and oppressed people on the other. The prophets attacked this. Hence their clashes with what is nowadays called the establishment, which tried to silence them. So what Jeremiah experienced was by no means unprecedented, any more than was the execution of the prophet Uriah some time afterwards.

These events also had an effect later. In Ezra's penitential prayer recorded in Nehemiah 9 one of the sins which Israel confesses is: 'Our fathers killed your prophets who warned them to return to you.' This becomes a fixed theme in the penitential prayers of the Jewish people.

Matthew and Luke cite a saying of Jesus which begins, 'Jerusalem, Jerusalem, who kills the prophets and stones those who are sent to her...' It is important to know that in using this description Jesus is taking up a centuries-old Jewish tradition.

Now we may ask whether the members of the Sanhedrin which declared that Jesus deserved the sentence of death also knew this tradition. Certainly the scribes were familiar with the story in Jeremiah 26 in which Micah and Uriah are mentioned. An answer to this question will have to show that in the eyes of these priests and scribes Jesus could not be a real prophet, i.e. someone who proclaimed something new in the name of God. For them, all that God wanted to communicate to his people had been already set down in the Torah. By Torah they did not just mean the biblical text which had been transmitted but at the same time the oral interpretation of it which had been handed down in an unbroken chain of wise men and scribes over the centuries. A Jew who taught men and women something about God outside that framework could only be a deceiver and had to be rejected from the community of Israel.

This attitude on the part of the Jewish authorities is understandable. That time teemed with people who claimed to have received personal revelations from God. One might think for example of the circles in which apocalyptic visions were related, but also of messianic prophets who recruited followers in order to drive out the Romans with God's help. The man from Nazareth with his foolish and dangerous talk about the kingdom of God might have been regarded by a group of followers as a prophet, but they were people without theological training. They did not realize that the time of the prophets was past. They were also politically naive. They had no idea what kind of careful manoeuvres were necessary with the Roman governor to secure the continuance of capital and temple.

Jesus had announced the destruction of the temple. As he said according to the beginning of Mark 13: of that resplendent building 'not one stone shall remain on another'. Some witnesses appeared during the session with the Sanhedrin. According to Mark they had heard him say: 'I shall destroy this temple made with hands and in three days build another temple not made with hands.' Matthew renders this saying as: 'I can destroy the temple of God and in three days build it up again.' Luke omits this testimony, but in Acts 6 he reports what witnesses say about Stephen, who is being judged by the Sanhedrin:

> This man does not cease speaking against the holy place and against the Law. For we have heard him say that the Nazorean Jesus will destroy this place and change the laws which Moses has handed down to us.

According to John, right at the beginning of his ministry Jesus drove the merchants out of the temple. When the Jews asked him for his authority he replied: 'Destroy this temple and in three days

I shall raise it up.' It seems probable that a saying of Jesus has been preserved in these different versions. What did Jesus mean by it? In Jeremiah it was clear that he was announcing the end of the temple because there 'religion' was being practised by people who treated their fellow men and women badly. So this went completely contrary to what Yahweh really wanted. For Jesus, God's dearest wish was even clearer. It was not just a matter of avoiding murder, theft, adultery, false witness and other such crimes. What God really wanted had to be expressed in much more radical terms: real love towards all fellow men and women. Jesus put that briefly and powerfully in the so-called golden rule: 'Whatever you want men to do to you, do so to them.' The coming kingdom of God was to consist in a community of people who would find one another in love. The few times that Jesus refers to this future he uses images like a wedding or a banquet. That is how the Father wanted to associate with his children. A temple would no longer be necessary there.

It was not unusual in the time of Jesus for a close community of people dedicated to God to be called a temple. We know that from the writings of the Essenes who lived by the Dead Sea. They spoke of their group not only as 'the community of the new covenant', but also as 'the temple of God'.

Jesus' saying could be understood in that sense: the temple of Jerusalem will no longer have a function; it can disappear. But after three days, the usual term for a change for the better, God will put a new one in its place, a community of fulfilled people.

There are further passages in the book of Jeremiah which make a Christian think of Jesus. The prophet came from a priestly family in Anathoth, a few kilometres north-east of Jerusalem, on the other side of the Mount of Olives. As a result of his preaching in the capital Jeremiah compromised his fellow villagers there. Hence their plan to kill him. He was unmarried, but joined in celebrating family feasts and shared in the joy of bridegroom and bride.

Other prophets received their commission in an overwhelming vision which shaped the rest of their lives. Jeremiah did not. According to the account with which his book begins, one day God told him that he was destined to appear as a prophet. Jeremiah did not then show signs of fright or surprise. He simply replied that he did not think that he was up to this task. He seems already to have been conversing with God for years, to have been a praying man from his youth.

This impression is confirmed by the prayers which are scattered through the book of Jeremiah. From them too we can see how firmly Jeremiah felt himself to be tied to God and at the same time to his people, God's people of which he himself was a part. To his own sorrow he had to threaten them with disaster in the name of God. He felt himself as it were bound to both 'parties', as a kind of mediator.

His sensitivity towards imagery and symbols is also very striking. All that he sees and experiences can become for him an expression of what is going on between God and his people. It can be a blossoming almond tree; a pot on the fire which boils over so that what is cooking in it runs away; two baskets of figs which he sees in the market; the way in which a potter deals with the clay; the girdle which the prophet has left lying too long in a damp chest; an earthenware pot which breaks into fragments, and so on. His style of speaking is also often extremely full of imagery.

Thus in many respects Jeremiah is a 'prefigurement' in the eyes of those who regard Christ as the fulfilment of what God had done earlier in dealing with his people. It is not, then, because Jeremiah foretold the coming Messiah but through the way in which he dedicated himself to the task of proclaiming the will and purposes of God while at the same time standing up for his people. In other words, it is through the way in which he functioned as a 'mediator' between God and his people. It has been suggested that we should use the term 'preliminary study' instead of 'prefigurement'. It is a term which suggests the sketchbooks of great painters and exhibitions in which sometimes preliminary studies of paintings that have become famous are put on display. Such sketches have a beauty and artistry independent of whether the planned painting ever came into being. It can also happen that such preliminary studies show different possiblities of which the artist has finally chosen one. The choice of the term has the advantage that the person and work of Jeremiah can be evaluated and admired as a high point of the history of God with his people without making it all subordinate to what Christians regard as the clear fulfilment of it.

One can also regard Psalm 22 as such a preliminary study. Its first words are, 'My God, my God, why have you forsaken me?' They make any Christian think immediately of the dying Jesus on the cross. In fact the suppliant here describes his distress in increasingly powerful imagery. Finally it seems as if his enemies are about to put him to a cruel death. Quite suddenly his prayer then turns into a thanksgiving for his salvation, in which he involves other believers. After that the perspective shifts: all people on earth and also generations to come will take part in that salvation which consists in Yahweh becoming king over all nations: the kingdom of God. In other words, God evidently brings about that universal salvation for all humankind by raising one individual from the dead. It is quite amazing that all this is sensed and expressed by a Jew some centuries before Christ.

For these reasons too it is a good thing to read this amazing text closely. Unfortunately the basic Hebrew text is not always clear. That is partly because of its poetic character, the powerful imagery and expressions which we can no longer understand. Moreover we have to remember that Hebrew texts are written without vowels. The Jewish scribes who translated this psalm into Greek already had difficulty with some passages. I shall attempt a translation, interspersed with some comments about the structure of the text and the possible significance of uncertain details. All this is in the hope that the reader will go on to read the prayer uninterrupted in his or her own Bible:

> My God, my God, why have you forsaken me,
> (you remain) far from helping me,
> from the cries which I utter.
> My God, I cry in the daytime and you do not answer,
> by night and I find no rest.

Now the thoughts of the suppliant turn to the temple, the place where the Holy One 'dwells' and where his people praises him without ceasing for his creative and redeeming activity which began with their liberation from Egypt. The suppliant feels himself involved in this; he no longer speaks of 'I' and 'me', but of us.

> Yet you are holy, enthroned on the praises of Israel.
> In you our fathers trusted,
> they trusted, and you delivered them,

to you they cried and were liberated,
in you they trusted and were not disappointed.

Then the poet returns to the distress in which he finds himself.
It is not clear what blow has struck him. He could feel deeply
humiliated by his surroundings, that he is crawling in the dust,
talked out of his trust in God.

But I am a worm and no man;
scorned by men and despised by my kinsmen.
All those who see me mock me,
they grin and shake their heads:

'He committed his cause to Yahweh, to deliver him, to liberate
him:
For he loves him.'

But he did not abandon that trust. He had had it from his birth,
as was characteristic of Israel since the deliverance from Egypt.
To begin with, it was 'our fathers', now for him it is 'my mother'.

Yet you are the one who took me from the womb,
you kept me safe on my mother's breasts;
on you I was cast from my birth,
and since my mother bore me you have been my God.
Do not be far from me,
for trouble is near and there is none to help.

The threat which is already coming on the poet now takes the
form of great, primaeval, powerful animals.

Many bulls encompass me,
strong bulls of Basan surround me,
they open wide their mouths at me
like a ravening and roaring lion.

He now goes on to describe his feelings, his inward state, with
equally strong imagery. The last line is directly addressed to God
and seems to conjure up the image of a pot which is put on
smouldering ash:

I am poured out like water,
and all my bones are out of joint;
my heart is like wax,

it is melted within my breast;
my strength is dried up like a potsherd,
and my tongue cleaves to my jaws;
you lay me in the dust of death.

The evil powers press constantly closer to him and it seems as if they are pressing for his execution. It is impossible to make out from the Hebrew precisely what is happening to his hands and feet. The standard text reads, 'like a lion my hands and my feet'; the Greek translator renders this 'they have dug out, hollowed out, my hands and my feet'. One of the many conjectures is that the writer is using a verb which means 'make short, cut off'. In torture, limbs were cut off so that the victim was deprived of the last possibility of defending himself or fleeing, so that they could quietly count his bones. For biblical people clothes were much more closely connected with those who wore them than they are for us. Dividing them indicates that the victim has no future.

Yes, dogs are round about me,
a company of evildoers has encircled me
...my hands and my feet.
They count all my bones,
they stare and gloat over me.
They divide my garments among them
and cast lots for my mantle.

Now comes the last prayer, taking up the lamentation at the beginning, over the distance of 'my God', here referred to with the kindred Hebrew expression 'my power'. This final prayer ends with a verb the vowels of which have been read by the Greek translator as 'my distress', in the sense of 'me, a person in distress'. But the Hebrew standard text reads it as a form of the verb, 'you have answered me', and in this way prepares for the second part of the psalm, the thanksgiving for deliverance.

But you, Yahweh, are not far off!
You are my power, hasten to my aid,
Deliver my life from the sword,
my own from the power of the dogs.
Save me from the mouth of the lion and from the horns of the buffalo,
my distress (or: you have answered me).

The beginning of the second part is characteristic of a thanksgiving; an explicit plan to relate the deliverance to the 'community' which embraces all Israel. But finally all people will belong to it and in this way the kingdom of God will become reality.

I will tell of your name to my brothers,
in the midst of the congregation I will praise you.
You who fear Yahweh, praise him,
all you sons of Jacob glorify him,
and revere him, all descendants of Israel.
For he has not despised nor abhorred the affliction of the afflicted,
nor has he hidden his face from him,
but he has heard when he cried to him.
From you comes my praise in the great congregation,
I will pay my vows in the presence of those who fear him.
Poor men shall eat and be satisfied,
those who seek Yahweh shall praise him,
your hearts will live for ever.
All the countries of the earth shall think of Yahweh
and turn to him.
And all tribes of the people shall worship him,
for to Yahweh belongs the kingdom
and he is ruler over the peoples.
Yes, all those who sleep in the earth (?) shall worship him,
before him shall bow all who go down to the dust,
and he who cannot keep himself alive (?).
Posterity shall serve him:
men shall tell of the Lord to the coming generation,
and proclaim his deliverance to a people yet unborn.
He, Yahweh, has done it.

Christians who read or hear read aloud the whole of this psalm for the first time in their lives are often amazed: how can it come about that a Jewish poet some centuries before the birth of Christ should describe his suffering so impressively and could also foresee what happened next: how, delivered from death, he called into being the worldwide community of grateful people? Amazement at this need not become less when it becomes clear that this prophecy did not drop down from heaven. It had a prehistory. Here are a few comments on that.

In the first part of the psalm vigorous laments and cries of distress alternate with expressions of trust and urgent prayers for deliverance. We find all these forms of prayer in other psalms and also elsewhere in the Old Testament. Peculiar to Psalm 22 is the order of themes and above all the way in which the suppliant expresses the intensity of his feelings and the hopelessness of his situation.

It is not clear who is meant by the 'enemies' who seek his life. It seems as though they are intent on attacking his piety and his trust in God and precisely in so doing want to test him with all their power. Such 'enemies' also appear in psalms which consist predominantly of laments. Sometimes the suppliant expresses the hope that these evil men will be punished by God. This expectation is connected with a very strong sense of God's justice. The enemies of the pious man are enemies of God; he himself has an obligation to avenge their crimes against the weak. In this judgment of vengeance God comes into his own and the pious person can now already rejoice at that. It is striking that in Psalm 22 there is no trace of such feelings.

In the second half of the psalm the suppliant suddenly begins an invitation to a festival with which a meal is associated. Although we feel the transition to be abrupt, even if one reads 'You have answered me' (we are not told how that happened), the transition from petition to thanksgiving was not unprecedented. One can see from several psalms what believers did who had prayed to God in their distress and had been heard. Such a person went with his family and friends to the temple to offer a thanksgiving. An essential part of this ceremony was his 'story' of how afflicted he had been and what had happened; how he already found himself in the grip of death and how he had then prayed to Yahweh. So that story could take the form of a prayer in the utmost distress. After that he invited those present to join him in eating the meat of the sacrificial animal that he had brought with him, an animal from his herd or one that he had purchased, either way a part of himself. He did that with others in delight at the life that had been restored to him.

The distress from which the suppliant had been saved could have been many things: sickness, the burden of debt, suspicion, persecution, imprisonment, torture, in short all the things that threatened life. Here we must remember that for biblical people 'life' meant what we would call fullness of life, happy life, in other words health, prosperity, reputation, a good name, a happy family and so on. If any of that was substantially missing, then the person affected already felt himself to be in the grip of death, the underworld, experienced as a satanic power which stood in the way of the purposes of the God who gave life. Here the pious Jew often attracted the mockery of those who identified him so closely with God and his laws, the 'godless'. They assaulted the unfortunate person with their sarcastic questions. 'Where is your God now? But you trusted in him! Why does he not help you?' This was a terrifying trial which further intensified the sense of godforsakenness.

That sense is expressed more strongly in the first part of the psalm than in any other biblical prayer. But the second part also goes beyond the familiar limits. The suppliant does not restrict his thanksgiving for deliverance from the distress of death, as was customary, to his 'brothers', the community to which he belongs and which he mentions twice. He makes this circle much wider and really includes the whole of humanity in it. He does not do that without preparation. For the thanksgiving festival takes place in the temple on Zion. There great expectations were kept alive in the liturgy: at this place where God dwells, his universal kingship will one day be made manifest. For the psalmist, that was the occasion for including at the end of his hymn all peoples in the praise and thanksgiving for his deliverance from death. Although it is not clear whether he also sees the dead as taking part in this festival, it is certain that coming generations will do so.

The psalm must have been written some centuries before Christ. We do not know precisely how many. Far less is it clear how the book of Psalms received its final form. Probably, to begin with, smaller collections came into being which were slowly brought together into the present book. These collections will have functioned like hymns in a Christian community.

Anyone who came to the temple to thank God for his deliverance from a situation of distress, and thus for his petitions to be heard, did not have to seek his own words to tell his story and invite his fellow believers to the festal sacrificial meal. There were texts for this with very varied imagery which to our minds is sometimes extravagant. Precisely because of the 'symbolic', wide-ranging character of these songs anyone could use them to express what he himself had experienced and felt. The poets and authors of these psalms had also expressed in an evocative way, on the basis of their own experience, what a believer was accustomed to think an feel in such a situation.

There is no doubt that pious Jews knew such psalm texts by heart and that these texts spontaneously came to mind when they were talking with God or wanted to address him. Many believers have experienced how good it was to have such ancient words in mind when they felt completely alone and in dire distress. According to Mark's story Jesus prayed with the first words of Psalm 22 when he was in extreme distress, and he did so in Aramaic, his mother tongue: 'My God, my God, why have you forsaken me?' There is no point in asking questions here: for example whether Jesus went on to pray more lines from this psalm. There is no point in doing so because no answer is possible, and moreover it would be a sign of considerable disrespect.

All we can say is that those who first related the crucifixion of Jesus had the text of Psalm 22 in mind. They took their description of what the soldiers did with Jesus' clothes from it, and also the detail that the passers-by who challenged Jesus with their mockery shook their heads at him. That is what Mark tells us. Matthew adds another sentence to this which he takes from the psalm. The mockers say that Jesus saved others and now cannot save himself. If he is the king of Israel, let him now come down from the cross and then they will believe. Matthew goes on to quote what the mockers in the psalm said:

> He trusted in God, let him now deliver him if he is pleased with him; *for he said, 'I am the Son of God'.*

The line in italics is not part of the quotation from Psalm 22. It seems to have been taken from another passage in the Jewish Bible which must irresistibly have made a Christian reader think of the sufferings of Jesus.

### 'Son' of God

The book of Wisdom was written in Egypt in the last century before Christ by a very educated Jew. It continued to be part of the Christian Bible until the Reformers rejected it. Their reason was that the book of Wisdom was written in Greek and therefore did not belong to the Bible of the Jews of the time.

In the second chapter of his book the author describes the mentality of those who live without God. They enjoy as much as possible of their life which is so short and transitory. The criterion for their action is power, not justice. Those who believe in God and act accordingly are a thorn in their flesh. The author makes them speak as follows:

> Let us lie in wait for the righteous man,
> because he is inconvenient to us and opposes our actions;
> he reproaches us for sins against the law,
> and accuses us of sins against our training.
> He professes to have knowledge of God,
> and calls himself a servant of the Lord.
> He became to us a reproof of our thoughts;
> the very sight of him is a burden to us,
> because his manner of life is unlike that of others,
> and his ways are strange.
> We are considered by him as something base,
> and he avoids our ways as unclean,
> he calls the last end of the righteous happy,
> and boasts that God is his father.
> Let us see if his words are true,
> and let us test what will happen at the end of his life;
> for if the righteous man is God's son, he will help him,
> and will deliver him from the hand of his adversaries.
> Let us test him with insult and torture,
> that we may find out how gentle he is,
> and make trial of his forbearance.
> Let us condemn him to a shameful death,
> for according to what he says he will be protected.

It is understandable that the Greek-speaking Christians regarded this passage as a prophecy of what had happened to Jesus. Centuries earlier God had already revealed that to King Solomon. For the author of Wisdom presented himself as being this king, though without using the name Solomon. In Jesus, what the wise king had written here was now fulfilled, had become reality: the righteous man *par excellence* who had rightly called himself the son of God was mocked when he hung dying on the cross; his Father should have rescued him from this mortal distress!

Our text confronts us with the question what inspired the anonymous writer of Wisdom to write the passage I have quoted. The answer to this must be that he wanted to demonstrate to his readers how they could confess their faith in a very perplexing situation. Chapter 2 above describes what the invasion of Hellenistic culture had brought about in Judaea. Many Jews, above all from the upper classes, were delighted with it. They rejected the ancient customs and thus the view of faith of which these were the expression and for which at the same time they were the protection. Hence their distaste and even hatred of those few Jews who continued to observe them.

There were also such apostates among the Jews in Egypt, especially among those who had many contacts with the non-Jews among whom they lived. The author devotes the first five chapters of his book entirely to the opposition between these apostates or godless and the pious or righteous. Here most of the emphasis is on their final fate. In very picturesque language he keeps describing how the godless have no future, how they will be annihilated and perish, while the relationship with God which the pious now already have will culminate after their death in endless happiness with him.

Those who immerse themselves in this book of the Bible will become increasingly amazed at the gifts of the author. He is fully at home in the literature of his time and has a command of the language in which educated people were accustomed to express themselves. At the same time, however, he has made the writings of the Jewish community so much his own that whole sentences from them or allusions to them occur to him automatically. Where he says at the end of chapter 1 of the godless that they have made a covenant with death, he is quoting literally a text from Isaiah 28 in which the prophet is protesting against the Jerusalem politicians who want to make a treaty with Egypt (the pagan land in which the author is living!). It would take too long to analyse the passage from Wisdom that I have quoted in terms of the concepts and words from other books of the Bible which are used in it. Hence my limitation to one instance which is connected with the theme of 'fulfilment'.

The godless accuse the righteous man of dealing familiarly with God, and even of calling himself a son of God. This expression has a very long history. One might recall the story of the exodus from Egypt in which Moses has to go and say to Pharaoh: 'Let my son go'. The prophet Hosea quotes as a word of God: 'When Israel was a child, I loved him, and out of Egypt I called my son.'

Here we have to remember that in Hebrew the term 'son' often has a wider significance than it does in our language. We can

184

understand how a teacher can say 'my son' to his pupil, and how a king can address a subject in this way. But the word also served to indicate that one belonged to a group. The prophet Amos is driven out of the temple of Bethel in the northern kingdom of Israel. He has to go and eat bread and prophesy only in Judah. Thereupon he proudly retorts: 'I am not a prophet or son of a prophet, but I am a herdsman and a dresser of sycamore trees...' Yahweh has called him from that work to prophesy against his people Israel. 'I am not a son of a prophet' means: I do not belong to that guild of professional prophets, but I was called by God himself.

When Jesus is suspected of driving out devils with the help of Beelzebul the prince of the devils he refers to the pious Jews who also drive out devils by asking, 'By whom do your sons drive out devils?' 'Sons' means 'those among you'.

Since the exodus from Egypt and the making of the covenant Israel has belonged to Yahweh and so can be called the 'son' of Yahweh. Thus Israelites could also be addressed in the plural as sons of Yahweh. The first word of God in the book of Isaiah begins: 'Sons have I reared and brought up, but they have rebelled against me...' And Deuteronomy 14 begins with the words: 'You are the sons of Yahweh your God...'

Kings from the dynasty of David had a special relationship with the God of Israel. They had to rule in the name of Yahweh, as it were give his kingdom form in their government. The king had to defend his people against enemies from outside, but above all see to just relationships, to the maintenance of justice and righteousness and to maintaining it especially for widows and orphans, the most vulnerable people in his kingdom. Hence the fact that a scion of the dyansty of David was in a special way a 'son of' Yahweh. According to II Samuel 7 the prophet Nathan had promised a successor to David in the name of God and said of him: 'I shall be his father and he shall be my son.' Hence a scion of the dynasty of David was in a special way 'son of God' when he was anointed at the time of his accession. Psalm 2 seems to contain elements of such an enthronement. In it God says: 'I have set my king on Zion, my holy hill', and after that the newly anointed king asserts that God has blessed him: 'You are my son, today I have begotten you.'

In the centuries after the exile, when there were no longer any anointed kings, 'son of God' was used to denote particularly pious

Jews. In chapter 4 of his book Jesus Sirach gives some instructions for a life that can be called truly pious. Anyone who wants that must be open to the needy and to beggars and free the oppressed from the hands of their oppressors. The last instruction runs:

> Be like a father to orphans, and instead of a husband to their mother;
> you will then be like a son of the Most High,
> and he will love you more than does your mother.

By that stage the time was long past when all Israelites could be called 'sons of Yahweh', in contrast to other peoples. Fidelity to the covenant has now become a matter of personal choice, and only those who really are willing to obey it are referred to by this title, as are the righteous in the passage from the book of Wisdom quoted above.

Of course this use of the term 'son' of God does not envisage physical descent, although the term 'beget' is sometimes used, as in Psalm 2. But the consequence was that God was called the 'father' of his people. Moses calls God 'father' according to the song that Deuteronomy 32 puts on his lips. He accuses his people of being a wicked and corrupt generation, since it fails to see what it owes to its God:

> Is he not the father who created you,
> who made you and established you?

In Jeremiah 3 God says, very much in the style of the sensitive prophet:

> I thought how I would set you among my sons,
> and give you a pleasant land,
> a heritage most beautiful of all nations,
> And I thought that you would call me 'My father',
> and would not turn from following me.
> Surely, as a faithless wife leaves her husband,
> So you have been faithless to me, O house of Israel.

In the passionate prayer of Isaiah 63-64, the Jews twice say to God, 'You are not our father!', and the third time,

> And yet, Yahweh, you are our father,
> We are the clay and you are the potter,
> We are the work of your hand.

186

The author of Psalm 89 records God's promise to David in a very poetic way in which the line occurs, 'He shall call to me, you are my father'.

Some centuries later Jesus Sirach, no David nor a son of David but a wise teacher, makes this appeal to his readers in the thanksgiving psalm with which the last chapter of his book begins. Anyone who reads all that poem will be surprised at the many parallels with Psalm 22. After he has described how close he was to death, completely without any human help, and how he then thought of God's former mighty deeds, he goes on:

> And I sent up my supplication from the earth,
> and prayed for deliverance from death.
> I appealed to the Lord, 'You are my father,
> do not forsake me in the days of affliction,
> at the time when there is no help against the proud.
> I will praise your name continually,
> and will sing praise with thanksgiving.'

The extent to which the passage quoted above from Wisdom 2 is as it were loaded with 'tradition' may have become clear from what I have just said. The relationship between the pious Jew and his God is described there in terms which had been in use for centuries and thus conjured up associations with great figures from the Jewish past. That could be illustrated further from the accusations by the godless against the pious man, namely that he calls himself a 'servant of the Lord'. This designation is given to Moses more than forty times. Moreover there are many texts in which God speaks about 'my servants the prophets'. The term especially suggested the figure in the second part of the book of Isaiah, who is introduced by God in chapter 42 in unforgettable terms and who then in chapter 49 himself talks about his call as prophet and about the efforts in which he found consolation. In chapter 50 he speaks again and describes the ill-treatment that he has to endure; after this, chapter 53 describes his martyr death in which he gives his life as an atonement and the justification which he subsequently receives from God, again for the benefit of sinful humankind. These descriptions are an account of all kinds of experiences. First of all, as is suggested by some interpreters, they are a description of the anonymous prophet himself, the end of whose life would then have been described by disciples and to be interpreted in his spirit. But the experiences of Jeremiah have also played a part in the descriptions of this servant of the Lord.

Two consequences are important for the subject dealt with in this book. One characteristic of Jesus was his strong sense of the nearness and love of the Father, especially for people who no longer had any future, because of their poverty or because they had been written off. His familiar converse with God also emerged from his manner of praying and the way in which he wanted to involve his disciples in this familiarity. If a dedicated believer could be called a 'son of God', that term applied particularly to him. Secondly, it took on an unprecedented new dimension when God rehabilitated him after his shameful death and he proved to be the 'Lord's anointed', the Messiah, to whom this designation 'son of God' had been given from of old.

### 'One humanity new born'

Finally I should like to add some comments about a theme which occupied many Jews in the centuries before Christ. They experienced their existence as members of 'the chosen people'. Only with Israel had the one true God made a covenant and only with that people had he so to speak begun a communal history. This belief raised questions like: in that case, what is the situation of other peoples? God also created them and there is no one in the world who falls outside his care; do they then have no connection with him, and does Israel have nothing at all to do with them?

A very elaborate text about this election occupies a central place in the Torah. In Exodus 19 the people finally arrives at Sinai from Egypt. Moses ascends this mountain and there hears Yahweh say to him:

Thus shall you say to the house of Jacob, and tell the people of Israel:

You have seen what I did to the Egyptians, and how I bore you on eagles' wings and brought you to myself.

Now therefore, if you will obey my voice and keep my covenant, you shall be my own possession among all peoples; for all the earth is mine.

And you shall be to me a kingdom of priests and a holy nation. These are the words which you shall speak to the children of Israel.

The whole earth belongs to Yahweh, with all the people who dwell on it. From it he has chosen Israel as his own precious possession. This privilege does not contain any guarantee. Israel has to implement it through its obedience to the laws and precepts which God will give through the mouth of Moses. Through this election Israel is a 'holy people'. In the Old Testament this designation does not primarily have a moral significance, as it does with us. 'Holy' is that which is designated for the cult, for the service of God, and is thus withdrawn from secular usage, separated. In this sense the temple is holy, as is everything to do with the cult, including the priests. Israel is a kingdom of priests, in other words a priestly nation. That means that it is a people destined for the service of God. But just as priests in Israel had a kind of mediating function, by offering the sacrifices of the people to God and also pronouncing the blessing of God upon the Israelites, so Israel as a whole fulfils a priestly function towards the other peoples.

This was probably also the view of those who edited the beginning of the book of Genesis. The ancient texts which are incorporated into it were about the beginning of everything. They were attempts from former times to explain the world and everything in it in terms of its beginning: not only what we call nature or the cosmos but also the fact of humankind and ultimately also the function of the people of Israel within it. The theme of this series of stories is known well enough. The first human couple transgresses the commandment and is driven out of paradise. An older son murders his younger brother and subsequently evil takes on increasingly gross forms. So God resolves on the flood, from which only Noah, his three sons, and their wives are saved. They become the tribal ancestors of the new humanity, divided into the descendants of Shem, Ham and Japheth. The names of these peoples, lands and cities are given in Genesis 10: there are seventy of them. Then follows the story of the tower of Babel, which is meant to explain why the countless peoples no longer understand one another. Humankind, intended by God to be one great family of Adam's children, has now fallen apart into all these peoples who no longer understand one another. Finally, from the family of Shem emerges the family to which a certain Abraham belongs. With him in chapter 12 a new story begins:

Yahweh said to Abraham: 'Go from your country and your

kindred and your father's house to the land that I will show you. And I will make of you a great nation, and I will bless you, and make your name great, so that you will be a blessing.

I will bless those who bless you and him who curses you I will curse; and by you all the families of the earth will bless themselves.

Here Abraham stands for the people of Israel, and it is clear that the same thought is expressed as in the text from Exodus: Israel is elected to be a source of blessing for all humankind. In other words: humanity, originally intended as one family which has now been split into many peoples, will be made a new community through the election of Israel.

But the developments after the exile also meant that the Jews had increasingly to put the emphasis on their vocation to be holy, separated for the service of God, set apart. That was necessary to preserve their identity in the midst of the other peoples and to continue to bear witness to the one God. Hence the importance of the customs which set them apart, so clearly expressed by the high priest in the letter of Aristeas: 'Therefore Moses has surrounded us with hedges without breaches and walls of iron, so that we should not mix in any way with the other peoples...'

However, there continued to be an awareness that Israel was called to be a blessing to all humankind. As well as in the passages from the Torah which I have quoted, this commission was also expressed in prophetic texts. Called to serve Yahweh, to be his 'servant', Israel had to be 'a light for the nations'. Sometimes that was a matter of course, when Gentiles felt attracted to the God of the Jews. That must already have happened in the first years after the exile, according to a telling saying of the prophet Zechariah:

In those days ten men from the nations of every tongue shall take hold of the robe of a Jew, saying, 'Let us go with you, for we have heard that the Lord is with you.'

But the initiative often came from pious Jews, above all in the Diaspora. Sometimes they were merchants who in their contacts with Gentiles aroused interest in Jewish belief. But things could not just stop at interest: someone born a Gentile could only call himself a worshipper of the true God if he had joined the Jewish people as a proselyte, in other words had become a Jew.

190

The conviction that this should be so and not otherwise was so strong that it also found favour among Jews who had joined the new community around Jesus Messiah. As I described in the previous chapter, it was Paul above all who powerfully challenged it with an appeal to the Scriptures. He showed that it had always been God's desire to give his blessing to all peoples. Therefore the separation of the Jews must have been a temporary measure on the basis of the Torah, done away with by God himself through the sending of his Son, who obediently gave his life for all men and women. So through what happened in Jesus a perspective was fulfilled which had been indicated in many Old Testament texts.

The Dutch writer Huub Oosterhuis recently published a 'Hymn of Paul' in which he makes the apostle himself say how he has come to see and experience this new truth. Here to end this chapter are some quotations from this masterly poem.

> I saw sitting at one table: Jews
> and Greeks, mixed up together, as though that were possible.
> Then I saw that it was possible, from now on...
> I saw what many people had seen before me:
> the God of our father Abraham,
> the God of Isaac, the God of Jacob,
> who first loved Israel,
> is the light and source of life for all nations,
> wills to be all in all. And I thought:
> no one need become a Jew in order to go with this God
> in spirit and in truth.

In the next strophe he evokes the picture of Jesus, the Jew who would have nothing to do with the discrimination in his milieu. Jesus blew away all these laws and rules because he lived from the God of Israel who seeks contact with everyone. For that reason he was crucified, but this death bore fruit. Since he has been taken up into God's own life, he has also broken down the wall which all over the world separated Jews from non-Jews.

> I saw humankind, a crucified slave,
> a seed sown, dead – I saw Jesus
> living in this way as the God of Israel.
> He blew on the trumpet of the covenant, broke down

the dividing wall which splits the world. After seven
blasts it fell down; about his feet
tombstones, rubble. The breath of his mouth
blew them away as though they were bits of fluff.

In this way a new society could come into being, which already
took shape in the meals of the first communities, the first beginning
of what God intended for his people.

I saw us at one table, men, women,
gentle, unveiled, without hard eyes,
servants and masters, and no first places.
And all drank from the same cup.
I saw that – God will credit me –
what is not yet: his spirit which makes many
one body, one humanity new born,
messiah-body, beyond death.

# Postscript

That's my story, for that is what it is meant to be. I wanted to describe how within the Jewish community around the unexpected figure of Jesus of Nazareth a group arose which slowly but surely grew away from the mother 'church'. My concern has been to describe this development as objectively as possible, by means of information from this time, material which is accessible to anyone who wants to investigate. Unfortunately this information is relatively sparse and sometimes difficult to fit together because of the lack of connecting links. That is why I have so often used words like perhaps, possibly, probably. Hence, too, differences from other accounts of the same subject.

For all my attempts at objectivity I have probably (!) not been able to conceal the fact that I feel myself to be a convinced Christian. Descended from many generations of Catholic forebears I perhaps have a tendency in this direction in my genes. But as a Dominican, for many years I have had the privilege of being able to immerse myself critically in all the aspects of our faith, also through great thinkers from the distant and nearer past. That was on the theoretical side. But Christian belief would deny its origin from Moses and the prophets and above all from its 'ownmost spokesman Jesus' if it did not put practice above theory. In that respect, too, it is a privilege to be able to stand in a centuries-long liturgical tradition which recalls the 'saints' each year on their festivals.

Under the title *We are not the First*, the Protestant theologian Niek Schuman recently produced a modernized version of such a liturgical calendar. Alongside saints of former times other people have a day on which they are remembered: non-Christians and people of our own century who have put their lives at the service of their fellow men and as a result have become witnesses to Jesus. Looking at them sharpens our insight into others who live that kind of life nowadays. To be able to know and recognize such silent witnesses is also a challenge not to limit one's activities with 'the faith' to thought and discussion.

While I was toiling over this book some friends and acquaintances offered to read and discuss with me passages which I had finished. I was grateful for that but have to regret that I did not take up their offer. I did, however, send the outline of chapter 2 to Professor A.van der Woude, who did me the kindness of making critical comments on it, for which I am most grateful. I owe most thanks to my publisher, Ton van der Worp, for his unceasing involvement, help and above all endless patience.

# *Notes*

The figures at the beginning of each line refer to the page numbers.

1: Mark 9.1–13; 14.21; 14.27.
2: Mark 14.49; 8.31; Luke 24.25–27; 24.44–47.
3: Luke 22.36f.; 18.31; Matt. 25.56; 26.52–54.
4: Matt. 1.21–23; 2.15.
5: Matt. 2.17f.
6: Matt. 2.23; 4.14–17.
7f.: Matt. 8.17; Isa. 53.17; Matt. 12.15–21; Isa. 42.1–4. This long quotation does not follow the Hebrew precisely nor the usual Greek translation. Only the last sentence is a literal rendering. Perhaps this is an indication that the quotation circulated earlier among Greek-speaking Christians and that Matthew added this sentence about the Gentile nations.
8: Matt. 13.13–15.
9: Isa. 6.9f.; Matt. 21.4f.
10: Zech. 9.9; Matt. 27.9f.; here words from Jer. 32.6–10 are combined with Zech. 11.12f.
11: John 1.45; 5.39, 46; 12.37–41; Isa. 53.1; 6.9f.
12: John 13.16–19; Ps. 41.10; 15.24f.; 35.19; 69.5.
13: John 17.12; 19.24; Ps. 22.19; John 19.28; Ps. 69.22; John 19.33–37.
14: Ex. 12.46; Ps. 34.21; Zech. 12.10.
15: Here is a list of 'traditional' messianic texts:
– paradise promise, Gen. 3.14f.
– promise to the patriarchs, Gen. 12.1–3; 18.18; 22.18; 26.4; 28.14.
– Jacob blesses Judah, Gen. 49.10 (cf. 8).
– Balaam, Num. 27.17.
– Prophet like Moses, Deut. 18.15.18.
– Nathan to David, II Sam. 7.11–16.
– 'Immanuel', Isa. 7.14, cf. 8.10; 9.5f.; 11.1f.
– Servant of the Lord, Isa. 42.14; 49.1–6; 50.4–11; 52.13–53.12.
– The 'branch' of David, Jer. 23.5f.; 33.15f.
– Shepherd alongside God, Ezek. 34.24f.; 37.24f.
– Born in Bethlehem, Micah 5.1–3.
– Gentle king, Zech. 9.9.
– 'Son of man', Dan. 7.13f.; 9.26.
– Messianic psalms, 2; 72; 110; 45; 89.
17: Historic framework, Luke 3.1f. Cf. Jer. 1.2.
18: Reading of the Torah, Neh. 8.

Sending away non-Jewish wives, Ezra 9 and 10; Neh. 13.1–3, 23–27.

37f.: Prov. 8.22–31. As well as worker or artist one also finds the word translated as 'darling', 'dearest child'.

40: Sirach 24.8, 23; Baruch 3.37; 4.1.

42: Wisdom 7.22–8.1.

45: Ps. 73.24; 49.16.

46: Isa. 2.2–5; also in Micah 4.1–3.

47f.: Isa. 25.6–9.

48: Enoch is mentioned in Gen. 5.18–24.

49ff.: Quotations in italics from Dan. 2.44; 6.27; 7.13–14, 17–18, 27.

51: Gabriel in Dan. 8.16: 9.21.

52: Resurrection in Dan. 12.2–3.

55: Deut. 18.15,18; Gen. 14.17–20; Ps. 110.4.

57: Mal. 4.5 (Hebrew 3.23).

59: Bas van Iersel, *Belichting van het bijbelboek Marcus*, Katholische Bijbelstichting, Boxtel 1986; G. Zuntz in the collected volume *Markusphilologie*, Tübingen 1984, 207.

62f.: Jesus in the temple, Luke 2.41–50

63: Women from Galilee, Mark 15.40f.; Eunuchs, Matt. 19.12.

64: Luke 10.23f.

65: Beelzebul, Luke 11.14–20.

66: Fall of Satan, Luke 10.18.
Temptation in the wilderness, Mark 1.11–13. Matt. 4.1–11. by Peter: Mark 8.32f.
'Prince of this world', John 12.31.

67: Peter's mother-in-law, Mark 1.29–31; Luke 4.38f.
The woman bent double, Luke 13.10–17.

68f.: 'Sermon on the Mount', Matt. 5–7.

70f.: The rich man, Mark 10.17–27.

71: Daughter of the Gentile woman, Matt. 7.24–30.
Roman officer, Matt. 8.5–13.
Seed growing secretly, Mark 4.26–32.

72: Leaven (yeast), Matt. 13.33: I Cor. 5.6–8.
Family of Jesus, 3.31–35.
Alternative society, Mark 10.42–44.
Jesus means to 'gather', Matt. 12.30.
Hen and her chickens, Matt. 23.37.

73: His own generation, Mark 9.1.
Noah, Matt. 24.37–39.
Dishonest steward, Luke 16.1–8.

74: Unscrupulous judge, Luke 18.2–7.
Treasure in the field, Matt. 13.44.

75: Prodigal son, Luke 15.11–32.

76f.: Workers in the vineyard, Matt. 20.1–15.

77f.: Good Samaritan, Luke 10.29–35.

79: John the Baptist's question, Matt. 11.2–6; Luke 7.18–23.

Solomon and Jonah, Luke 11.31f.
80: Son of man, cf. Matt. 16.13 with Mark 8.27.
81: Children at play, Luke 7.31–34.
No place of his own, Luke 9.58.
Task of a prophet, Ezek. 2.1–7.
82: Son of man in Daniel, see note on p. 15.
Come to minister, Mark 10.45: Matt. 20.28; Luke 22.27; John 13.1–17.
85: C. F. Burney, *The Poetry of Our Lord*, Oxford 1925.
Journey to Jerusalem, Luke 9.51: 13.31–33.
88f.: Zechariah 9.9 in Matt. 21.5; John 12.15.
90: Question about his authority, Mark 11.23.
Request for a 'sign', John 2.18.
91: Disquiet of Sanhedrin, John 11.47–50.
92: One version of the word over the cup is in Mark 14.24 and Matt. 26.28; the other is in Luke 22.19 and I Cor. 11.25.
93f.: Ellis Rivkin, *What Crucified Jesus?*, Abingdon Press 1984 and SCM Press 1986.
98: The twelve thrones, Matt 19.28: Luke 23.30.
101: God's breath of life, Ps. 104.29.
102: 'Firstborn of the dead', Col. 1.18; Rev. 1.5.
Experience of the Spirit, Gal. 3.1–5 Heb. 6.4–5.
103ff.: Appearance of Stephen, Acts 6f.
106: No man unclean, Acts 10.28.
106: Paul persecuted, Acts 13.45.
109: Crispus, Acts 18.8; I Cor. 1.14.
Forty-less-one, II Cor. 11.24; Deut. 25.1–3.
Stumbling block and folly, I Cor. 1.23.
110: Formerly without God, Eph. 2.12.
113: Scripture addressed to our time, I Cor. 10.11: Rom. 15.4 (Ps. 69.10).
114ff.: Peter's sermon, Acts 2.22–31; quoting Ps. 16.8–11; Ps. 32.11.
116ff.: Paul's sermon in Antioch, Acts 13.16–41; quoting Hab. 1.5.
121: The rejected stone, Acts 4.11.
124: I have discussed these methods of interpretation in more detail and with sources in my *A Bible for our Time*, SCM Press 1979, 14–23.
132: Secret followers, John 12.42.
Hatred of 'the world', John 16.1–4.
133: The word goes forth, Isa. 55.8–11. What John says in his prologue about the role of the world (in Greek masculine, the Logos) in the relationship between God and his creation corresponds closely to the role of wisdom. As I said in chapter 2, Jewish thinkers said that wisdom had come on earth in the form of the Torah. Over against this John, following other Christians, said that this was now embodied in the person of Jesus. Hence in his Gospel he so often expresses the significance of Jesus in the terms and images which pious Jews used to say what the Torah meant for them. Did he prefer the male term

Logos to the female Wisdom (Sophia) because Jesus was a man?
Equal with God, 5.18.
Before Abraham, 8.58.
One with the Father, 10.30f.
134: Before Pilate, 19.7.
Joseph of Arimathea, disciple, Matt. 27.57.
Secretly, John 19.38f.
For fear of the Jews, 20.19.
135: Children of the devil, 8.42–47.
136: Instructions to the Twelve, Matt. 10.17.
'Ekklesia', Matt. 16.18; 18.17.
137f.: In the service of Beelzebul, Mark 3.22: Matt. 12.24; 9.34.
Cries of woe, Luke 1.52.
138: The little ones, Matt. 18.1–5.
139: Wisdom, Luke 11.49.
140f.: Mark 15.6–15 compared with Mark 27.15–25.
141: Washing hands in innocence, Deut. 21.7f.
Prohibition to the Twelve, Matt. 10.5.
Gentile woman, Matt. 15.24.
Last commission, Matt. 28.19f.
142: The centurion, Matt. 8.5–13; cf. Luke 13.28–30.
Wicked husbandmen, Matt. 21.33–43.
143: Lord, lord!, Matt. 7.21–33.
144: Last judgment, Matt. 26.
144f.: I Thess 1.9f.: 2.13–16.
145: 'Murder of prophets', Neh. 9.26: Matt. 23.37.
150: Paul's own words, Gal. 2.20f.
Blessing for all, Gal. 3.14.
151: Fullness of time, Gal. 4.4–7.
Abraham's two sons, Gen. 16. 21.10.
152f.: Taunts, Phil. 3.2; 3.18f.
156: Request for prayer, Rom. 15.30–33.
157: Simeon, Luke 2.25–35.
'all flesh': Luke 3.6.
158: Sermon in Nazareth: Luke 4.35–40.
158f.: He weeps over Jerusalem: Luke 19.4–44.
'Visitation' also in 7.16; 1.68.
159: Siege and downfall of Jerusalem: 21.20–24 (revision of Mark 13.14–20).
160: Quotation from Zech. 12.3.
To the weeping women, Luke 23.38–31.
161: Paul's explanation, Acts 13.46f.; 18.5f.
162: To the Jews in Rome, Acts 27.23–30.
165f.; Jon D. Levenson, 'Is there a counterpart in the Hebrew Bible to New Testament Antisemitism', *Journal of Ecumenical Studies* 22, Spring 1985, 242–60.

166: Amalekites: Ex. 17.2–16; Deut. 25.17–19; I Sam. 15. Esther 3.1.

167: Moldavian: this account was in *De Bazuin*, 27 March 1987. John Barton, *Reading the Old Testament. Method in Bible Study*, Darton, Longman and Todd 1984, 101. The phrase in fact originates from C. F. Evans.

169: From the temple speech, Jer. 7.8–14.

171: Micah 3.9–12.

172: Neh. 9.27: Matt. 23.37; Luke 13.34.

173: The temple-saying Mark 14.58: Matt. 26.61; Acts 6.13f.; John 2.19.

174: I gave a detailed description of Jeremiah with illustrations from the text in *Rediscovering the Bible*, SCM Press 1978, 200–6.

184: A covenant with death, Isa. 28.17.

185: Israel 'son' of God, Ex. 4.22f.
Successor to David, II Sam. 7.14.

186: A pious Jew son of God, Sirach 4.10.

186f.: God as Father, Deut. 32.6, 18f.; Jer. 3.19f.; Isa 63.16; 64.7.

187: Ps. 89.27; Sirach 51.9–11.

188: Election of Israel, Ex. 19.3–6.

188f.: Call of Abraham, Gen. 12.1–3.

190: The ten men, Zech. 8.23.

191: 'Hymn of Paul' is in Huub Oosterhuis, *Nieuw bijbels liedboek*, Baarn 1986, 166f.

192: For the dividing wall cf. Eph. 2.14.

193: Our 'ownmost spokesman Jesus' comes from the 'Hymn of Paul'. Niek Schuman, *Wij zijn de eersten niet*, Meinema, Delft 1985.